The Instrument Pilot's Library
• Volume Eight •

Aircraft Systems

by
The Editors of *IFR* and *IFR Refresher*

Belvoir Publications, Inc.
Greenwich, Connecticut

ISBN: 1-879620-38-3

Printed and bound in the United States of America by Quebecor Printing, Fairfield, Pennsylvania.

Contents

Preface

Flying IFR is one of the more complex tasks most of us are required to perform. While not as confoundedly mind-boggling as, say, doing your taxes (or, some would argue, programming a VCR), flying a high-performance, IFR-capable modern aircraft demands much of the pilot. A well equipped airplane is a very complicated machine, and the pilot must know how to properly operate it.

While automation is slowly finding its way into general aviation cockpits, by and large most systems found in small airplanes are dauntingly complex. And, for IFR flight, there are a lot of them.

An instrument pilot is not just an aviator. Just as important is his or her ability to manage the many systems on board the aircraft. From the simplest navcomm to complex engine controls to pressurization, the IFR pilot is required to assume the role of systems manager.

In this eighth volume of the Instrument Pilot's Library, we'll take a close look at the major systems an IFR pilot deals with. Here you'll find not only the nuts-and-bolts anatomy of aircraft systems, but a wealth of information on how to efficiently and safely operate your aircraft. Previous volumes of the series have concentrated on pilot technique and the tasks associated with operation in today's ATC environment. This book is different; it covers the hardware we use whenever we fly.

• Section One •

The Airplane as a Whole

The Book
of Instructions

Rather than begin with detailed examinations of specific parts of your airplane, let's first look at the machine as a whole, and how it is operated.
As students, we pore over aircraft flight manuals as if they were holy books. Familiarity breeds comtempt, however, and all too often a pilot with a lot of time in type will not bother opening the book on a regular basis.
First up is test pilot Bill Kelly on the niceties of the aircraft flight manual.

Flying by the Book

To begin our discussion of the machines we fly, let's get back to "basics" and consider an important resource at every pilot's disposal: the *flight manual*, be it an FAA-approved airplane flight manual (AFM) or a pilot's operating handbook (POH).

Some of the older airplanes certified under CAR 3 come with a thick book that's a combined pilot's operating manual (POM) and FAA-approved AFM. These manuals tend to be confusing, because the FAA-approved portions may be buried within the book, between "unapproved" sections.

Best of the manuals are the newer "GAMA-format" versions, which are somewhat standardized to an arrangement adopted by the General Aviation Manufacturers Association.

Information appears in nine numbered sections that follow a standard order, typically: general information; limitations; emergency procedures; normal procedures; performance data; weight and balance, and equipment list; systems; handling, service and maintenance; and supplements.

If your manual is a real "oldie," it may consist only of a few pages of browned and weathered typing paper, usually stating only the limitations. You may not have even that, since some airplanes were certificated on the basis of cockpit placards, alone. There may be an unofficial "owner's manual" or such available, providing the only source of general, performance and systems descriptions.

If the need-to-know information is out there, in *any* form, the FAA expects you to know it. FAR 91.103 states, "Each pilot in command shall, before beginning a flight, become familiar with all available information concerning that flight...."

Before you fly *any* airplane for the first time, it's essential that you read, from cover-to-cover, any "flight manual" material that is available.

That holds even if you are going to take formal ground and flight training in that airplane. There are specialized training courses available for many of the "complex" airplanes out there, which may even include simulator time. But, taking such a course does *not* negate the need for you, yourself, to *read the whole book.*

No transition or refresher course can possibly cover everything in the applicable flight manual. So, read the "book," take notes and ask questions of a qualified instructor or a manufacturer's rep if there are questionable areas.

Tricky Transitions

Too many pilots today seem to figure that an instructor can teach them everything they need to know about operating a certain type of aircraft.

Some pilots who've been at it awhile may figure that lots of flight time and previous experience make them immune to the need to study each particular airplane.

That is asking for trouble if you transition from, say, a Piper Lance to a Cessna Centurion or a Beech 36 Bonanza and treat the electric fuel pump the same in the Cessna or Beech as you did in the Piper.

The Piper's Lycoming engine, with Bendix fuel injection, can handle the operation of the electric pump while the engine-driven pump is also working. But, with the Continental injection system, full high-pressure operation of the electric pump can "flood out" the engine in normal operation.

That example is just one of the many "funnies" which can get a pilot into trouble when he or she tackles an unfamiliar airplane without taking the time for a careful reading of the flight manual.

Funnies abound in fuel tank and fuel selector operation, electrical system operation, hydraulic systems and, especially, emergency landing gear extension. You just have to read that flight manual and memorize some of the most critical procedures.

Often, while giving biennial reviews or refresher training, I find airplane *owners* who haven't read their flight manuals for years. It soon becomes obvious that they have forgotten or, maybe, never really learned some important information that's provided in the manual.

So, even if it's your own airplane, the only airplane you ever fly, and you fly it 50 or 100 hours per year, there's still something to learn or remember through occasional re-readings of the flight manual.

Hapless Harv

I remember "Harv," who had been flying a big turboprop twin for almost three years when he asked me for a "refresher." That he certainly needed it became evident when he started the engines.

He violated the flight manual procedures several times. First, he turned off the starter motor too soon while cranking one engine (and ran the risk of an rpm "hang-up" and "over-temp"). Then, he engaged the generator without advancing the power lever, as required, to well-above idle rpm (risking overloading the idling engine with a big battery re-charge load and getting another over-temp).

Harv hadn't read the flight manual since his initial checkout at the factory, and he had *not* memorized the standard start procedures. The *only* checklist he ever used was the "before takeoff" list.

We changed our plans about flying after that engine start and spent the next two hours in a review of the AFM.

Especially if you fly turbine equipment, you *must* memorize the starting procedure *completely*. Things happen too fast to rely on a step-by-step reading of the procedures *during* the start.

Even if your airplane has a piston engine, you've got to know the engine start procedure *cold*.

Speaking of cold, does your AFM prescribe different procedures for the first start of the day versus a warm-engine start? Or warm-day versus winter starts? Better read that part of the flight manual.

A long time ago, I got to fly a variety of military airplanes (mostly USN and USAF jet fighters, but also Beech 18s, Grumman S-2 anti-submarine patrol planes and other "oldies"). Usually, if the airplane was still in active squadron service, there was a dedicated ground school available and required before first flight.

But, once the airplane was beyond active duty as a warplane and into a proficiency flying role, the primary ground school consisted only of a study of the flight manual, followed by a short written exam and flight check.

I got pretty good at "learning" an airplane from a day's worth of flight manual reading, followed by *my own* cockpit ground training time, comparing the "book" to the instrument panel and controls.

Later, while ferrying GA airplanes overseas, I frequently had to do the same kind of self-training.

Self-Checkout

There's a wealth of knowledge in most flight manuals—information you *need* to know if you're going to be flying the airplanes.

Although it's not the *best* way to get a checkout, you *can* learn the airplane pretty well by just reading the good book and putting in several hours of cockpit and outside walk-around time.

Here are some suggestions for a self-checkout:

Start with general information (Section 1 in GAMA-format manuals). Then, study Section 7 (systems descriptions). Then, read Section 4 (normal procedures) and compare this to what you have learned from Section 7.

Also, read the engine limits in Section 2 and compare these to both Sections 7 and 4.

Then, read the remaining sections and study the information in Section 9 (supplements) on any modifications or optional equipment installed in the airplane. If the airplane has an autopilot, essential information on that autopilot (including operating limitations) will be in the supplements. This is information you really need to know.

If you have any questions about the airplane's systems after studying the manual, schedule some "ground" time with a qualified instructor. Also, read the maintenance or service manual. Even many of the more modern flight manuals are a little skimpy on systems descriptions, and you may need the expanded explanations in the mechanics' manuals.

Most FBOs will let you use the microfiche files in their maintenance shops and, maybe, charge you only for any paper copies that you make. Some shops even maintain a hard-copy file of maintenance publications.

Manual Run-Through

Let's leaf through a 1981 "information manual" for a Cessna P210N (pressurized Centurion) that I have on hand.

The first page states that this book was an exact duplicate of the official POH and FAA-approved AFM when issued. But, it cannot be used as an official replacement for the airplane's "real" AFM because it has a soft cover and isn't kept current with revisions from the factory.

So, during a real "self-checkout," use the approved manual, so that you'll be sure to know the revisions and the supplements that apply to the particular airplane you'll be flying.

For our run-through of the P210N information manual, we'll hit some highlights in chronological order, *not* in the recommended order of studying a new flight manual.

Section 1 ("General") takes only a few minutes to read, but there are a few items of note, such as:

• The Continental TSIO-520-P engine has a five-minute takeoff rating of 310 horsepower at 36.5 inches MAP and 2,700 rpm. MCP (max continuous power) is only 285 hp, at 35.5 inches MAP and 2,600 rpm.

This little bit of advance knowledge will help explain the engine instrument markings given later in Section 2 and those small MAP and tachometer yellow arcs you'll see when you climb into the cockpit.

• Minimum fuel grades of 100LL or 100/130 are also stated, along with the maximum percentage of fuel deicing additive allowed.

There's still a lot of look-alike airplanes out there (usually normally aspirated) that are powered by different engines—some that can use 80/87 fuel, others with higher-compression that can use only 100-octane fuel. And, many airplanes do *not* have decals by their fuel filler caps.

• Fuel capacities of each tank and total usable fuel is need-to-know information. But, also check Section 9 ("Supplements") to see if any "add-on" aux fuel tanks have been installed. If so, read the procedures for using the extra gas.

• Engine oil type and grade are stated in Section 1 and in Section 8 ("Airplane Handling, Service and Maintenance"). Of particular note, ashless-dispersant (AD) oil *must* be used after the first 50 hours of engine-operating time.

• The last four pages of this section are a dictionary of "symbols, abbreviations and terminology." Sure, you probably know the difference between KIAS and KTAS, and Vno vs. Vne. But, if you should run across an unfamiliar term while studying the manual, this "dictionary" might come in handy.

Know the Limits

Section 2 ("Limitations") is of paramount interest to the FAA and contains some of the most important information for pilots.

For the P210N, limits are given for Vne, Vno, Va, Vfe, Vlo and Vle, and the values are stated both in KCAS and KIAS. There also is a table of airspeed indicator markings—the "arcs" and the "redline." For this airplane, the markings are in KIAS (knots, indicated airspeed).

Remember, some of the older planes have limits *and* airspeed indicator markings expressed as CAS (calibrated airspeed). For example, my

1972 Piper Chieftain pilot operating manual and 1966 Cessna Skyhawk owner's manual provide CAS limits.

It's worthwhile in such cases to refer to Section 5 (performance) and check the calibrated stall and Vne airspeeds vs. the airspeed (position error) correction chart or graph.

Your cockpit airspeed indicator needle is showing *indicated* airspeed, and you really should know how this correlates with the stated stall and max-limit CAS values.

Other need-to-know information from Section 2 includes:

1. Engine limits and powerplant instrument markings.

2. Weight and c.g. limits. Very important stuff; but, you'll spend more time with this subject later when you get to Section 6 (weight and balance). You'll need to do some careful calculations based on the data provided in the *approved* flight manual for the airplane you are going to fly.

It's sometimes difficult to determine the latest "empty" or "basic empty" weight for a particular airplane. There may be a ream of Form 337s (and, hopefully, revisions in Section 6, itself) to account for equipment changes and modifications.

So, a little time may have to be spent checking the dates on the 337s to come up with the "current" one.

For an airplane such as a Cessna 150/152 or 172, Beech Musketeer or Piper Cherokee 140, certified in both the Normal and Utility categories, Section 2 will state the tighter limits for Utility operation, as well as the "maneuver" limits for both categories.

Especially if spins are allowed in Utility category configuration, check those weight and c.g. limits closely.

Ops Limitations

It's also important to check the operations limits.

The P210N manual indicates that the airplane comes with standard equipment suitable for "day VFR" operation and "may be equipped for night VFR and/or IFR operations." The manual refers to the minimum equipment standards in FAR 91, which should be checked against the particular airplane's equipment list (Section 6).

Maybe you noticed that the airplane you intend to fly has a "hot prop" and "heated windshield," maybe even wing and tail boots. So, it's OK to launch into known icing conditions, right? Maybe (probably) not.

The P210N manual states quite clearly that "flight into known icing conditions is prohibited" *unless* the airplane is suitably equipped. Better go to Section 9 and look for the "Known Icing Supplement," and then check the equipment list to ensure that *all* of these items are installed.

Just boots, hot prop and hot windshield do not a known-icing airplane maketh. In the case of a 1981 P210N, you also need a 95-amp alternator, static discharge wicks, ice detector light and high-capacity, heated stall warning vane and pitot tube.

Sure, FAR 91.527 on "Operating in Icing Conditions" doesn't apply to single-engine airplanes and small, non-turbine twins (see "Legal Matters," Jan. 1), but FAR 91.9 certainly does. It requires you to abide by the operating limitations published in the AFM and/or by markings or placards in the airplane.

You can tempt fate by flying in ice all winter long without all the needed equipment, but should you be involved in an ice-related emergency, incident or accident, you will be facing FAA for probably at least a "609 check ride."

Also of interest in Section 2 for those with a turbocharged and/or pressurized airplane is the maximum operating altitude limit. For the P210N, it's 23,000 feet. Sure, the airplane probably can climb much higher (other turbocharged and pressurized Centurions *are* certified to higher max altitudes); but, in the P210N, it would be violating the rules (91.9, again) to do so.

There just might be a valid reason for the limitation, such as a potential fuel system problem. "Yours is not to question why."

Digging for Gold

The P210N manual has a rather nebulous subsection in "Limitations" on the use of an EGT gauge for engine leaning at various power settings, altitudes and OATs.

Better make a note to *carefully* check the information on leaning in Section 4 ("Normal Procedures") and Section 5 ("Performance"). You could burn up your engine if you get this one wrong.

Unfortunately, you'll have to do lot of "digging" to find those little notes. For instance, under the chart of cruise performance data at 22,000 feet, there's a note that states, "Use of an EGT indicator to set mixture is prohibited for power settings above 65 percent when OAT is above standard." Another note states, "Recommended lean mixture ... to set mixture using an EGT indicator, refer to Section 4."

Note that we've learned a lot about a P210N just by perusing Section 2. The leaning limits forced us to a cross-check with Sections 4 and 5. We discovered that we can't just leisurely lean to peak EGT, or a little richer than peak, like we do in "Old Bessie." We had to refer to other parts of the flight manual.

Before we leave Section 2, let's look at the placards (which usually are much easier to read in the manual than in the airplane—*any* airplane). There's one stating minimum fuel flow and maximum manifold pressure at max continuous power at various altitudes. Some other airplanes have a rather confusing set of blue or green arcs on the fuel flow / fuel pressure gauge to denote desired values.

We've covered a lot of ground already, but we're only through the first 22 pages of the P210N flight manual. And, we did hit on some rather important "funnies" of this particular Cessna.

Best to know about these items *before* you fly, not *after* you have done some damage to the engine, airplane, innocents aboard or on the ground, or the FAA's "bible" of regulations.

On Your Own

By now, hopefully, the point has been made that there *is* a lot of critical, need-to-know information in your flight manual. So, we'll close the P210N manual and spare you a run-through of Sections 3, 4, 5, 6, 7 and 8.

One suggestion for doing your own self-checkout, though: When you have finished with each individual abbreviated checklist of emergency and normal procedures (Sections 3 and 4), leaf back a few pages to the associated "amplified procedure," as given in the GAMA-style manuals.

This may even lead you into further perusal of systems descriptions, including cockpit switches and instrument panel layout (Section 7).

If the airplane is available, a lot of this reading is best done *in the cockpit*, where you can search for the control, switch, lever or gauge mentioned in the flight manual.

By the time you are ready to fly a "new" airplane, you really should know where every control and gauge is located. Better look over the circuit breaker panel(s), also, and know where the "essential" breakers are located.

I remember an investigation that I worked on several years ago. It involved an unreported in-flight "incident" that, fortunately, just scared the owner of the big turboprop and his two pilots.

Apparently, there was frozen water in the tail cone that was impeding elevator control cable travel while operating "on autopilot" at high altitude. The airplane got into a mild "porpoise," and the pilot tried an improper means of disconnecting the autopilot. As a result, the autopilot didn't let go of the controls.

For several minutes, both pilots "fought" their control wheels while searching for the autopilot and electric trim circuit breakers. The pilots' control wheel inputs only aggravated the porpoising by running the elevator trim, since the autopilot hadn't really been disconnected.

Finally, after several minutes, the copilot found the appropriate circuit breakers and disconnected the autopilot. The porpoising stopped, but manual elevator control remained stiff. At lower altitude, the ice apparently melted, and all controls were normal.

Plugged Drains

Next morning, several tail cone drain holes were found blocked. When they were cleared, much dirty water drained onto the hangar floor.

Airplane/maintenance problem? Yes. Pilot problem. Double yes. Neither of the "pro" corporate pilots knew that the control cables ran under the cabin floor and were only about two inches above the tail cone belly skin where they passed through pressure seals.

They didn't know that there were large drain holes in the tail cone that exited into the ventral fin, and that the additional ventral drain holes were supposed to be checked to ensure that they were "unobstructed" before flying.

With a plugged ventral drain, lots of water can accumulate at the forward end of the tail cone, immerse the control cables and freeze at altitude.

Mechanic foul-up, you say? Well, maybe, if the drains were plugged at the last 100-hour check and the mechanic failed to notice. Even if so, a preflight checklist for this airplane (and many others) requires the pilot to check that the drain holes are open.

In addition, neither pilot had read the autopilot supplement in Section 9 of the GAMA-style AFM. They didn't know the proper procedures for coping with an autopilot or electric trim "runaway." They didn't know that their autopilot *required* a preflight ground check; they had never performed one!

More basic, neither pilot knew that autopilot procedures were *not* covered under Section 4 (normal procedures) and that they would have to refer to the applicable supplement in Section 9.

That's typical of almost all airplanes. Optional or "after-market" equipment almost always has its own supplement, and you *won't* find the procedures and limitations for this equipment in Sections 2 and 4.

Neither pilot had any idea where the autopilot or electric trim circuit breakers were located. This airplane had several breaker panels, and the pilots spent several valuable minutes searching for the applicable little black buttons. All the while, the airplane was "porpoising" severely enough to scare the heck out of the owner, who was riding in a back seat.

As I've noted previously, another "professional" crew (as well as 15 other line pilots interviewed) did *not* know about an important revision concerning icing that had recently been inserted in the AFMs of the airplanes they flew.

Result: a hard crash-landing following a probable stall of the horizontal tail after it picked up light icing. In this particular case, the boot system had been placarded "inop due to a puncture in the left wing boot"; so, the crew didn't even try boot inflation when they picked up a little ice during the ILS approach.

Had the pilots been a little more familiar with their AFM and the associated training manual, they would have learned, via the diagram of the pneumatic boot system, that the tail boots are independent and *would* have operated normally.

Yes, there's good stuff in that flight manual. Stuff that can save your life. Better read that manual thoroughly. And, even if it's for "Old Bessie" or "Little Betsy," how about re-reading the good book again, at least once per year?

Before the Flight

*I*t's a little ritual we all do (or, rather, those of us who want to live a long time do): the preflight inspection. It's easy to let the preflight go; you may have flown earlier that day, or the weather might be terribly cold and/or wet, and you'll get your suit dirty.

But the preflight is a simple and direct way to increase the safety of your operations. You won't find any problems if you don't look, but that won't make them go away.

This chapter was written by Clint Lowe, an A&P and Skyhawk driver.

The Best Preflight

You had to know Jerry to understand our grins anytime he showed up to fly. Always in a hurry, he'd fairly race around his airplane, throwing off the tie-downs, and then jump in and fire up.

Once, he didn't realize he had left the tail tied down until a lot of throttle failed to get his airplane going. Another time, he left the rudder gust lock in place and, after seeing several people on the ramp waving and pointing, had to stop his takeoff roll to remove it.

No doubt, Jerry's antics were an extreme example of how *not* to perform a preflight. But, all of us have forgotten to do something during a preflight inspection that we're not proud of.

As with anything in aviation, the benefits derived from your preflight depend greatly on your attitude. If you look at the preflight as an opportunity to discover potential problems (even if not of immediate concern), you'll be well ahead of the individual who pulls ropes, checks the oil and blasts off.

A properly conducted preflight increases your confidence in your aircraft and provides timely warning of items that will soon be in need of maintenance. My experience has shown that thorough preflights work and that they provide the bonus of avoiding some costly repairs later.

To gain the most benefit from your preflight, the recommendations in your owner's manual should be thought of as *minimum requirements* and as a guide to an orderly method of reaching all the critical areas of the aircraft.

Inserting photocopies of the preflight checklists from the manual— or, better yet, the homemade checklists you have developed from the manual—into a plastic sleeve you can use as a carry-along guide will eliminate the need for toting around the entire owner's manual and trying to open or protect pages on a windy or rainy day.

Along with your checklist, you should have available a phillips-head and a flat-tip screwdriver, fuel sampling cup, flashlight, tire pressure gauge and a rag (for pilots of high-wing airplanes, a short ladder is helpful, too).

With our checklist and tools ready, let's begin our preflight with one caveat: If anything suggested hereafter is contrary to what is recommended by your aircraft manufacturer, *follow the manufacturer's recommendations*.

Starting in the cockpit, the first thing to check is the fuel gauges. Verify their accuracy by looking into the tanks.

If you have electric flaps, extend them for inspection. Then, make sure the master switch and ignition switch are off; you may have to turn the propeller later in the preflight, and you don't want any accidents. Before leaving the cockpit, check that your fuel selector is "on," so any water collected at the valve will get to the sump drain.

Empennage Examination

Next, the tail. While moving to the rear of the airplane, take a quick look at your antennas and fuselage for any signs of bird-strikes (I once found my VOR antenna bent from a sparrow strike), missing inspection plates or attachment screws/bolts, and signs of vandalism (my father once found two .22-caliber bullet holes in the vertical stabilizer of his Cessna 180).

Check each hinge point on the tail to ensure proper attachment. This may require using the flashlight to see them adequately. If a bolt holds any particular hinge point, check that the nut is in place and won't back off. The nut should be of the self-locking variety or have a cotter pin locking a castellated nut in place. If it is a piano hinge, ensure that the hinge pin has not backed out.

At each hinge point, move the control surface up and down through its full travel and watch for any binding or chafing of the hinge mechanism. Check for secure attachment of the control rods and cables to the rudder and elevator bellcranks, and look for any sign of chafing or deterioration.

Move the surfaces again while watching these attachment points to ensure that they aren't binding, and listen to your rudder and elevator systems carefully for any unusual noises. About the only noise you should hear will be that of the control wheel moving in the cockpit. Any grating, scratching, screeching, etc., should be investigated.

Look at the trim tab hinge and actuator rod to ensure good security. Move the elevator full-deflection in both directions; the trim tab should move in proper relation to the elevator.

While undoing the tie-down rope, look at the underside of the tail surfaces and rear fuselage to ensure that you aren't missing any inspection plates and to check for damage from objects thrown up from the ground.

If the airplane has tricycle gear and has been exposed to rain, carefully push the tail completely to the ground (find out where to push, and get help, if needed) and listen for water movement. Frequently, drain holes don't work; they become plugged, and water gets caught in low spots. Lowering the tail allows the trapped water to move to areas where it will drain away. (I've seen as much as two gallons of water drain from the tail of a Cessna 150 after several days of sitting on a ramp in a slow rainfall.)

Wing Check Points

Moving from the tail group, take a quick look across the aircraft from wing tip to wing tip for ice and frost in winter, and unusual distortions or bending year-round.

If you pass a strobe light or antenna on the bottom of the fuselage along the way, take a look at its condition. These bottom-mounted accessories take considerable punishment from thrown rocks and moisture.

At the right wing, check your flap-extension rod and flap guide rails or hinges for security, as done at the tail. (Helpful hint: Have your mechanic put a torque seal on the jam nuts of your control surface adjustment points. This material cracks and breaks at the slightest turn of the jam nut, telling you the locking feature has been tampered with and should be checked.)

On aircraft with guide rails (like most Cessnas), check the rollers to make sure they are turning and not developing any flat spots. Better to get the rollers replaced than to have to replace all the other things they were designed to protect.

Also, on Cessnas, check for wear on the top of the flap, where it meets the wing. On most models, little plastic wear "buttons" are attached to the top of the flap, where it meets the wing, to prevent metal-to-metal contact. If they're missing or worn out, get new ones. They're cheap compared to a complete skin.

Moving to the aileron, look carefully at the hinges and move the ailerons through their complete travel. Check to ensure the hinge pins aren't backing out and that the hinge bolts aren't loosening up. Listen to the aileron system for unusual noises while doing this. Check the actuation rod for security at the aileron while making sure the jam nut is tight (again, a torque seal is helpful here). Check any trim tabs for security and proper operation in relation to the surface.

Check the wing tip for security and that any vent holes aren't plugged. See if the nav light assembly is in good repair and that the screws holding it in place haven't backed out.

Moving along the leading edge, check for dings caused by birds, hangars or fuel trucks. Stop somewhere en route to the fuselage—perhaps, while disconnecting the tie-down rope—and scan the entire bottom surface of the wing, paying particular attention to inspection plates, screws and fairings.

If your cabin vent system source is at the leading edge, check the openings for nests (bugs or birds) and, if transitioning from winter to summer operations, that the tape is removed.

On a high-wing airplane, take a look at the strut to make sure some 300-pounder didn't place all his weight on it at mid-point and buckle it.

If refueling is complete and several minutes have elapsed to allow the water to settle, now is the time to drain the fuel sumps. Use the fuel sample cup, paying attention for water, contamination and proper fuel color.

Wheels, Brakes and Tires

On low-wing aircraft, check not only for tire inflation pressure, but that the scissors are secure and the oleos are properly inflated. Any leakage of oil or low inflation of the struts should be serviced promptly. On all aircraft, tires should be checked *with a gauge* once every week or so (proper pressures are in the owner's manual).

Check behind the tire, on the brake assembly, for evidence of leakage of brake fluid. Check gear actuation mechanisms for evidence of binding and hydraulic leaks.

On aircraft with wheel fairings, grab the fairing at front and rear and gently attempt to rotate it both ways around the axle. It shouldn't move at all. Look behind the fairing to determine if any attachment screws are backing out.

Only because you're already down there, take a look over the forward portion of the belly for excessive oil (as in *leaks*). And, while you're at it, wipe off the little transponder antenna with your rag. Without a doubt, one of the biggest contributors to poor transponder performance is a dirty antenna.

Front-End Features

Approaching the engine cowling, take a look at all of the fasteners to determine that they are still there. Now, grab the lip of the cooling inlet holes—or some other convenient spot—and shake the cowling to determine if it feels firm (desirable), rather than loose (undesirable).

Grab the spinner and give it a quick shake to see if anything is letting loose or developing cracks. This is especially important for spinners on variable-pitch props.

Look at the air filter to see if it isn't excessively dirty from that last trip to so-and-so's oh-so-dusty airstrip.

Look just behind the cowling at the static ports for cleanliness (one or both sides of the plane). Though a little small for most bugs, the ports can get plugged by wax and dirt and cause some bad errors in your static-system gauges. If they're up front, the landing lights also should be checked.

On to the propeller. Check each blade for nicks, dents, bends, etc. *Any* nicks and dents can develop into cracks, so get them tended to as soon as practical. Your prop should be smooth to the touch; anything else is unacceptable. If you don't want to be constantly "blending" your prop blades (that is, filing out the nicks and pits), take more care in where and how you operate your prop.

On variable-pitch propellers, check the hub area for evidence of oil leakage. *Any* leakage is too much and means the prop should be looked at. Attempt to twist the prop at the tip and shake it fore-and-aft. Any looseness should be brought to a mechanic's attention.

Moving on down, look at the nose gear for proper inflation of the tire and oleo. As with the mains, check the nose tire pressure once a week. Check the security of the rudder pedal linkages, making sure the bolts are secured. Check the shimmy dampener for security and look for any oil seeping from the seals housing the piston assembly.

On retractable-gear airplanes, check the gear door linkages, retraction mechanisms and other items for cracks, binding and security. Look over the hydraulic lines for leaks.

While you're here, pull your fuel sample cup and take some fuel from the engine sump drain. Again, check for water, sediment and proper fuel grade. Quickly look at the little open lines extending from behind the cowling (crankcase breather line, battery overboard vent, etc.) to see they aren't half-clogged shut from dirt. If you have them, the cowl flap linkages should be checked to see that they are secure (you may need the flashlight).

Look up your exhaust pipe(s) to see how the engine is burning. They should be a powder tan or gray. If there is more than one pipe, they should look alike inside. On turbocharged aircraft, check for imminent turbo failure by looking for oil spots in this area.

Under the Cowling

No doubt, the older aircraft have the best preflight-friendly engine cowlings. By merely looking through a cowl ring or popping a couple of quick-release fasteners, the entire engine opens up to you.

Newer aircraft, though, frequently offer only a 12-inch by 12-inch opening through which to examine things. Considering the restriction, a little flashlight will help you see a lot.

Open the access panel(s), pull the dipstick and check the oil level as detailed on the checklist. If you haven't run the aircraft or moved it in the past hour or so, you should get a true reading of what the oil level is. However, if your line personnel just bumped it out to the flight line for you, or if it was parked on an uphill slope until just a minute ago, wipe the dipstick off, replace it and pull it again to get a true reading.

Check and *double*-check the dipstick or filler cap for security. They are often forgotten or poorly replaced and then lost. Don't rely on the full-service FBO personnel to get it right. (We left a cap on the taxiway many years ago after a young line guy put a quart of oil in our Cessna 337.) If you need a quart, leave the door open as a reminder; but, then, before closing the door, reach in and check all that stuff again.

Besides oil, pull out the flashlight and take a look around the visible portions of your engine. Look at the battery box for security of the lid and make sure the leads have grommets around them at the box. Check any viewable fuel, oil and electrical lines for contact with hot or sharp objects that may chafe or burn them.

Check for obvious looseness of nearby fasteners. Look for leaks on valve covers and accessories on the back of the engine, and at connections of fuel and oil fittings. If you have a turbocharger, look for hot-gas leaks which, especially around the flange areas, will show up as black, sooty material. Look for bird nests above the cylinders and for tools left behind during the last inspection or maintenance (they are yours to keep).

When everything has been looked over, oiled up and rechecked, make real sure the door is closed properly (as a student, my instructor pointed out my mistake when we cranked and the 150's door started waving bye-bye to all the other planes) and that *it* is attached to the cowling securely.

On the Other Side

Essentially, the left wing and left main gear are a mirror image of the right, except that the fuel vents and pitot tubes are usually on this side.

So, remove or open the pitot tube cover (*What? You don't have a pitot tube cover?*) and station an observer, if one is available, to read the airspeed indicator while you blow *gently* into the pitot. Just blow *at* it; don't wrap your mouth around it. The observer should report a small deflection.

Bidding the observer adieu, take the flashlight and check for obstructions in the tube. (Remember, pitot tube covers aren't foolproof. A determined little bee once managed to get past my loosely installed cover and make a wax plug that required me to take apart the entire tube assembly. Another time, during a fuel stop in Flagstaff, Ariz., a small wasp managed to crawl into the pitot tube and caused bad airspeed readings for the two hours it took to get home. A very dazed and out-of-breath wasp emerged at the home aerodrome on shut-down.)

Since most fuel systems have only one vent, it should be checked carefully for stoppage. A clogged fuel vent can cause the engine to be starved for fuel at the time when you most need the power. Near the fuel vent is usually the stall horn sensor. Though they vary in operation, you can check them by either blowing across them a certain way (consult your flight instructor for details here), or you can push gently on the switch-style sensors, with the master switch on, and listen for the horn.

If the landing lights are located in the wing, check the lenses for cleanliness. One last thing to do before mounting up: Grab a wing tip (where you won't squish something) and give a couple of good, solid shakes to the airframe. Other than some squeaks, the airframe should respond solidly, with no mushiness and no "looseness." Here, we're checking for solid attachment and health of the spar (especially important in wooden-wing planes) and for any items (such as tools and parts) laying loosely in the airframe.

If you'll be flying at night, check all of your lights, paying particular attention to the landing lights. Cowl-mounted landing lights are especially important to check, since the engine vibration is hard on them and their wires get disconnected and reconnected every time the cowling comes off.

Easier Done Than Said

Everything discussed in this article I do on a daily basis. As pointed out in various places, I've found problems while performing these checks, and I've found problems when it *didn't* perform the checks.

Regardless, the procedure is really very simple, and my preflight takes from 10 to 15 minutes—about twice what I see most other pilots take.

With practice, you'll get comfortable with the procedure, and it will become normal to wipe off the transponder antenna and check the exhaust pipes. It will also become normal to never second-guess your aircraft's airworthiness.

When I occasionally rent an airplane, I find greater confidence with these procedures, because I haven't placed all of my faith in an unknown mechanic or previous renters who may have been too much in a hurry to report a problem—or, maybe, didn't *want* to report it.

Now, back to Jerry. Some time after I first saw his antics at the airport, he came up to me and asked if I knew where he might locate a prop, cheap, for his 172. The airplane was sitting in Chicago, and he needed to get it back home. It seems that in his haste to get out of the airplane, he had left on the master switch and run down his battery. Then, instead of taking the time to get the battery charged, he had decided to hand-prop the plane. But, he didn't check for chocks or tie-downs, or even set the brakes. When the Lycoming came to life, the airplane rolled into the gas pumps.

Jerry's quite an inspiration.

After the Flight

*A*nyone who's been involved in the ownership and maintenance of an airplane knows that the best, safest, and (in the long run) least expensive way to keep flying is to catch problems before they become critical. Like the oil filter commercial says, "You can pay me now...or pay me later."

After a flight, many pilots simply taxi to the parking spot, secure the airplane and walk away. They're missing a good opportunity to check on the health of their airplane.

Postflight Checks

You've been waiting for this vacation for months. The rising sun shines brightly as you pull your bird from the hangar and start your preflight. You couldn't have asked for a better day for your flight. You cheerfully work your way down the preflight checklist, mentally ticking off each item as you systematically walk around your pride-and-joy.

Your fingertips glide over the propeller and you make a mental note to get that little pit tended to at the next oil change. Then it happens. You're practically past the prop and on to the next item when you realize that you felt something that wasn't quite right. And it wasn't just a small pit. It was a big nick. Worse, it has a crack starting from it. Well, there goes your nice day. What a way to start your vacation.

The sad thing is, your day didn't have to be ruined. That nick didn't just suddenly appear since the last time you flew. Like so many other problems, big and small, that we find on our preflight inspection, it was there when you walked away from the airplane after the last flight. If you had caught the problem then, you could have had it taken care of already.

From a practical standpoint, it makes a lot of sense to do a thorough postflight inspection. There are good reasons the military and airlines require such inspections. The benefits are obvious.

From the standpoint of safety, the most obvious benefit is that there won't be the pressure to launch despite something found on the preflight that may be marginal. The outright broken or damaged stuff shouldn't be a problem. Hopefully, we all have the sense not to fly when we find something that's really bad.

It's the judgment calls that can be a problem: the ever-so-slightly weeping hydraulic fluid; the low but not nearly collapsed strut; the tight but not quite frozen control bearing.

These are the potentially dangerous sort of discrepancies that we may convince ourselves to put off attending to until after we return from the trip. But if these types of discrepancies can be found on a postflight inspection, there's a lot more time to have them taken care of and less of a risk of making a potentially poor decision due to pressure to get going.

Save Time and Money

No matter what problem you may find on a postflight inspection, you will have more time to get it taken care of properly.

You also can use the time to find the right shop and, maybe, save yourself some big bucks. Rushing around to get something repaired so you can take off ASAP doesn't lend itself to arranging for the best work at the best price. Even if you find that there isn't enough time to have the problem fixed before your next flight, you'll have lots more time to prepare an alternative.

If you fly frequently as the sole pilot and keep your plane in a secure hangar, then you can save time on your next preflight. Some of what you normally check on preflight will need little or no attention since it will not have changed since you postflighted the aircraft. This doesn't mean you can skip your preflight, only that it can be a little quicker, if you want.

As a rental or club pilot, or as a partner in an aircraft, it's in your best interest to ensure the aircraft is in flying condition for the next pilot. After all, wouldn't you want that pilot to do the same for you? Some clubs and partnerships require a postflight.

So, now that you may be convinced that a postflight inspection is a good idea, let's examine what we should be looking for.

Pre-Shutdown Checks

The following checks should be performed before shutting off the engine:

First, as you taxi in, check your gauges. Is idle rpm correct? (Have you checked the accuracy of your tach lately? Mechanical tachs are notoriously inaccurate.)

Are cylinder head and oil temperatures dropping as you would expect? Does the oil pressure gauge register above minimum at idle?

Check that the vacuum (suction) gauge is in the green at the appropriate rpm. Be aware of vacuum instruments that don't stay erect while taxiing in. Any aberrations should be checked.

Then, when the aircraft is stopped, check for proper magneto grounding. Switch off all electrical equipment and reduce throttle to idle, taking note of the rpm. Switch both mags off momentarily and check whether rpms drop rapidly and that the engine stops firing.

If the engine continues to run while the switch is off, have a mechanic check for a hot magneto.

Check that your idle mixture is set properly. If leaning the mixture slightly from full rich at idle or low rpm causes a slight rise in rpm, then it's probably set correctly.

If engine speed rises 100 rpm or more, there's a good chance that the idle mixture adjustment is over-rich. If there is no change in rpm, or if the rpm drops when you lean it out, then it's possible the mixture is set too lean or that there are other problems affecting the fuel/air ratio, such as manifold or vacuum leaks.

If you fly a turbocharged aircraft, be sure to allow sufficient time for the turbo to cool down before you shut off the engine (and stop the flow of oil to the turbo bearings). Check your manual for the manufacturer's recommendations.

Don't "goose" the engine and then shut it down. Contrary to popular myth, studies have shown that this does not help increase lubrication of bearings above levels normally found at idle and it may actually promote additional wear as well as fuel fouling. Turbos are particularly sensitive in this regard. If the engine doesn't quit smoothly when you move the mixture to idle/cut-off, there may be problems requiring the attention of a mechanic.

Finally, there are two non-mechanical items that should be on any pre-shutdown checklist. First, cancel your flight plan if you haven't already. Then, tune a comm radio to 121.5 MHz and make sure your ELT hasn't been activated. You'll be doing a lot of people a big favor.

Saving the Sparks

According to Larry Peth, owner of Spirit Aviation in Tucson, you now have the opportunity to prevent the most common problem found during preflight inspections: a battery depleted of charge by a master switch left on.

One way to help prevent this is to use a written checklist. But let's face it, most pilots are not likely to do so. A good alternative is to borrow a trick that many charter pilots use to keep from embarrassing themselves. Instead of turning off the rotating beacon with the rest of the electrical items, leave it on as you shut down the engine. If you fail to turn off the master switch, the flashing beacon will remind you.

Now that you've shut down and taken care of that pesky master switch, it's time to do a walk-around. Essentially, you need to look at the same sort of things you would on your preflight. The difference is that some problems will be more obvious now.

The first area I check is the engine. The smell of burning oil always provides a hint of something amiss. Take a look underneath for oil on the belly of the fuselage or beneath the wings. It may be more than that same old persistent weep. It could be that the weep is getting more serious or that a significant leak is developing. Obvious oil leaks are sometimes easier to trace when they are fresh, and the trail of fresh oil is easy to distinguish from older oil deposits covered with dust and dirt. These leaks may clear up and virtually disappear once the engine cools down, the metal contracts and the oil thickens.

A word to the wise: Clean engines make problems easier to find. Another suggestion is to wipe off any oil from a non-serious leak found on the belly so that its presence won't disguise a bigger leak that may develop later on.

Look for Leaks

The smell of fuel or an obvious fuel leak point to potential problems that may not be as obvious later when the fuel evaporates and the lines depressurize.

Again, it's a good idea to wipe off any stains you find once you have assessed the problem.

A leaking propeller seal will deposit fresh oil near the hub. Be sure to check the back side of the prop. Prop nicks should be attended to immediately.

Check belts and electrical leads for tightness and condition. An acrid smell or wisps of smoke coming from the area of the generator or alternator can signal wiring or bearing problems.

Next, check your fluids. Any losses of hydraulic or brake fluids can point to areas that may require more intense scrutiny. Any excess oil consumption should also raise a warning flag. It's worth taking a look at fuel levels, too. Not only does it allow you to better evaluate the accuracy of your gauges and calculations, it also can disclose leaking lines or vent problems that might be forcing fuel overboard.

If you've been through wet weather, a check of the sumps might point out fuel cap seal problems that need attending to.

On to the undercarriage. You should look for the usual sorts of things: leaking hydraulic or brake fluid; broken pieces; cracks in the gear; seized rod end bearings; chafed lines; and damaged electrical switches or lines.

Low struts are easier to find after you've unloaded the aircraft. A slightly deflated tire could portend a problem. Have it inflated and check the valve for leakage. If the valve is OK, make sure to check the tire later, preferably *before* your next preflight. If it's lost a significant amount of air, it's time to have the leak repaired (or the tire replaced).

Don't forget to check the tire tread—not just for wear or flat spots, but also for cuts and embedded foreign objects.

Control Checks

Next, it's on to the airframe. The control surfaces should be checked for freedom of movement and the hinges and bearings examined for either too much play or for having frozen up.

A rod end bearing that doesn't freely move in all axes means that the rod, the pin or bolt, and the attachment point are all being subjected to loads they aren't designed to handle.

You can see but a small portion of all the bits and pieces that hold the aircraft together. But, at least you can make sure that these bits and pieces are in good shape. Hinge pins and bolts have been known to fail and come out. Is there a wire showing at both ends of the piano hinges? Are there nuts still attached to all the bolts? Are there cotter pins still in place on all the castellated nuts?

Check the limit stops to ensure that they are doing their jobs. If the control surface doesn't reach the stop, it may indicate a problem elsewhere.

Obviously, you will want to check for any damage to leading edges and fuselage and wing panels. Cracked plastic and fiberglass fairings and wing tips are common problems. And don't forget to look for loose rivets. These items bear particular attention if you've experienced bad weather or significant turbulence on the flight.

Carefully examine the antennas. Make sure they're all still there. Check that each is still firmly attached and that there are no obvious broken pieces. The belly antennas are particularly susceptible to damage if you fly out of rough strips.

Finally, is the aircraft subject to any recurring airworthiness directives or service bulletins that you can check without too much trouble? We cannot expect that failures or incipient failures are only going to show up conveniently at the 100-hour or annual inspection. If you can check it yourself, it's a good idea to keep an eye on these things between inspections.

So, have a safe flight and leave yourself a few minutes afterward to postflight the aircraft. In the long run, you might save yourself a good deal of time, aggravation and, most importantly, the pressure to make a poor go/no-go decision later on.

Maintenance

A subject near and dear to our pocketbooks, maintenance is absolutely vital to the ongoing safety of flight in IFR conditions. Shortcomings you could get away with in a puddle-jumper can be life-threatening hazards in an IFR-capable airplane.

But, who's really responsible for the airworthiness of the airplane? The owner? The pilot? The mechanic who may well be the only one to actually lay eyes on parts of the airplane?

Here, corporate pilot Brian Jacobson makes the case for the buck stopping with you, the pilot.

Taking Charge

Although many of us tend to regard our aircraft as living beings, they are, in truth, machines. They require regular maintenance like any other machine or piece of equipment. The FARs are quite explicit about how maintenance is to be performed and the time limits allowed for its completion.

The responsibility for assuring compliance with maintenance regulations rests on several shoulders. Traditionally, the owner or operator of an aircraft has the primary responsibility for maintaining his or her aircraft in an airworthy condition. The owner/operator must have the prescribed inspections completed, ensure that maintenance personnel make appropriate entries in records and have any inoperative instrument or item of equipment repaired.

The mechanic making repairs or conducting an inspection must meet certain quality standards and make required entries in the maintenance records of the aircraft before returning it to service.

Finally, FAR 91.7 requires the pilot in command to determine whether the aircraft he is to fly is airworthy.

If a particular airplane were never flown, it wouldn't matter if it were in airworthy condition or not. However, once a pilot approaches that aircraft with the intention of flying it, he must meet the requirements of FAR 91.7, which states, in part, "The pilot in command of a civil aircraft is responsible for determining whether that aircraft is in condition for safe flight."

Therefore, while the FARs delegate airworthiness requirements to several parties, the ultimate responsibility for airworthiness rests squarely on the shoulders of the pilot in command.

Unfortunately, not all pilots meet that responsibility. For example, I recently asked a pilot why he didn't do a preflight when he came to pick up his aircraft after an annual inspection. He said it wasn't necessary because the mechanic who completed the inspection was better qualified than he is, and he expected that there was nothing wrong with the airplane. It never occurred to him that the mechanics who had worked on the machine may have made a mistake somewhere along the line.

Last Resort

The accident files show that mechanical malfunctions immediately after scheduled or unscheduled maintenance do occur more often than we would like to believe.

A friend of mine was able to preclude such an occurrence by doing a thorough preflight after an annual inspection. She discovered that the mechanic had not replaced the oil in the engine. Had her preflight been hasty or nonexistent, the engine would have seized shortly after she applied full power. She was rightfully upset and let the mechanic know it. Her own inspection saved her from experiencing a very dangerous situation.

Another friend was not so fortunate. She had a complete electrical failure at night after maintenance was done on her aircraft's alternator.

Several years ago, I ferried a Cessna 150 to a mechanic for a pre-purchase inspection. When the cowling was removed, we found a half-inch-drive ratchet resting on top of the engine.

There are other stories of mechanics not safety-wiring oil plugs, leaving cotter pins out of wheel nuts, leaving jack pads attached to the aircraft, tying cable bundles to a vacuum line, thereby constricting the line, and rigging ailerons backwards after a cable change.

Your mechanic is not infallible. He is human and can make mistakes, too.

With this in mind, I always ask the mechanic to accompany me during a preflight after maintenance. If I should spot something that doesn't look right, he can explain the apparent anomaly or make repairs. Sometimes, the mechanics find something they missed earlier, before I see it.

Even if there is nothing to be found, having the mechanic accompany you on the preflight inspection will enable you to learn more about your aircraft. My experience has been that mechanics enjoy the opportunity to explain the workings of airplanes and their systems to customers.

Check the Records

Before flying an aircraft you are unfamiliar with, assure yourself that the required maintenance is complete and up to date.

Last summer, while pursuing a purchase of a Cessna 172, I ran across two airplanes that had not been inspected within the last 12 months. Neither owner told me his airplane was not airworthy, and both had flown their airplanes recently.

One of the airplanes was two years out of annual. When I asked the owner why it had been three years since the last annual, he explained that he had been "ripped off" by the mechanic who had done the last inspection and wouldn't allow that to happen again.

The owner of the other airplane, which was six months out of annual, claimed the inspection had been done but not recorded in the logs.

Potential Disaster

Many pilots don't preflight their airplanes or only do cursory walk-arounds. There is a potential for disaster here.

One airplane I fly is kept in a community hangar where each aircraft owner may move others to get his own airplane out. It is possible that someone could do some damage to another airplane and not say anything about it. If I were to fly that aircraft without preflighting it, I would be inviting Mr. Murphy to knock on my cockpit door.

Good preflights can also alert you to problems that require immediate attention, or discrepancies that could become problems in flight. If you find a discrepancy during a preflight, have a mechanic look at it.

Not long ago, I was preflighting a Cessna Citation and noticed that the oil in one of the engines was almost black. Jet engine oil is usually clear or straw-colored and seldom changes color very much. Suspecting a serious engine problem, I grounded the airplane and sought out a mechanic. It turned out that one of the engine's main bearings had "coked," contaminating the oil in the process. The engine had to be disassembled and the bearing replaced. That engine would have failed in the next several hours, had it been flown in that condition.

Another point to be made regarding preflight inspections is that one time around the airplane at the beginning of the day is not enough. At the very least, you should walk around the aircraft before subsequent takeoffs. Once, a pilot taxied his Cherokee into the tail of my Cessna 310. While he was inside looking for me, I was outside getting ready to leave. Had I not walked around the airplane, I might have taken off without knowing about the damage done to the tail section.

Fuel Checks

If you are not present when your airplane is refueled, make doubly sure you check the fuel and security of the caps.

If jet fuel is put into a piston engine airplane's tanks, the engine will most likely quit shortly after takeoff. Jet fuel is clear and has a thick, oily touch and smell. The best way to avoid a mixup in fuels is to stand by the airplane while servicing is in progress. Check the decals on the fuel truck and drain the airplane's sumps. Check the color and smell of the fuel samples.

Being there during refueling will prevent the need for a time-consuming draining and cleaning of the tanks, to say nothing of the mess you would have if you took off with jet fuel in the tanks and had a forced landing just off the airport.

Several times a year, we hear stories of airplanes that hadn't been flown for long periods of time, being involved in mishaps and, too often, fatal accidents. A lot of the crashes are caused by fuel contamination or lack of maintenance.

I remember a pilot who showed me an aircraft he had just purchased. He boasted about the low-time engine and how it would last him years and years. A month later, he was doing a top overhaul because of a lack of compression in most of the cylinders. Piston engines that are not flown regularly will deteriorate. Cylinder walls can rust from lack of use, causing excessive ring and cylinder wear when put back to work. This particular engine was overhauled 10 years before and had only been flown 50 hours since.

Most engine operating manuals provide recommendations that should be followed if an airplane is not flown for long periods of time.

If you must fly an airplane that hasn't been flown for a long time, get a mechanic to inspect it and sign off the logs. He will check the fuel system for water or other contaminants, the engine for proper compression and the airframe for control continuity, bird nests and other things that might present a problem during flight.

If you are not a licensed mechanic, don't do it yourself. There are many reports of pilots who drained fuel until they were satisfied that there was no more water, only to have the engine quit on takeoff.

Complying with ADs

Another thing to be aware of in any aircraft is compliance with applicable airworthiness directives.

AD notes can be issued at any time and may ground an aircraft immediately or at some point in the future. Several months ago, a Cessna 180 took off from my home airport only to crash just off the airport property. While the official word is not out yet, it is possible the AD note which affects most Cessna seat rails was overlooked. Investigators are checking the possibility that the seat had not latched and slid backwards during the takeoff.

Mechanics must check AD notes during each annual inspection. Some mechanics are more thorough than others when it comes to this tedious job. However, an AD note issued against an aircraft or accessory will affect its airworthiness. It becomes the pilot's responsibility if he flies an aircraft affected by an AD that has not been complied with in the required time frame.

Similarly, if you fly an aircraft after maintenance has been completed but before the appropriate entries have been made in the log books or aircraft records, your aircraft is not airworthy.

As mentioned earlier, the FARs require that a mechanic make the appropriate entries in the aircraft records before returning the aircraft to service. They also require an owner or operator to insure that those entries have been made.

An occasional review of the log books for the aircraft you fly will alert you to maintenance inspections that are coming due. It can also serve as a reminder for altimeter and encoder certification dates, and other items that are often forgotten.

After maintenance has been done, make sure the mechanic has made the necessary entries. Be cautious when dealing with a "hangar queen" or an aircraft that has been sitting for a long period of time. Watch for AD notes that affect the types of aircraft you fly. The required work should be accomplished within the time frames set forth in the directives.

Before you fly any aircraft, it is up to you to be certain that it is airworthy. In reality, it is more than just following the rules for the sake of the rules. It is following the rules so that you will have a safe, uneventful flight.

Out in the gritty real world, there are lots of operators who don't quite pay enough attention to maintenance. The motivation is obvious: general aviation is beginning to rebound, but many airports are still pretty depressing places when it comes to money. The average operator has to keep rental rates low to attract business, and sometimes there just isn't enough cash to do what needs to be done.

The same crunch affects many private owners. It's expensive to keep up an airplane, and if your cash flow can't cover it, well....

So, how do you protect yourself? Brian Jacobson follows up with some real-world observations.

Keeping Track of Maintenance

It was a cloudy, windy, day typical of New England in winter. I was returning to my local airport after a test flight in my Alon Aircoupe following a carburetor overhaul. As I taxied to the ramp, I noticed a Cessna 150 tied down with its nose in the air.

Upon closer inspection, the reason was obvious. The nose wheel was bent backward with the tire almost touching the belly. It looked like a retractable gear just about to enter the wheel well. Also, the outer portion of the left wing was smashed, and both propeller blades were curled inward toward the cowling.

A student had taken the local aero club's airplane without his instructor's approval and had botched his first landing attempt in the windy conditions. He wound up in a snow bank alongside the runway.

The aircraft had been in a similar accident only months before and had not been back on the line very long. After the second accident, the club engaged a different mechanic to make the necessary repairs. It didn't take long for him to find that the previous repairs were not up to FAA standards.

The damage to the wings in the earlier accident was more extensive, and the mechanic who worked on the aircraft used "cherry" rivets for the entire job. Cherry rivets are similar to "pop" rivets. A gun-like device is used to install them, instead of a rivet gun and "bucking bar." In aircraft, they may be used only in certain non-structural areas where there is no load placed on them in flight.

The mechanic reported the illegal repair to the FAA and the club's insurance company. The FAA demanded the disassembly of both wings so that the extent of the poor repair could be discovered. Then, using the correct rivets and repair techniques, the mechanic reassembled the wings.

The club's insurance company refused to pay for bringing the wings up to standard, saying they paid for the original repair and that was the limit of their obligation.

Their position was that the club, not the insurance company, contracted for the work and should have been more careful about who was repairing the aircraft. The club had to pay for all of the rivet work.

In the club's defense, I will say that they had no reason to think they were dealing with a disreputable mechanic. He had been maintaining their aircraft for some time, and they had not had any problems with his work prior to this incident.

Scuttlebutt around the airport was that the FAA took action against the mechanic who made the illegal repair and that he switched to working on automobiles.

Ignoring the Rules

Fortunately, most of those involved in aviation take pride in following established standards, whether they are mechanics, pilots or others who have responsibilities governed by the FARS. But there are those who ignore the rules.

What keeps these shoddy operators in business? Customers. Some people think they are getting a deal when someone offers them flight instruction, rental aircraft or maintenance cheaper than the "going" rate, not knowing until too late that what they are getting is substandard.

Initially, these people refuse to believe (or don't stop to consider) that they may be buying a service that is not up to standard. They justify their thinking by saying that the person or company they are dealing with has to be certified by the FAA, so they must be performing competently.

Unfortunately, that is not always the case. For example, several years ago when I was looking for a flying job, I heard that a local freight operator needed a pilot for an airplane in which I had logged many hours.

The operator expressed an interest in me and asked that I accompany him on his next trip. I did. Had I been an FAA inspector, I would have put the man out of business. His airplane had many defects, a couple of them serious. Some of his procedures violated the FARS.

He explained to me that the only way to make money in the air freight business is to "get the trip done as quickly as possible." He also said their unwritten policy was to "fly IFR only as a last resort." I declined his offer of work and kept looking.

Today's aircraft are highly reliable, and that is what keeps some operators going when they intentionally skip required maintenance or skimp on it when they do have maintenance performed.

But skipping maintenance for the sake of making or saving a few bucks will only cost you money over the long run.

Appearances Can Deceive

Appearances can deceive. Turbine aircraft engines, for instance, may have the appearance of being in good condition when they are not. Items such as fuel injector nozzles have required service intervals. They must be removed, cleaned and flow-checked to be certain they are spraying the fuel in the proper pattern.

Skipping this inspection can cause a nozzle with a faulty spray pattern to create "hot spots" within the burner section of the engine. That leads to premature wear of hot-section parts. If more than one nozzle is faulty, more damage can be done.

Any higher-than-normal temperatures inside a turbine engine, including those caused by faulty nozzles, will cost big bucks to fix.

Yet, some operators will skip required maintenance because a quick test run shows the engines are putting out normal power levels and give the appearance of being okay.

I suspect such discrepancies existed in a Mitsubishi MU-2 that I flew for about a month for an operator who was skimping on maintenance. The airplane was old and had its interior removed so that it could carry freight. The logbooks showed that the engines had their mid-life ("hot section") inspection only 400 hours earlier. During a hot-section inspection, inspectors can discover and repair any hot spots or heat anomalies.

But the engines did not put out the proper power levels, and I always wondered if that inspection had been done correctly, or at all. There were other problems, too. A week after I quit, one of the engines on that MU-2 decided it didn't want to run anymore.

What You Pay For

I have found the old saying "you get what you pay for" to be particularly true in aviation.

I have seen many people take their airplanes to purveyors of fifty-dollar annuals for several years in a row. Then, when the "specialist" who they normally used was not available, they'd go to someone else, only to become angry at the bill presented to them.

Invariably, these bargain-hunters would claim the shop ripped them off and that they would never go there again when, in reality, nothing more was done during the inspection other than make up for several years of neglect.

For example, there was a Cessna 172 owner who was trying to sell his airplane. The airplane did not look good. Even with the engine warm, there wasn't much compression in the high-timer. There was oil all over the inside the cowl and along the belly. There were many little things inside that showed neglect.

Looking through the logs, I discovered that the airplane had not had an annual inspection for more than two years. I asked the owner why. He told me that the last mechanic who did the inspection charged him $1,045 (he even showed me the bill), and he swore he would not pay that much money for an inspection again.

So, he just didn't bother to have his 172 inspected. Did he fly the airplane? Well, the engine was warm when we got there to look at it, and he said he had taken the airplane around the patch to "shake the cobwebs" out of it.

Another time, I looked through the logbooks of another Cessna 172 and found no entry for an annual. The owner told me it was done but the mechanic forgot to sign the books. Although I know there are mechanics out there who hate to do paperwork, I thought that neglecting to sign off an annual was unusual.

A few months later, I was looking at a Cherokee Six that was undergoing an annual. The owner, who is not an A&P, had opened up the airplane and was waiting for the mechanic to come look at it.

According to the owner, the mechanic would inspect it and give him a list of things that needed to be corrected. Then, before closing the airplane up, the mechanic would return and look at the repairs.

I asked him when the logs would be signed, and he said the mechanic would come back "when the airplane is finished." It turned out that his mechanic was the same person who "forgot" to sign the 172's logs. You can come up with all kinds of scenarios for that, including one in which the mechanic never came back to see the completed work.

I am in favor of an owner doing the maintenance on his aircraft, providing that the mechanic who is going to sign off the job supervises the work properly.

FAR 43.3(d) requires that the mechanic personally *observe* the work and be readily available while the job is in progress. According to an FAA inspector I talked with, the arrangement between the owner and mechanic mentioned above would not meet a test of the rule.

Cheap Overhauls

Engine overhaul is another job where "cheap" usually means poor work.

With the manufacturing burdens of product liability and relatively low demand, parts for any aircraft engine are extremely expensive. If one shop quotes an overhaul on your engine of $10,000 and another shop says $5,000, investigate carefully. There will be some major differences between the work done for the price.

A couple of years ago, I read about an engine shop that was doing cheap overhauls. The FAA got many complaints from operators whose engines failed after a very short time. My impression of the place was that they were doing nothing more than disassembling, cleaning and reassembling the engines.

Looking through *Trade-A-Plane*, you will find many prices for an overhaul on the same type of engine. Are there differences? You bet!

To be considered a major overhaul, the work must meet the requirements set forth in the manufacturer's overhaul manual. Some shops meet the minimum requirements, while others go beyond the minimums to bring the engine back to new limits. Still others, like the shop mentioned above, don't even bother looking at the manual.

A "new limits" overhaul will cost more than a "minimum requirements" overhaul. A "firewall forward" overhaul will cost even more. Such an overhaul usually encompasses everything under the cowling, including engine accessories, hoses and exhaust components, as well as the propeller.

A factory remanufactured engine will be even higher-priced after you add the cost of removal, shipping and installation.

When you shop for an overhaul, compare quotes from different shops and be certain that you understand what each shop is promising. Get references from people who have had work done by the shop you decide is going to do your work.

A friend of mine had a valve break in his Cessna 210's engine a couple of years ago. He landed at a large Florida airport and engaged a shop to repair it. They installed a new cylinder assembly and returned the airplane to service.

Approximately five hours later, the engine failed completely and had to be replaced. The mechanic who had done the repairs in Florida hadn't found all the pieces of the broken valve.

When you have taken your airplane to a new shop, how can you tell that the work has been done satisfactorily?

First, make sure you ask beforehand to see any parts they replace. Then, look them over carefully and have the mechanic explain exactly what was wrong with them. If he shrugs off your inquiry or goes into a diatribe that makes no sense, he may be trying to hide something.

Examine the log entries carefully. I am suspicious of any mechanic who merely writes something like this for an annual inspection: "Performed annual inspection this date according to manufacturer's recommended inspection." A logbook entry should include a complete description of the work.

Some shops, mostly FAA-certified repair shops, may put a simple entry in the log but provide a complete written description of the completed work on a separate work order. While this practice is legal, it gives no information about the inspection or repair to someone, like a prospective purchaser, who is looking at the logbooks.

It does not take long for a shop or a mechanic to make a reasonable logbook entry. You should insist on it.

After maintenance, look your airplane over carefully. Did the mechanic take the time to clean up all evidence of his work? Are there greasy fingerprints on your seats or cowling? Check the oil. Is it up to the correct level? Look at the tires. Have they been serviced?

Little things mean a lot. If a mechanic fails to attend to them, he may not have pride in his work; and that could mean trouble with the quality of the work that he did.

You might also want to keep an eye on the work as it progresses. If you don't like the looks of something, ask about it. If the mechanic ushers you to the lobby and tells you that his insurance company requires you to remain there, find another mechanic.

Renters' Woes

If you rent airplanes, you will be told little about the maintenance work that has been performed on them.

Make the operator prove to you that the airplane you're renting has had its necessary inspections. It is *your* responsibility as pilot-in-command to ensure that required inspections have been performed.

Recently, while waiting for some passengers at a small FBO, I heard the beginning of an oral exam for a private pilot applicant. It didn't get very far. The examiner wanted proof that the airplane was "in license."

There was much paper shuffling done before they called the student's instructor into the room. None of them could find an entry confirming that the airplane had a current annual inspection.

The instructor called back to his school and verified that, somehow, they had missed the inspection—three and a half months earlier. The school had to dispatch another airplane to pick up the now-stranded pilots.

I have no doubt that an FAA inspector would have issued a violation against the instructor on the spot for flying the aircraft in its unlicensed state.

In addition, the school or the aircraft's owner could be taken to task for each flight the airplane made after its annual ran out. Technically, every pilot who flew the airplane during those three and a half months had violated the FARs.

So, look over rental airplanes very carefully. Sometimes, the ones that lack proper maintenance are dirty, have a poor appearance and equipment such as radios and instruments that don't work properly. But, as suggested earlier, appearances can be deceiving, and it's important to check the logbooks, yourself.

Seeing Dollar Signs

Many aircraft owners don't realize that the work they are paying for is shoddy.

All they see are dollar signs when someone says they'll do the annual much cheaper than anyone else.

Beware of this type of activity. Not all mechanics who are working for less than the going rate are doing poor work. But, remember, a shop can't lose money on every job unless, of course, it is planning to make it up on volume.

Okay, your shop has just finished a job for you. Everything should be just fine, right?

Not necessarily. Making any sort of assumption about your airplane is particularly dangerous when it's just come out of maintenance. Mechanics are human, and can drop the ball with the best of them.

The classic case of pilots failing to double-check on the mechanics occurred several years ago. Two professional pilots died when the big piston twin crashed just after takeoff. The ailerons had been rigged backwards, and they didn't notice until it was too late.

A pilot should bear in mind that if he or she is the first one to fly an airplane after maintenance, the role of test pilot must be assumed.

Clint Lowe, an A&P mechanic, here offers some advice on how to make that post-maintenance test flight safe and productive.

Post-Maintenance Shakedown

There was a week's wait before the mechanic had time to work on your airplane. Then, another two weeks in the shop. You've developed a rash for the lack of flying, and you've become such a grouch that your spouse has been content to let you eat in front of the TV for the past several days.

Finally, word comes that the maintenance is completed, and you set off to go flying.

But wait. Before you go off boring holes in the sky, it's time to take a few steps to ensure that the airplane really *is* ready to fly again.

Why? Well, consider what happened to a local crop duster who had a mechanic perform a complete rebuild of an airplane over the winter some years ago. In the spring, with the spraying season rapidly approaching, the mechanic proclaimed the airplane ready to work. Anxious to get the aircraft back to his home strip, the pilot quickly preflighted and taxied out.

It wasn't until he was airborne that he discovered the mechanic had rigged his elevator backwards, and the freshly rebuilt airplane ended up in a heap at the departure end of the runway. Fortunately, the pilot wasn't hurt badly.

He could have caught the problem quickly by doing the part of every preflight checklist that says, "controls free and correct," or words to that effect.

It is very important to realize that flying the airplane for the first time after maintenance makes you a test pilot. This may seem rather extreme, but it's true. Every time a mechanic works on your plane, there is some chance that the work was performed incorrectly or that something was left somewhere it shouldn't have been left.

The pilot who flies an aircraft fresh from the shop without taking time to ensure that it really is ready to fly is taking an unwarranted risk. I once found an inspection plate missing from the bottom of the horizontal stabilizer and loose screws in two valve covers after an annual on my Cessna 150.

Test Pilot Tactics

So, *you* are the test pilot. *You* can and should take some steps to ensure that the maintenance was performed properly. If your mechanic objects, perhaps it's time to find another mechanic.

Following an annual inspection or other major work, schedule a "maintenance flight." To perform the flight, you'll want to have a nice, VFR day and a couple of hours of your time to go through what follows.

Here's how to prepare for the maintenance flight:

1. Ensure that you are qualified to fly. Occasionally, as with an engine overhaul or when the airplane has been waiting forever for hard-to-find parts, long periods of time may pass and the owner will do no flying at all.

Why not either rent an airplane to maintain your proficiency or take along a current, experienced safety pilot for the first ride after a hiatus? After all, many in-flight emergencies occur right after maintenance, and a lack of proficiency could make handling the emergency that much more difficult.

2. Review the maintenance performed. Before accepting the keys to the aircraft, go over what was done in the shop, so you can determine what is flight-critical and what is trivial, as well as what portions of the aircraft were worked on. If you are not familiar with a certain maintenance item, have the mechanic show you what was done.

Consider *any* engine work as flight-critical. This includes oil changes, magneto adjustments, carburetor work, etc. Any work with a flight control also is flight-critical, as is any fuel system or hydraulic system repair.

3. Look over the areas where maintenance was performed. If light maintenance was performed and nothing was done in any hidden areas, you can look things over on the ramp or in your hangar. If the maintenance was extensive, then it would be a good idea to tell the mechanic beforehand that you want to look everything over prior to buttoning up the cowling and/or the inspection panels. Decide on times when things can be looked at.

While discussing upcoming maintenance work with your mechanic, it's a good idea to have a copy of the aircraft maintenance manual (available from the manufacturer and other sources) to determine what the he will be doing and what follow-up maintenance actions are necessary.

Here's a helpful checklist for looking over the areas in which work was performed:

• *Engine:* Check all fuel lines and electrical wiring for proximity to vibrating parts and hot surfaces. Pay special attention to where lines and wires pass close to exhaust system components. Look for evidence of burning, and make sure these items show no signs of chafing or other deterioration.

Check the mountings for the magnetos, alternator or generator, vacuum pump and other accessories. If the magnetos were adjusted, for instance, make sure the bolts securing them to the case are tight and the clamps are seated properly. Make sure the electrical connections are tight (you can lightly push on the terminals to see if they move).

Check the carb-heat, throttle, mixture and propeller linkages for freedom of movement. Make sure the cables are securely fastened. If provision is made for safety wiring (i.e., small holes drilled in the bolt heads and nut hex),make sure they are used. If no provision is made for safety wiring,ensure a self-locking device of some sort has been used (you can ask your mechanic about specifics here).

Check the oil filter or screen for security and make sure it is safety-wired. Ensure that any oil pressure or oil temperature probes have been reinserted and are tight. Make sure that no tools have been left in the baffles or on top of the cylinders (these are convenient spots to lay tools during maintenance).

If permissible with the cowling off, run the engine for a couple of minutes and check for leaks around the oil filter/screen and in other areas. Do a magneto check, as you would in the run-up area. Report any problems to the mechanic.

• *Airframe:* If necessary, open access panels to the areas where work was performed and, with a flashlight, look them over. Ensure that control cables are properly routed in their pulleys and not chafing against each other. Look for any tools that might have been left in the belly of the airplane.

If work was performed on fuel and/or hydraulic lines, pressurize the lines (by either running the fuel pump, engine or by pressing the brakes—whatever is necessary) and take a peek to see if any leaks occur where the lines were disconnected during maintenance.

If work was done behind the instrument panel, take a flashlight and look around for wiring or air lines chafing against control cables, chains or control wheel linkages. Look for loose connections on the various components. Make sure cannon plugs are fully seated to instruments and radios. If you find a problem, have your mechanic correct it.

If a sheet-metal repair was performed on the control surfaces, ask your mechanic if he statically balanced the surface following the maintenance. Such balancing is sometimes required to avoid flutter at high airspeeds.

4. Perform a thorough preflight. Refer to the owner's manual while doing a walk-around preflight inspection. Fuel valves, electrical switches and all manner of things can be left in unusual positions.

Don't just glance in the direction of an inspection item. Take a close look. If you are inspecting the elevator, look into the hinge areas and at the bellcranks and exposed cables to ensure that they aren't binding or missing locking devices, such as cotter pins, lock nuts, safety wire, etc.

Satisfy yourself that the tires haven't become deflated. Drain all of the fuel sumps to get rid of any water that may have accumulated.

Do at least what the "book" calls for. One item not typically included in a POH or AFM, but a good one to attend to, is to grab one wing tip and vigorously shake the airframe. On a quiet ramp, you'll very likely hear any loose tools knocking around inside the fuselage or wing. And you can check the wing spar and attachments for security. The airplane should follow your strokes solidly, without any "mushiness."

5. Prepare carefully for the "maintenance flight." If you're going to be testing the radios or the engine, doing any unusual maneuvers or making unusual requests to ATC, give the tower a call beforehand to discuss your intentions. A "heads-up" of this nature will greatly enhance their cooperation with you. In the event a problem should occur, ATC might be able to help you isolate it (as they did recently when I had a transponder problem) or help you get back to the field faster.

Again, using the book, go through all the "before-start" and "before-takeoff" procedures. Pay special attention to the various switches, knobs, valves and gauges referred to in the book. After starting the engine, turn everything on to give it a chance to fizzle on the ground before you need it in the air.

Unless you are sure you know them intimately, review the emergency procedures listed in your manual. Know not only the engine-failure procedures (including glide speeds and restart procedures), but any procedures that may be remotely related to the work performed, such as electrical failures and in-flight fires.

During the run-up, be especially critical of anything not meeting the book's specs. Take off the headset and listen to the engine. Set all of your instruments as if you were going on a 200-mile cross-country over a remote and hostile area.

Make plans for aborting the takeoff, if necessary. Especially when operating from a short runway, pick a point down the runway where you will abort the takeoff if something is amiss.

If work was done on the engine, maintain takeoff or maximum-continuous power until reaching a safe altitude from which you can either glide back to the airport or land somewhere with a good chance of survival. From there on, throttle movements should be slow and carefully monitored. Many power failures occur during throttle transients (especially in turbines).

In a safe maneuvering area, check out anything that might be remotely related to the maintenance performed. If new spark plugs were installed or the magnetos were repaired, turn off the squelch control for your radios and listen for the fast snapping or buzzing that may indicate an ignition leak due to improper shielding. If radio work was done, track a VOR for a few minutes or check your comm radios a good distance away from the ground facility.

When you run out of things to check, why not do a little slow flight, a couple of stalls and, maybe, some ground-reference maneuvers? You'll get some good practice while putting time on the repair.

If all of this seems like a lot of trouble, consider what happened several years ago when a Beech Duke took off from Minnesota, bound for Illinois, a couple of weeks after a "simple" repair had been performed in a fuel tank. The pilot encountered a line of thunderstorms, and, while coordinating with ATC to find a hole in the line, he screamed that his shoe was on fire.

None of the occupants survived the subsequent crash. Investigators discovered that a large punch had been left in the fuel cell and had ruptured the tank and the cabin wall during the turbulence encounter. Fuel had poured into the cockpit and had then been ignited.

Now, how much faith do *you* want to put into even a simple repair?

• Section Two •

Powerplants

Why
Engines Fail

There are many things that can fail on an IFR airplane that, while serious, won't end the flight right away. An IFR pilot can get by without radios, and is trained to survive gyro or other instrument failure.

But, when the powerplant dies, the airplane is going to land...right now. While practicing for that eventuality is certainly wise, it's best to avoid it entirely.

This section of the book presents, from different perspectives, many ways to make sure your engine keeps doing what it's supposed to.

Causes and Cures

We didn't notice it at first, what with the excitement of preparing for vacation. We were putting luggage in the back of our Cessna 180 when one of the relatives hollered, "Look! Down there." It was the tail of a Mooney sticking up from the rocks and weeds. We went to investigate.

The airplane wasn't damaged too badly, considering it had skidded with collapsed gear about a hundred feet across the desert's rock- and brush-strewn terrain. We found out later that the engine had quit late in the takeoff roll and the pilot, trying to figure out what was wrong, had his head down when it should have been up and ran off the runway. Fortunately, no one was hurt, and the airplane was trucked out of the small desert strip a few days later for repair.

They were lucky. Roughly one out of every 20 reportable accidents involves an engine problem on takeoff, and in about one-third of these cases, the occupants of the aircraft are killed or seriously injured.

To examine how and why this type of mishap occurs, we asked NTSB for a recent two-year sample of reports on accidents involving power loss on takeoff or initial climb. The sample included 273 accidents, and it was a real eye-opener. An overwhelming number of the cases proved the truth in the old Air Force saying that "accidents are caused and, therefore, preventable." Poor maintenance, cockpit management, operating technique and/or decision-making played roles in many of the accidents.

Right up front, we should mention that the investigators' findings do not support the belief that a power loss on takeoff is most likely to occur at the first power reduction. This happened in only four of the 273 accidents. What actually caused these power losses could not be determined, although in one case, the pilot admitted that he hadn't turned on the fuel boost pump, as recommended in his Navion owner's manual, either before or after the engine quit.

We'll consider power reductions in more depth later; but, first, let's take a look, in detail, at what leads to accidents involving powerplant failures or malfunctions on takeoff.

Where's the Gas?

In spite of the warnings throughout our primary training, fuel-related problems appear to play the biggest role. Nearly one-third of the accidents (85 of them) in our sample were caused by fuel contamination, fuel starvation or fuel exhaustion.

Fuel system problems that could be classified as unpreventable—or, at least, not easily identified—were involved in 19 other accidents.

Water was the culprit that doused the fires of internal combustion in 18 of the accidents. Sources included water-contaminated fuel trucks and other dispensing tanks (five gallons of water were found in the sump of one such tank following an accident), and wash water and rain that entered through bad seals on gas caps. In only one case did the pilot report that he'd performed a preflight check of the fuel prior to takeoff.

Twelve other accidents were caused by fuel contaminated with some form of foreign matter, such as rust from corroding aircraft fuel tanks and residues of various fuel additives.

In most cases, however, the pilots simply ran their tanks dry. One flew a Cessna 150 three times on training flights without refueling; only unusable fuel was found in the tanks after the crash. In many other cases, very little or *no* fuel remained. Some accidents occurred when pilots attempted to fly to nearby airports to gas up.

Besides those who exhausted their fuel supplies were several pilots who starved their engines for fuel by positioning the selector valves on empty tanks. Miscellaneous problems relating to fuel lines, fuel pumps and carburetors caused the early termination of several other flights.

In one case, a homebuilt builder/pilot discovered that one does not use automotive-style vinyl fuel hose in proximity to an airplane engine. Another pilot took it upon himself to replace the rubber gasket in his gascolator bowl, only to have it float downstream and clog the line at the carb. The investigation of one accident turned up a clogged jet in a brand-new carburetor, apparently the fault of the factory. A few cases of fuel pump failure and/or poor pump operating technique completed the list.

Blocking the Flow

Twenty-seven accidents (10 percent) involved induction system difficulties. As may be expected, carburetor icing headed the list, but clogs/restrictions from other sources contributed significantly.

Carburetor icing was identified in 19 accidents. In most cases, either no carburetor heat control was available for use or the pilots failed to use carb heat at appropriate times. One problem, which should have been detected on run-up, was a disconnected carb heat hose.

The other cases of choked induction systems were primarily a result of poor maintenance and inspection. A shop rag was found in a carb airbox following an annual inspection of one airplane. Deteriorated and loose components in the inlet area contributed to the remainder of the accidents. For example, a Brackett air filter had not been properly installed, and filter remnants blocked the carb venturi.

Mechanical Problems

Problems directly related to the engine's mechanical workings contributed to 55 (20 percent) of the accidents in our sample.

In 17 cases, cylinders and associated hardware fell prey to poor maintenance and/or poor operating technique. Only one engine failure was attributed solely to metal fatigue, which resulted in a broken rocker arm and a consequent valve failure. In several cases, valves stuck because of excess varnish build-up between the guide and valve stems. In some cases, excess heat broke, deteriorated, burned or otherwise damaged valves (likely, after warning signs of impending failure were ignored).

Some takeoff accidents involved low compression, cylinder cracks and total cylinder failures. One airplane, a Cessna 170, was four hours out of an annual inspection which had revealed that *two* of the six cylinders had compressions of 25/80 and 24/80, respectively. This is incredibly far below limits. Two fatalities resulted when the airplane lifted off but was unable to climb over the terrain ahead.

Ignition problems were involved in 13 accidents. Three resulted from spark plugs that were oil- and lead-fouled, and severely eroded; two from improperly timed magnetos. Other problems included P-leads shorting against exhaust components, bad ignition harnesses and failures of various internal magneto components (points, condensers, etc.).

Sixteen accidents resulted from miscellaneous mechanical problems. In two cases, mufflers came apart internally and blocked the exhaust system sufficiently to produce excess back pressure and, consequently, low power output.

"Hard Core" Failures

There also were the types of "hard core" failures we've heard so much about, including two connecting rod and two crankshaft failures. In almost all cases, obvious deficiencies existed in maintenance or operating technique.

One particularly noteworthy case involved a Cherokee 180 that had been purchased only a few weeks prior to the accident (which proved fatal for two of the three occupants). Engine tear-down revealed excess wear on all main/rod bearings and several main bearings and caps installed backwards. The crankshaft was worn out, as were all the piston rings (one was broken). Mag timing was three degrees off, plugs showed rich fuel condition, and the carb was worn and dirty in several areas. The intake/exhaust rocker arms were improperly installed. Metal flakes were discovered in the oil filter, which also clogged the prop governor screen. The engine must have been running poorly for some time.

In another case, a Cessna 210 owner had noticed odd vibrations coming from the engine. When consulted, the manufacturer, Continental, advised that the engine be torn down and examined immediately. The pilot elected to fly anyway. The crankshaft broke and, upon examination, showed signs of fatigue in several areas.

Other failures included burned pistons and associated hardware (wrist pins, rings) damaged by poor operating technique (running over-rich or over-lean), and a failed fuel pump drive.

Four takeoff mishaps resulted from power losses due to lubrication problems. All but one involved large leaks that depleted the oil supply. In one incident, oil gushed through a "hole" left when a rented Cessna 152's vacuum pump was removed *three days earlier*. With insufficient lubrication, the engine was capable of producing only 1,200 rpm on takeoff. In another case, a flying club's airplane caught fire when a severely deteriorated oil supply tube blew out and sprayed oil on the exhaust manifold.

Blowers and Props

Turbocharger problems figured in five of the accidents. Several occurred in heavier twins, and the sudden reduction of power caught the pilots by surprise, resulting in improper engine-out technique that led to off-airport forced landings.

In only one incident did a turbo come apart, resulting in pieces of the impeller damaging the engine. A worn exhaust clamp and a broken controller linkage were the cause of two accidents.

Propeller problems played a role in only three accidents. All were controllable-pitch props and had something to do with poor maintenance or manufacture. In one case, both props on a King Air went to near-feather position due to misadjusted ground idle stops. In another accident, a homebuilder decided to shorten a propeller without examining the consequences or contacting the manufacturer. An overspeed condition (lots of rpm with no "bite") resulted.

Other Problems

Many of the accidents involving power loss on takeoff defy characterization. For example, a primer was left unlocked and caused an over-rich mixture. In another case, the pilot of an Ercoupe apparently was filming with a camcorder on takeoff when his passenger inadvertently retarded the throttle.

However, 12 of the accidents were ascribed to "improper operation." To understand what that means, consider the pilot of a B55 Baron who apparently ignored the prohibition against taking off with less than the requisite amount of fuel in the tanks. He banked the airplane to the left at about 100 feet, and the left engine quit when fuel in the left tank moved away from the engine feed port. Then, in an effort to return to the field, he banked right, unporting the right tank and starving the right engine for fuel, too. Fortunately, no one was hurt; but there was considerable damage.

In another case, a Cessna 421 was seen flying low over trees with gray smoke trailing from the left engine. It then rolled inverted and crashed into trees. Both engines ran satisfactorily on a test stand. A service letter to disable the "automatic" feature of the auxiliary boost pumps had not been complied with.

Following 70 of the accidents in our sample, investigators could come up with no probable cause. Frequently, post-crash fires and impact damage made determination impossible. In some cases, parts were removed from the wreckage before investigators arrived.

Avoiding Missed Beats

Normally, takeoff and initial climb are among the easiest maneuvers for the pilot; but they are the most difficult for the engine. You are asking your engine to go from idle to full power in a few seconds and expecting it to accelerate you to flying speed in the shortest possible time ... all without missing a beat.

The engine is, of course, designed to give you this performance *if* it is fed and maintained properly. Let's look at just what that means. A lengthy discussion with the chief engineer at Lycoming, Rick Moffett, revealed several things that can be done to reduce the possibility of engine failure on takeoff (or any other phase of flight, for that matter):

1. Keep your engine oil clean. Gums, acids and lead sludge that form in the oil cannot be removed by the filter, and they cause sticking valves. The only sure way to get rid of contaminants is to follow the recommended oil-change schedule. Typically, oil with screen filtration should be changed every 25 hours (every 50 hours with full-flow filtering) or every four months—whichever comes first. Check your operator's manual, and follow the manufacturer's recommendations.

2. Never use automotive oils or oils with automotive additives. Air-cooled aircraft engines have significantly different lubrication needs than automotive engines. They get operated less frequently, get exposed to different loads and temperatures, and require oil specifically designed for this operating environment.

3. Avoid automotive fuels. Primarily, aviation fuels meet across-the-country "uniformity-in-product" standards set by Uncle Sam. Automotive fuels are governed by state standards which vary a lot. Automotive fuels deteriorate more rapidly than aviation fuels (avgas is designed to sit two years in your tanks without loss of quality, though it's not recommended). Those who insist on using auto fuels should follow the STC provisions precisely (i.e., make sure you put in the recommended amount of 100LL).

4. Avoid *sudden* changes in power. Yanking the throttle back from max power places undue loads on the crankshaft, rods, etc. It has been found to cause failures in counterweighted engines. Ease in the throttle on takeoff and ease it out during your power reductions.

5. Avoid shock-cooling your engine. Another consequence of quick power changes is to heat/cool those portions of the engine that cool rapidly, especially in colder temperatures. Shock-cooling is a major contributor to cylinder failures.

6. Put your engine on an oil-analysis program. It has been proven that oil analysis can find problems within the crankcase long before they become major.

7. *Fly* your engine. An engine that is not used is getting almost as much damage done to it as one that is operated improperly. Atmospheric moisture corrodes magneto components and creates bearing-etching acids in your oil. Moisture rusts cylinders, which may make your piston rings take a set on the cylinder wall. Extended ground runs may get your oil warm, but the inadequate cooling may damage the very components you want to save.

Only flight operation can get temperatures up to levels that can rid the oil of moisture-induced contaminants while assuring proper cooling. Optimum engine life can be reached at 15 or more hours per month of operation, according to Lycoming.

Harbingers of Trouble

Often, an engine will provide some sign of an imminent problem. Here's what to look for:

1. Abnormally rough running immediately after start. An engine that rattles and shakes for even a few seconds after start and then smooths out may have sticking valves. The valve guides should be inspected for proper clearances and reamed, if necessary.

2. Oil in the exhaust pipe. Especially true of turbocharged aircraft, oil in the tailpipe is indicative of something not sealing properly. On turbos, oil in this area can mean real trouble.

3. Soot in the exhaust pipe. Black soot deposits indicate rich operation which leads to excessive oil contamination, fouled plugs, preignition and detonation, and poorer lubrication of cylinder walls. Properly operated engines should have exhaust stacks that are a light powder gray or tan.

4. Intermittent abnormalities in operation. Problems that "come and go" or that frequently require a full-power run-up to clear are definite indications that something is wrong. If necessary, take your mechanic along and show what's happening (mechanics are far more attentive when they are riding behind the problem).

5. Oil anywhere but in the crankcase. With the exception of oil loss through the breather during radical maneuvering, oil should remain in the crankcase during normal operations. Evidence of leakage may indicate a loose attachment, a bad gasket, a blocked breather or deteriorated oil lines or fittings.

6. Excessive oil consumption. Oil consumption in excess of that advised as normal by the manufacturer for your particular engine indicates you've got a problem. A jump in consumption over a 25-hour period, too, may indicate something is going wrong. Consult a competent mechanic for advice.

And, by all means, make sure the people who work on your airplane are competent. It's unfortunate that the FAA can't look into the soul of a mechanic during the testing process. Many of the takeoff accidents in our sample resulted from problems caused by mechanics' carelessness. Such problems as rags left in intakes, bearings installed backwards, compressions considered acceptable even though below limits all would have been prevented had the fellows with the wrenches been conscientious. It's in your best interest to screen the individual you're depending on to help keep your aircraft airworthy.

Preflight Strategies

We know all about annual and 100-hour inspections done by mechanics, but few of us seem to really recognize that the most important inspection of all is done by the pilot. So many of us gloss over the preflight by, maybe, checking the oil and ducking under the wings momentarily. I've been guilty of it, and so, probably, have *you*.

Focusing on what is revealed by the takeoff-accident record, let's see what shouldn't be glossed over:

1. Fuel quantities. Many accident reports had notes similar to this: "Since fuel wasn't available at the airfield, the pilot departed for a nearby airport with 'enough to make it that far.'" Some pilots used sticks to check their tanks; others didn't bother checking at all. Some knew their fuel gauges were unreliable and depended *solely* on their watches. All crashed.

Something that must be considered when you are low on fuel is that fuel moves to the low side of the tank when you rotate on takeoff. When you "stick" the tank, it is level. When you rotate for takeoff, all that gas moves to the back of the tank and can leave the fuel feed port high and dry. The fuel in the lines is quickly used up at full power and, at around 100 feet, the engine sputters and dies. It's better to make arrangements to add several gallons of fuel than to risk ending up in a heap.

2. Check for fuel contamination and water. Fuel-testing devices are inexpensive and readily available. Get one and use it before the first flight of the day and following *each* refueling. Check for proper fuel grade (color), no contaminants floating around (i.e., rust flakes, dirt, etc.) and, of course, for water. And, test *all* the aircraft sumps, not just the one(s) at the engine(s); the engine sump may not show the water that was just pumped in by the line truck.

If you find anything questionable, go out to the wing tip and shake the airframe and/or push down on the tail until you get a good, nose-high angle. This can jar loose water and contaminants that didn't settle right next to the sump drain. Test again. If anything appears, maybe a better inspection of the tanks is required.

(By the way, by performing these first two steps, you have just decreased your chances of a takeoff power loss by over 30 percent.)

3. Check the weather. It's likely that, during a briefing, you listen intently as the FSS specialist covers ceilings and winds, but yawn when the temperature and dew point are given. You shouldn't. That's your key to deciding whether you're in for a day of carburetor icing. It can be 90 degrees and sunny, but a muggy day can mean icing in the venturi.

4. Check your exhaust stacks. As pointed out previously, clean, light tan or gray exhaust stacks tell you the engine is burning fuel efficiently. Black soot is indicative of excessive richness, and oil stains may be foretelling problems.

5. Check fuel vents. The biggest problems are ice build-ups and insect nests. Listen for a rush of air when you remove the filler caps. Also, a small puff of air into the vent tube will usually determine if the tube is clear. A flashlight can aid in determining blockage near the end of the tube. Any hiss on cap removal or resistance to blowing into the vent tube should be investigated. Check the owner's manual for any information on this.

6. Inspect the air filter. Air filters are relatively inexpensive items and should be serviced frequently, especially if you're operating from dusty strips. Take a good look to satisfy yourself that the filter will flow all the air your engine will require.

7. Brief your passengers. It is pretty much standard procedure to give newcomers to flying a briefing prior to getting into the airplane. Indeed, most of us probably brief them all the way to the airport. Regardless, prior to boarding, it is a good idea to include specific instructions not to touch anything without asking first. Airplanes are completely foreign to newcomers, and, as the fellow with the camcorder found out, what looks like a throttle to us may look like the vent knob on a '63 Chevy to them.

Before-Takeoff Tips

During starting, taxi and run-up, there are several things you can monitor to help determine engine health prior to takeoff:

1. Pay attention on start. Remove your headset and listen to the engine. Listen to the starter groan. Listen for irregular compression cycles and for misfiring and roughness. The engine should quickly settle into a stable idle, and oil pressure should be up within a few seconds (longer in winter, but always within handbook time limits).

2. Stay below 1,000 rpm during the first few minutes of operation. Revving the engine before the oil has a chance to lubricate everything

contributes significantly to engine wear and, under extreme conditions, can cause failure of bearings, pistons, cylinders, etc. Especially for an 80-octane engine running on 100LL, lean the mixture as soon as a stable idle is reached. This will reduce the amount of lead contamination that fouls plugs and contributes lead sludge to the oil. Watch the gauges for fluctuations in oil pressure, fuel flow, etc. Everything should be stable.

3. During the first few minutes of operation, avoid using excessive power to move the aircraft. If pulling out of the chocks is difficult to do without a lot of power, it is a good idea to shut down and move the aircraft by other means. Otherwise, not only would you abuse your engine, but your prop, as well. Keep in mind that while taxiing, engine cooling is poor; so, monitor your cylinder head temperature closely.

4. Be critical during the run-up. This is the last chance to check everything prior to asking the engine for all it's got, and you want to make sure it's got it. Just prior to advancing the throttle for run-up, put the mixture to full rich. Advance the throttle slowly and perform the mag check as pointed out in the operating handbook.

The carb heat check should be made as follows: Pull the heat control out and observe the drop. *Hold it there* for 10 to 15 seconds and watch for any rise in rpm. If a rise in rpm occurs, you had carburetor ice. Keep the carb heat on until no further rise is observed. Then, turn off the carb heat and note the rise in rpm. Check oil pressure and other engine instruments for proper indications. Return the throttle to idle.

It is important to note that if carb icing conditions exist and you have a long hold, waiting for traffic or a clearance, following the run-up, it's cheap insurance to run up the engine a little and apply carb heat just prior to taking the active (be sure to turn it back off, too). Under certain conditions, ice can build up quickly, leaving you without all the engine can deliver.

Moment of Truth

Takeoffs are pretty much whatever your particular application requires, but I'd like to point out a couple of items worthy of attention regardless of your situation:

1. Unless stipulated otherwise in your owner's manual, leaning the mixture may be necessary at density altitudes above 5,000 feet. Just prior to takeoff, find a debris-free area, run the engine to full power and lean the mixture by reference to either the EGT or tachometer. Try to minimize the time at high power, though. Bring the throttle back and proceed with the takeoff.

2. Avoid sudden throttle movements. When applying takeoff power, apply it gradually to give the oil system time to catch up with the higher

lubrication requirements and to minimize acceleration loads on the crank, rods and other internal components. This is especially important for counterweighted engines, which can be damaged in short order by snap accelerations.

3. Minimize engine heating. At takeoff, the engine is putting out all the heat it is capable of. As soon as obstacles are cleared, the nose should be lowered and airspeed increased to improve cooling of the engine, whether you reduce power or not. Best rate and angle of climb figures are only short-duration maneuvers; when you don't need them, don't use them.

First Power Reduction

It's been proven that engine health (read *safety*) is improved in the long run by minimizing the use of high power as much as possible. This isn't to say *don't* use high power, but physics, metallurgy and general engineering principles tell us that the more you ask of something mechanical, the quicker it will wear and stress, the end result of which is higher maintenance and/or earlier component failure.

If each of us could see the high-speed photography sequences done by major industrial engine manufacturers of engines being operated at max power, the heaving and pulsating in cylinder and head areas due to high power loads would certainly change the minds of naysayers on this.

Contrary to the beliefs of many, piston engines never reach a "steady state." The virtually instant reversal of directions, ever-changing combustion chamber pressures, power pulses and other dynamics hardly fit a steady state definition. The earliest possible power reduction will benefit the engine and decrease the possibility some undetected flaw will decide to give out.

Only one thing orchestrates a power reduction: a change in manifold pressure (by opening an air valve—the throttle valve). Nowhere does anything disengage, shift gears or otherwise perform "automatic" functions that might disable the engine. The results of the air valve movement are decreased fuel flow and a decrease in combustion chamber pressure which reduces the amount of force being applied to the pistons and cylinders. It's actually a relief to the engine to get the throttle pulled back a little.

Lycoming uses statistics to deny that one has any more chance of an engine failure due to a power reduction immediately after takeoff than in any other phase of flight. In fact, the engine-maker *encourages* power reduction to cruise-climb as soon as all obstacles are cleared, especially for larger turbocharged, geared and other complex powerplants.

The brute force of high rpm and chamber pressures, etc., can, indeed, hide or overcome abnormalities within the engine ... for a time. These may show on the first power reduction, especially when the reductions are not gradual. Valves in need of attention may "hang" when they become hot during the takeoff roll, and a power reduction reduces the forces pounding them through tight guides. Full throttle may be overcoming high frictions generated by deteriorated cylinder/piston assemblies; when power is reduced, these frictions may become more apparent in poor operation or failure.

Yes, problems *do* occur on power reductions, but only when something drastically wrong is going on to begin with. Power reductions are not the *cause* of engine failures.

Reducing power shortly after takeoff is a good idea. Like many other aspects of flight, though, it has a time and place. The wrong time to practice power reductions is when your takeoff will carry you over densely populated areas, forests, rocky terrain or any other place with undesirable landing areas. The right time is when you've got several thousand feet of runway directly ahead of you and a forced landing is easily accomplished. Common sense dictates the use of the power.

One final thought on this subject: Continental derived the GO300 (175-horsepower, geared engine) from the 0300 (145-horse, direct-drive engine). Behind the geared section, the engines are virtually identical. Because of the direct drive, the O300 operates consistently at lower rpm than the GO300. Solely because of this difference, the GO300's TBO was reduced from the O300's 1,800 hours to 1,200 or 1,400 hours (depending on model).

Operating an engine at higher power than necessary simply wears it out faster.

Inside
the Engine

*I*n the last chapter we saw some of the reasons that *engines fail. Much of the grief that those pilots came to could have been avoided had they operated their engines better on a consistent basis.*

It's tough to avoid abusing your powerplant in today's IFR environment: ATC wants all the speed they can get out of you, which is hard to do if you want to avoid, say, shock-cooling your engine.

One key to fending off future engine failure is to have a better understanding of what goes on under the cowling. Here's a detailed look.

Understanding the Engine

Have you ever really considered what goes on inside your aircraft engine?

While cruising along at, say, 2,400 rpm, each piston travels up and down 40 times a second, the valves open and close 20 times each, and each spark plug fires 20 times.

In an hour's time at cruise, your crankshaft will make 144,000 revolutions and the pistons will reverse direction 288,000 times.

Between overhauls, the propeller will turn 259,200,000 times.

The common air-cooled aircraft engine is a marvel of strength, simplicity and engineering. Considering that most designs originated well over 50 years ago, it's amazing the foresight the designers had in those days.

It is equally amazing that many of us still don't know how to properly operate our engines.

One of the highest-cost items which aircraft owners face between engine overhauls is cylinder maintenance brought about principally by poor operating technique.

Because of the need to create a lightweight engine, designers maximized the use of light materials (aluminum, mostly) and minimized the use of heavy materials (such as steel).

Though they came up with very light engines for the purpose, there is a penalty for the use of aluminum. This relatively soft metal stretches and shrinks with temperature changes far more than steel.

Offsetting that penalty somewhat is aluminum's good ability to transfer heat.

The superior heat-conducting and high expansion characteristics present something of a dilemma: Our engine will cool itself well through conduction, but it will shrink into itself (like a balloon when you let the air out slowly) while doing so.

Metals heat and cool unevenly. The surface of the metal will cool quickly, while deeper down, the heat takes more time to get out.

This develops stresses within the metal where the outside (cooler) portion shrinks faster than the inside (warmer) metal.

In areas where the metal is of uniform thickness, the stress is more spread out and is not as critical as the stress that occurs when large layers, such as crankcases and accessory drive cases, are cooled.

Strength vs. Weight

The cylinders in your aircraft engine are made of a combination of steel and aluminum.

This is necessary because of the high pressures of combustion, the higher wear resistance necessary to accommodate piston movement, the lower shrinkage involved and other factors.

Basically, the cylinder, itself, is made of steel and has fins for cooling. The cylinder is attached to the cylinder head, which is made of aluminum. The cylinder head also has fins for cooling.

The cylinders on a common aircraft engine, then, are steel sleeves within which the pistons travel. These steel sleeves are mated—very firmly, by heating the whole arrangement and bolting it together—to an aluminum cylinder head which contains the valves and associated hardware.

This design allows the cylinders to be strong, yet retain their light weight, but it causes some problems.

The aluminum cylinder head is cast, then machined into shape. Though the engineers did all they could to minimize the problem, all cylinder heads are plagued by having thick metal in some areas and thinner metal in other areas.

As we learned earlier, this means the head cools faster in some areas than others, and different levels of stress are created.

Because an area of high stress has about the same effect as bending a piece of metal back and forth (it will soon start to crack and weaken), cylinder heads are very susceptible to cracking, especially in areas where high heat can turn to low heat in a hurry—as in the combustion chamber.

Like running a bad balance in your checkbook, the problem gets worse as time goes on.

One means of reducing stress cracking is to *slowly* heat and cool the cylinders, so heat transfer in the thicker areas can "catch up" to the thinner areas.

Not only will this reduce the risk of a power loss while in flight, it will reduce your maintenance costs.

Cylinder maintenance is expensive. A rebuilt cylinder will cost $350 and up. To have a cylinder crack welded will cost well over $150. Include the mechanic's time and labor, and you can easily spend $500 or more *per cylinder*.

Easy on the Throttle

Here are a few simple practices which can help you reduce the risk and cost of cylinder cracks:

To an engine, a throttle snapped to idle would be like you jumping into a frozen pond—everything sort of shrinks up and stresses out.

The name of the game is to minimize rapid heating and cooling of the engine, regardless of the type of operation.

Chopping the throttle from cruise to idle power is a definite no-no. Combustion temperatures can drop 500 or more degrees in seconds, and all that aluminum is trying to get rid of the heat and stressing itself out in the process.

Some other ideas:

1. Get a cylinder head temperature gauge. If you already have one, use it.

We typically make power reductions by increments of 50 degrees or less on the cylinder head temperature (CHT) gauge. Even in the pattern, it is possible to keep CHT power adjustments within these limits.

2. Plan to begin a descent from cross-country cruise altitude or even from the practice area way out (several miles), using only slight power reductions.

We normally use a 200-300 fpm descent rate and try to arrive at pattern altitude a couple of miles from the field. We have never had any trouble working out an early descent with Air Traffic Control.

3. Try to plan touch-and-goes and power-off stalls for warm-weather

days. Cooling of engines occurs more rapidly in low temperatures.

Our personal rule is no air work that will require idle operation of the engine in ambient temperatures below 40 F.

4. Wen very cold temperatures (say, below 25 F), try to carry at least some power through an entire landing approach.

We carry power to touchdown, if possible. Otherwise, We bring power to idle in the flare.

5. Use a "winterization" kit when appropriate.

But make sure you take the winterization kit off when the manual says to. Overheating an engine is no better than shock-cooling it.

6. When performing maneuvers such as power-off stalls and approaches to simulated emergency landings, pull the power off slowly.

Though you may not make the target 50-degree reduction increments on the CHT, you'll at least be doing *something* to allow temperatures to stabilize somewhat.

7. When descending from cruise altitude, keep the mixture leaned as long as possible.

We adjust the mixture full-rich just before leveling off in the pattern. The extra fuel provided by suddenly enriching the mixture cools the incoming charge and shocks the cylinders from the intake side.

Another benefit of this tactic is a small savings of fuel, which is nothing to waste at today's prices.

Avoid the Extremes

Really, what is good for the cylinders is good for the whole engine. Rapid cooling has bad effects on anything that shrinks and expands with temperature changes.

The cylinder sleeves shrink and expand around the rings a little bit. The front of the crankcase being blasted by the cold air cools a little faster than the back. The accessories meet even more abrupt temperature changes.

Think back to what we talked about at the beginning of this chapter. Looking at it another way, you can see that you get only so many revolutions before the propeller needs to be overhauled. The faster you use them up, the fewer hours you will get between overhauls.

The valves will only open so many millions of times before they are worn out of limits. The bearings will only support the load for so many revolutions before they need replacement.

Much like an automobile tire, if you abuse these engine components, they won't make their rated service lives. If you take care of them, they'll go the distance and beyond.

Operating Tips

Here are some more good practices:

1. Use the minimum power you need at cruise or for whatever mission is on hand.

An engine operated at reduced rpm not only makes valves, rings, accessories, etc., work less often, but the reduced combustion pressures in the cylinders reduce the load that's being put on bearings, pistons, rods, cylinder bases, etc.

If you're going out to the practice area or just seeing the sights, the extra 10 knots won't mean a thing to your logbook and can add a lot of life to the engine.

Even on cross-country flights, we usually use 50 to 60 percent power (or less at high altitudes) and find our trips taking only a few minutes longer.

The reward comes when your engine is still running strong at TBO (the engine manufacturer's established time between overhauls).

2. On takeoff, reduce power as soon as practical to a cruise-climb setting and let the nose down a little to improve cooling.

Though full power should be used on the takeoff roll (the engine mixture is full-rich and provides extra cooling), a slight power reduction as soon as a climb is established will go a long way in saving engine wear.

The book says our best climb rate is 65 mph, but we find that the CHT drops from 325 degrees to 275 degrees when we pull back the throttle a little and lower the nose to maintain 75 mph on a warm day.

3. Put your engine on a good oil-analysis program.

At each oil change, get the oil analyzed to get early indications of problems that can be fixed long before a failure can occur. Record each reading in your engine logbook; the readings can be compared to spot changing trends.

4. Abide by the engine and aircraft manufacturers' recommended maintenance intervals.

Oil changes and other routine maintenance is cheap compared to catastrophic engine failure. Such failures can almost always be prevented by detection of problems early on through good maintenance combined with oil analysis.

If you own an airplane, no doubt you know the high cost of keeping the engine healthy. The practices we've discussed we use, and we've seen others who've had 2,000-hour (TBO) engines go beyond 3,000 hours only because they always kept in mind how that engine is operating at any given time and operated the engine accordingly.

Over time, these practices will become habits that can have a very real effect on your aircraft's performance, reliability and cost of upkeep.

Like people, engine health is determined a lot by stress and TLC (tender, loving care).

Contributor Bill Kelly has been around the block a few times, and has seen more than his share of aviation blunders and dumb stunts.

Here he shares some of what he's learned about recip engines over the years, with some common-sense ideas on keeping them working well.

Engine Management

There is one (small) advantage to getting older: you pick up a lot of valuable experience along the way. You also begin to notice that people make the same mistakes over and over. Let me share some of what I've learned.

Let's start with one of the most common operating problems I've seen: the high-rpm engine start. I see this, and hear it, every time I'm at an airport. Some pilot fires up his recip and allows it to accelerate to 2,000 rpm before he retards the throttle, maybe only to about 1,500 rpm. Then he revs up again to start an immediate taxi.

By the time this guy gets to the run-up area, he has probably worn a measurable amount of hardened steel from the camshaft and valve tappets, and possibly has scuffed a few pistons against dry cylinder walls. Hopefully, the crankshaft bearings had enough of an oil film to prevent damage, but don't count on it. For sure, he has shot some of those precious TBO hours, and the next overhaul may be very expensive.

You can do hundreds of hours of wear and damage to your engine if you allow it to go to high rpm before the lubricant is flowing, especially if your bird has that infamous Lycoming O-320H engine that Cessna used for a few years in the 172. I've seen a camshaft from an H-engine with lobes scraped down to an almost circular shape.

Keep the starting rpm *low*, preferably below 1,000 rpm, and keep it there for at least one whole minute—longer if the ambient and oil temperatures are low. Be especially careful to keep the rpm down there if you are running "single-weight" straight summer-grade oil (with a viscosity index of, say, 50 weight). That stuff does not want to flow when outside air temperature gets down close to freezing.

The oil pump may cavitate (fail to pump) if the oil is too thick. The various oil passages may be partially plugged with the thick lubricant. Hydraulic lifters may not "lift" because they can't be filled quickly enough due to the increased viscosity of the cold oil. "Oil squirts" may be dribbling, instead of spraying cylinder walls and other wear-prone components. Bearings may run dry. Splash-lubricated components won't get much splash from oil that's as thick as cold honey.

I still remember the old Beech 18 that I ferried to Africa in the dead of winter. We knew that we would have to have an oil-replenishment system, because the Pratt & Whitney R-985 radials used a lot of oil, and there would be legs of up to almost 1,500 miles over water. The answer was a five-gallon can filled almost to the top with 60-weight oil and installed in the cabin with a hand-operated piston pump and selector valve to allow refilling each engine oil tank.

While en route to the northeast U.S., the cabin heater quit, and cabin temperature rapidly dropped to near-ambient (below freezing by the time I reached New Hampshire). After a quick stop for customs in Bangor, Maine, I headed on to Gander, Newfoundland. En route, I tried the oil-replenishment system for the first time while airborne. No luck. The oil in the five-gallon can had congealed to such a high viscosity in the frigid cabin that the hand pump wouldn't move it.

I had no problem getting to Gander; there was plenty of warm oil in the engine tanks for that trip. On the ground, I ran the engines every hour or so to keep them warm. I removed the five-gallon can from the cabin and drained it, very slowly, into the FBO's waste-oil bowser. That straight 60-weight oil was really "molasses in January." Then, I refilled the can with AeroShell 15W-50 semisynthetic multigrade oil. It did the trick. I was able to transfer oil to each engine during the long, cold trip to the Azore Islands.

Imagine the engine damage that might have been done had I allowed the 60-weight in the engine oil tanks to congeal during the overnight stay. The engines would have been starved for oil during the next cold start.

Flow Control

Moral of the story: If you are going to fly in cold climates, better either have sufficient engine preheat equipment available or keep the crank-case full of multigrade oil. Better yet, keep your airplane in a heated hangar.

Congealed or very thick oil just will *not* flow fast enough through the oil pump or the many oil passages. Even if the oil is still warm, or it's the middle of summer, or you have multi-viscosity oil, you have to give your engine some time to get the oil flowing everywhere. Give the squirters, splashers, drippers and flowers time to get their full head of pressure and flow rate.

Run that engine slowly after starting it. You can avoid one of the most common causes of early engine wear by giving the oil a chance to get flowing. If it's really cold, give the various metal parts a chance to come up to a decent operating temperature and expand to their normal dimensions.

Remember, also, that a quick rise to high oil pressure right after a cold start is not necessarily good. High oil pressure immediately after start probably means that although the oil pump is pumping, the oil passages are still filled with semi-congealed oil and not allowing full flow. Keep that rpm low!

Water Hazards

Let's switch from lubrication to carburetion and injection. Your big motor was designed to run on a proper mixture of fuel vapor and air. Sudden slugs of water through the carburetor or injectors won't do anything but cause loss of power—maybe *all* power.

Your engine can tolerate lots of moist air and rain entering through the air induction piping, but that's inconsequential when compared to the potential results of water getting into the fuel.

If you find a lot of water while draining your fuel system, there's a good chance that rain or wash water is getting into the tanks through the filler cap. Another possibility is that your fuel supplier has a lousy underground tank system with inoperative water separators.

Several years ago, I bought five dollars' worth of gasoline for my old auto at a local convenience store—right after a heavy rain. What I really purchased was $4.95 of rainwater, thanks to leaks in the underground tanks. Later, I had to buy a new carburetor, too. Since then, I have made a point of dribbling a few drops of avgas or autogas onto a finger before putting the nozzle into the fuel tank. I smell the sample, feel it and watch for it to evaporate rapidly. (Water evaporates slowly and doesn't cool the skin.)

Leaking Fuel Caps

If you park your airplane outside, expect water in the fuel tanks. The fuel caps are always on a top surface and are seldom protected by a hinged cover, as on your auto. Even the best caps leak, and every gas cap seal is suspect. Even after only one night in a heavy rain, expect that you have water in the fuel. If your bird has those modern, expensive flush fuel caps—the ones that always drip a teaspoonful of water into the tank when you open the cap after a rainfall—be suspicious. They may have been leaking water into the fuel for the last two rainy days.

Even the old-fashioned thermos bottle caps under flush cover doors (common on Comanches, Apaches and Aztecs) have been known to leak rainwater, especially if the scupper drain tube is clogged and allows the water level to rise around the cap, itself. Same with the domed fuel caps on small Cessna high-wingers. Just figure that *any* fuel tank cap exposed to the wind and rain is going to leak.

How about that old J-3 Cub with the thin wire rod (the fuel gauge) sticking out the top of the tank cap ahead of the windshield? I know from experience that water will enter the gas tank by dribbling between the rod and its tube in the gas cap. You had better drain the gascolator thoroughly if your Cub is tied down outside.

Don't figure that you will get *all* of the water out of your fuel system with routine preflight drainings of the tank sumps, low-point drains and gascolator. You may have that Cessna bladder tank problem, in which water is trapped by wrinkles in the rubber bladder. Apaches and Aztecs have been alleged to trap water in the aft end of their fuel tanks. Independent investigators have run tests on several other airplanes and were able to show considerable undrainable water in various airplane fuel systems.

Rain Shelters

So, what can a pilot do to be sure that he or she doesn't have a big slug of water just waiting for the right pitch/bank attitude after takeoff to send it on its way into the carburetor or injector?

Best thing: Do not park outside if rain is forecasted. Sure, I know that we can't all afford to hangar "Old Bessie" at the home field and that we often make overnight stops during cross-country flights. But you can ask your local shop to check the fuel tank cap seals. You can purchase temporary rain shields for your gas caps. One source is Norm Smith of Aerotrim, which has some nifty plastic and foam rubber rain shields for "flush" tank caps.

If I parked an airplane with protruding caps outside (Cessna 152, Cherokee, etc.), I would consider duct-taping an old coffee cup over each fuel cap for the overnight, rainy stays—anything to keep falling or blowing rain from getting to the cap seals.

You could shake Old Bessie's wing tips and lower and raise the tail during your tank drainings if the airplane has been sitting outside in the wet. (This procedure actually is required by an AD on many Cessna singles.) You could drain the sumps after *every* refueling. You could carry a quart jar and dump your drain tube or cup samples into it, instead of dumping them on the ramp. Then, maybe, you would be willing to drain three or four samples from the gascolator and other low-point areas to be sure that you had completely drained the fuel lines, themselves.

Even a few drops of water in the fuel sample is reason to shake, rattle and roll Old Bessie until the samples are free of any sign of water or crud. Then, drain four or five *more* samples. Expect that if you get water from the fuel tank low-point drains, there will be water in the fuel lines to the gascolator and engine—and that, maybe, it won't come out with just a single sample of fuel. You should drain sufficient fuel from the gascolator to at least equal the volume of the fuel lines between the tanks and the gascolator, itself. If there is a low-point drain between the tanks and the gascolator, give it extra attention; if it's low enough, it could trap a lot of water.

For severe cases of water contamination—where you continually get water in the fuel samples—be ready to drain and discard *all* of the fuel. Have your mechanic swab the fuel tanks dry and disconnect fuel lines in the low-point areas if there aren't sufficient drains there. Don't expect that water will flow uphill through a fuel line to the gascolator drain valve. The water may pool at the low point, while fuel flows over it to the drain. Remove and clean the gascolator filter. In some cases, you might even have to have the fuel tanks removed to get them dry.

Case in Point

That was a lot of words on the relatively simple procedures for draining and sampling fuel. But the record shows that a lot of crashes have resulted from contaminated fuel—mostly from water contamination.

I recently worked with a mechanic to re-skin the belly and left side of an old, all-metal high-winger that had been left sitting in the rain for many months. Several weeks earlier, on the airplane's first takeoff in many months, the engine had quit due to water in the fuel. It wiped out several citrus trees in the forced landing. And gave me a job as "Rosie the Riveter."

Bad fuel from the supplier? No. Condensation? No. The tanks had been left full. Bad tank caps? Yes. The seals were worn and cracked, and incapable of keeping out heavy rainwater. Poor preflight inspection? Yes. The owner didn't take the time to borrow a ladder and, therefore, couldn't reach the wing tank drains. He drained only a token amount from the gascolator. He missed the bucketful of rainwater in the tanks and fuel lines.

Remember, your carburetor feeds the engine almost from the very bottom of the bowl. Your injector servo will feed the engine any liquid that comes to it from the fuel pump. Less water than it takes to make a demitasse of spiced tea is enough to make your engine quit. And it won't run again until it gets pure fuel again. By then, you may be in the trees, right after takeoff. That's when contaminated fuel usually seems to strike.

Enough words on bad fuel. Just remember that it's a bigger killer than bad magnetos, blocked air filters and engine mechanical failures—combined!

Maligned Magnetos

Let's discuss "spark"—*ignition*, that is. Magnetos and spark plugs. Over the past few years, there has been lots of criticism of the ancient state of ignition art and bemoaning for the lack of solid-state, breakerless ignition systems for airplanes (except in the short-lived Porsche/Mooney PFM).

Sure, there are some disadvantages to the old-fashioned magneto. Coils do occasionally burn out. Condensers may slowly break down. Expensive points may burn and wear. Compared to the newest automotive electronic ignitions, the spark isn't as hot but is of longer duration, which leads to more rapid plug erosion. But the biggest advantages of electronic ignition are more applicable to high-rpm engines. There's not as much value for slow-revving airplane motors. Bendix and Slick mags generally do a good job of providing the right spark at the right time.

You get either a "retard breaker point" or "impulse coupling" to give retarded spark for starting, then a well-advanced spark for high power. Sure, it may not be quite the optimum spark advance for your particular power setting, and it may cost one or two percent in power or fuel economy—but it's *reliable.*

As a pilot, you just have to make sure that the magneto, high-tension leads and spark plugs are in good shape. Overhaul the mags when you overhaul the engine—maybe even sooner. Shell out a few bucks to replace worn and aged plug leads. Clean or replace the spark plugs when necessary.

That 100LL fuel has only half of the lead content of 100/130 avgas but way too much lead content for the older, low-compression engines. That lead is not only bad for your valves, it can mean slow or quick death for spark plugs, as well.

Get the Lead Out

If you fly an older airplane, or one with a low-compression engine designed for 80/87 octane avgas, you can help protect your plugs against lead fouling with proper leaning. That means leaning after starting the engine and before taxiing, and leaning during flight, after landing and while taxiing back to the ramp. You might want to consider mixing TCP with your 100LL, to help "scavenge" the lead.

Even if you have a newer engine with a higher compression ratio and fuel injection, you can help your spark plugs (and valves, too) by leaning the mixture a bit while taxiing. Maybe lean just a hair leaner than idle best-power for a minute or two before shut-down, just to clean the spark plugs for the next start.

Do it like this: Once in the chocks, set the rpm at 800-1,000, then very slowly pull the mixture farther back until the rpm peaks and starts to fall as the engine tries to quit. Keep enough fuel flowing to keep the engine running smoothly, but let it run for a minute with an oxygen-rich mixture in the combustion chamber. There won't be enough of a temperature rise to damage anything, but the slightly elevated temperature plus the extra oxygen will tend to clean plugs that may have been fouled while you were taxiing in.

Induction Air

So far, we have covered lubrication and high-rpm starts, and touched on fuel systems and ignition. Now, let's consider the induction system, which passes outside air to the carb or injectors, then on into the innards of that big, expensive motor.

Except in a few homebuilts, the induction air is going to flow through some sort of filter—either the folded-cardboard type or some sort of foam rubber or metal mesh. Almost always, that air filter is going to be exposed to whatever trash that's kicked up during taxi or in the air you fly through.

If there's any sand or dust on the taxiway or runway, some of it is bound to get "vortexed" up into the air filter by the propeller. (Next time the ramp is wet, take a look—from a safe distance—below a spinning prop. You may see a tiny water tornado reaching upwards from the ground.)

Now, take a look at the size of your airplane's air filter and compare it to the one on your automobile. Sort of small for such a big airplane engine, isn't it? Won't take much crud on the front face of the filter to make it start acting like a choke and restricting air flow. And it's likely that some of that crud is slowly leaking through the filter into the engine, itself. If you have a periodic oil analysis done, you may see a rise in silicon when the bad stuff gets inside that big motor. There, it acts like sandpaper, causing rapid wear of metal components.

I'll bet that most pilots change their auto air filters more frequently than they change or clean their airplane filters. It's easy to do with the auto. Just pull into one of those "fast-lube" establishments, order five quarts of 10W-40, new filter and lube job, have them check the differential and transmission, and replace the air filter while they're at it.

But what do you do with your airplane? I'll bet that many of you leave air-filter servicing for the annual inspection. At the very least, you should check the air filter frequently, especially if your engine doesn't have an oil filter. Dirty induction air *does* result in dirty and abrasive oil. So, it's a good idea to also change your oil much more frequently if your motor doesn't have an oil filter.

False Economy

Let's finish up with two "horror stories" of bad engine repairs to reinforce the point that you cannot afford anything but good repairs on something as expensive as an airplane engine.

First, there was the little Continental C-85 that "swallowed a valve" on a training flight. The valve head punctured the top of the piston and spread pieces of aluminum into the crankcase. The quick repair involved immediate replacement of cylinder and piston, then a flight to home base. By then, flakes of aluminum had flowed throughout the engine and contaminated all the bearing surfaces. Result: a complete and expensive overhaul.

Second, another small engine, a Lycoming O-235, that also swallowed a valve. This time, there was no piston damage. The engine got a new cylinder and piston, and was put back into service. Less than an hour later, a pilot taxied back in with a red-hot engine. The new cylinder was steaming and had the color of the blued barrel of an expensive shotgun. All the paint had been burned off. Reason? The cylinder and piston had been replaced without changing or checking the connecting rod. The rod had been bent by piston head contact with the wayward valve. Because of the bent connecting rod, there were large side forces between the new piston and new cylinder—very high friction and much heating. And ruined piston, rings and cylinder. There also was the possibility of damage to the crankshaft and main bearings.

Moral: Don't mess with halfway repairs to that expensive airplane motor. Get the repairs done properly and completely. Don't mess with less-than-adequate servicing, inspection, preflight or operation of any of the engine systems. That big chunk of metals up front is worth somewhere between $10,000 and $40,000. Treat it right. Your life and wallet depend on it.

Engine Ground Checks

I n the first section we touched on pre- and postflight
inspection procedures that can increase both your
safety and the longevity of your airplane. For that
discussion, we looked at the aircraft as a whole system, and we were thinking
of the entire thing.

Here, Bill Kelly will get more specific and concentrate on the powerplant.
There are many things a pilot can do, some of them not obvious, and few of them
taught anywhere, that can help to keep your engine from suffering a premature
death.

Beyond the Checklist

Drivers don't need to know much about their cars. If something goes
wrong, they can just pull off of the interstate and wait for help. Not so
if you are a pilot. There are no shoulders or rest stops on the airways.
Pilots have to have a little mechanical knowledge.

At the very least, being able to brief your mechanic about a problem
can save repair time and costs. Even more important, knowledge of
how your aircraft works can enable you to know when even a seem-
ingly minor mechanical problem is good cause to cancel a flight.

I suspect that many of the "unexplained" accidents involving engine failures could have been avoided if the pilots had taken their time
before takeoff to do a really thorough preflight and run-up. But there's
much more involved in conducting a good preflight than what's
included on the checklist. In this article, we'll go beyond the checklists
and try to get a little more familiar with our airplanes' powerplants and
the clues they can provide about our chances for a glitch-free flight.

Prop Tips

A good place to begin is with the propeller. You can get some important information about your engine by pulling the prop through a few strokes. This shouldn't be attempted, of course, unless you know how to do it safely. Several weeks ago, a friend scared me by walking up to the front of his homebuilt and pulling the prop through several times. We had just wheeled the little composite rocket out of the hangar—hadn't even started a preflight walk-around. No chocks. No tie-downs.

I felt justified in hollering, "Stop." A quick check of the cockpit indicated *almost* everything was OK for the pull-through: mixture off, ignition off. But the throttle was full forward. If just one mag wasn't grounded or the carburetor idle/cutoff setting was a little out of adjustment or a bit of fuel vapor lurked in an intake tube—he might have been chopped to pieces.

Don't mess around with that big fan blade unless you are prepared for it to kick over some day. Another friend, a mechanic, almost lost a leg when a big Cessna single fired while he was positioning the prop for some engine maintenance. Just one power stroke, but it cut his thigh clear to the bone. Sure, he was a little careless; but what about the owner of the airplane? He had flown many hours without knowing that one of his mags was "hot"—that is, it couldn't be grounded even with the ignition switch shut off.

Grounding Check

For any airplane you fly a lot, you should *know* that the magnetos are really dead when the ignition switches are off. You should have performed an ignition grounding check prior to the last engine shut-down. You won't find this procedure in your airplane's flight manual.

Most pilots end their flights as soon as they're finished taxiing by bringing the mixture control to the idle/cutoff position and switching off the ignition and master switches. Then they go home not knowing if one of the mags is still hot and the prop is just waiting for a little nudge to become a cleaver.

Pilots should put an ignition grounding check on their engine shutdown checklists. Here's how it's done: Let the engine cool as you taxi back at the end of the flight. At your tie-down or hangar, turn off all extraneous electrical and radio gear. Pull the throttle back to idle and note the rpm. Now, switch both mags off. Listen for the engine to quit firing and look for a rapid drop in rpm; but switch the ignition back on before you have lost more than a couple hundred rpm. If the engine begins to quit and the rpm drops when the ignition is turned off, the mag grounding is OK. But if the engine kept running, chances are you have a hot mag.

Over the years, I've had several engines keep right on running smoothly with the ignition switches off. Usually, the problem was traced to a bad "key" ignition switch; but once it was a broken magneto primary (P) lead.

Running Rough

Don't shut off the engine yet. After the grounding check, we have a few more opportunities to learn a little more about the condition and rigging of the engine, while it's still warm.

Check the tachometer and listen to the engine as it runs with the throttle at idle and the mixture full rich. It should idle smoothly and within the prescribed idle rpm range. If the idle is rough and (as is likely) on the low rpm side, it's quite possible that your idle mixture setting is too rich. That lead-laden 100LL fuel will be playing heck with your plugs and valves if this is the case.

Let's explore a bit further by gently leaning the mixture. If the roughness goes away and the rpm increases, you have just adjusted the mixture from an over-rich condition toward the best-power setting. Most engine manuals (but very few airplane manuals) specify a maximum and, maybe, a minimum rpm rise when you pull the mixture slowly toward idle/cutoff. A typical max rpm rise is 25 to 50 rpm, which is hard to see on the tach—but usually can be heard.

Yes, you want idle mixture to be slightly rich, but the tendency, especially with injected engines, is for the mixture to be excessively rich. If it's hard to get a good check when the engine is idling, ease the throttle up to 1,000 rpm and try the leaning procedure again. If you are seeing a 100- to 200-rpm increase when you lean the mixture at low power, that engine is probably way over-rich. Maybe it's time to head for the maintenance hangar, maybe not.

Mixture Control

You probably can handle low-power richness, if it's not extreme. Just lean the mixture a little before you start taxiing for takeoff and after landing.

How much to lean? Well, how far back was the mixture knob when you reached max rpm during the "richness" check? If it was, say, a little more than one knuckle's width from the panel, set the mixture just a little richer than that—maybe three-quarters of a knuckle—so that you get good acceleration from the engine if you add a little throttle. For quadrant-type controls, make a pencil mark or apply a piece of masking tape to mark taxi mixture.

But, what if there was *no* rpm rise when you ran the mixture checks? It could be that your idle mixture is set a little on the lean side. Or it could be that several of your intake pipes are leaking—sucking in air at low manifold pressure to give a lean mixture. Better have this one checked out by a mechanic. A too-lean mixture at idle could cause the engine to lose power on final approach or respond poorly if power is advanced to correct the glide path or to start a go-around.

Gauge Tales

Now it's time to shut down, right? Nope, not just yet. Let's check the idle speed on the tachometer. I used to fly a rented Cessna 172 that idled high—around 900 to 1,000 rpm. Lightly loaded, that Cessna just didn't

---

Pre-Shutdown Checklist

Grounding check
ThrottleIdle, note rpm
Electrical equipment   Off

IgnitionOff, momentarily
            (check for rpm drop)

Mixture check
ThrottleIdle
MixtureRich, note rpm
MixtureLean slightly, listen
            for rpm increase

Gauge, gyro check (during taxi)
Idle speed   Per mfr. specs
Oil temp, CHT Dropping
Oil pressure   Above minimum
Gyros   Erect
Suction gauge   In green
            (1,500 rpm)

Turbocharger
ThrottleIdle for 3 min.
            (to let spool down and
            cool before shutdown)

---

want to land, even with 30 degrees of flap cranked in.

Idle setting has to be checked with a *warm* engine. It's among the items that should be checked after each flight. If the airplane's idle speed is excessive, you might as well trash those landing distance charts in the manual. Trash the stall speeds, also; you'll be able to get "power-off" stalls well below the published figures.

Take a good look at the other engine gauges, too, after taxiing back to the ramp. Oil and cylinder head temperatures should have been dropping while you taxied and made the checks already discussed. Oil pressure doesn't have to stay in the green arc at low power, but it shouldn't drop below the yellow. If it does, you may need an oil and filter change or a switch to the proper oil viscosity for the season.

Similarly, the suction gauge for your vacuum system probably will read low at or near idle rpm, but if you goose the throttle up to 1,500 rpm or so, it should read in the green. If not, you should have the various hard lines and soft tubes in the vacuum system's plumbing checked. If the vacuum instruments (typically, the attitude and heading indicators) roll over and die while taxiing in (or are slow to erect after starting the engine), you should have the inlet filter checked. These things can clog in a hurry, especially if you allow smoking in the cabin.

Turbo Care

Last item before shutdown is the turbocharger—if your airplane has one, that is. Not a check, just a precaution, especially if your bird has a fixed waste gate, à la Seneca, Turbo Arrow or early Mooney M20K.

If you ran all of the checks outlined above, the turbine wheel has had plenty of time to slow down. But I see lots of pilots maneuver their turbo birds into parking spots with big bursts of power, then kill the mixture immediately. Boy! Zero engine rpm means zero oil pressure. But that turbine wheel has been spooled up again and is spinning rapidly without an oil supply. That's not good for the bearings and seals, or for the wallet when you have to go for an early turbo overhaul.

And just imagine what might happen if that abused turbocharger decides to pack it in suddenly on the next takeoff. Quite often there's panic and misidentification of the loss of turbo boost as an engine failure. Typically, when a turbocharger fails, the engine loses about 25 percent of its rated power. That doesn't sound too bad, does it? Well, the problem is that the power loss may be over *half* of the excess horsepower you need to climb.

Compression Check

We started this long discussion with caveats about touching your propeller. Let's get back to what an occasional propeller pull-through can tell you. For starters, it can let you know if you have a weak cylinder (but please be sure that the ignition system is off and that your bird passed a very recent grounding check).

If you have a *really* bad cylinder, you will probably be able to feel it while pulling the prop through one compression stroke for each cylinder. Best to do this when the engine is warm—not cold and not right after shutdown when it's hot (too good a chance of getting a firing from a hot spot inside a cylinder).

"Snap" the prop through four (or six) compression strokes. If you feel relatively little resistance on one of the strokes, try it again with a slow pull-through of each of the cylinders. If you still get indications of a weak cylinder, maybe it's time to call for the A&P and his compression tester.

A mechanic's differential tester is set to inject a small volume of air through a calibrated orifice at a pressure of 80 psi into a cylinder. That value is compared with the pressure that the cylinder is able to contain. A result of 75/80 means that the cylinder can hold 75 of the 80 psi. Not bad. But a reading of 60/80 could signal a problem. A reading of 40/80 would indicate there probably *is* a problem.

If you get a slightly low reading, such as 60/80, don't be in a big hurry to buy a new cylinder, piston, rings, valves, etc. Maybe it's only a valve that needs adjustment or a dirty valve seat. Or, it might be that the compression ring gaps on one piston are lined up and causing temporary, excessive blow-by. Go fly a few more hours and then get another compression check.

During the test, you may be able to *hear* where the pressure is leaking. If you have serious blow-by, the sound of the air rushing into the crankcase might be heard by holding your ear close to the top of the oil dipstick tube or the outlet of the crankcase breather pipe. Problems with exhaust valves or valve seats will give the sound of a viper's hiss through the appropriate exhaust pipe outlet. If the hiss is faint, the valve face and seat might just be loaded up with too much lead and soot from over-rich operation at low power. To check for leaks by an intake valve, have your mechanic unbolt the induction tube and listen at the cylinder head.

Get the Lead Out

A magneto check is among the most important items on the preflight checklist, but few airplane manuals provide any information on what may be amiss if the rpm changes noted during the check are not within the prescribed limits.

If the mag check reveals *no* drop in rpm, one side of the ignition system might not be grounded properly or mag timing may be too far in advance, which could cause destructive detonation in the combustion chambers. The problem should be corrected before flying.

But let's say that just before takeoff, the left mag shows a 200 rpm drop (when 150 is supposed to be the limit). No cause to scrub the flight, yet; it could just be a dirty plug. Run the engine for a minute at 1,000 rpm with the mixture leaned to just above where the engine begins to quit. Then go to full rich and try another mag check at the rpm specified in the manual. Still getting an excessive rpm drop on the left magneto? OK, if there's no one behind you and no loose gravel beneath the prop, go to full throttle for about 30 seconds with the mixture full rich. (If we didn't burn off plug deposits with the mixture leaned at low power, maybe we can blow off the deposits at high power.)

Now, back to the specified rpm and another mag check. If it's OK, then go fly. If you still have that big 200 rpm loss, then taxi back and consult your mechanic. Maybe it's not just a single fouled plug. Maybe it's a problem in the high-tension lead. Maybe it's a bad magneto.

Don't ever consider taking off after a bad and uncorrectable mag check. You would automatically lose 25 percent of your total power (in a four-cylinder engine) if the *other* plug should fail in the same cylinder. And you would probably lose additional power to pumping losses in the dead cylinder. Departing after a bad mag check puts you at risk of losing a considerable amount of your available climb power.

Plug Problems

As mentioned earlier, it's likely that a bad mag check could indicate just one ruined spark plug. If this is the case, you could save yourself a lot of shop labor charges if you could tell them *which* plug needs replacement. Select the left mag position again while you taxi back to the ramp and let that cylinder start to cool if the plug is still misfiring at idle. Shut down and open the cowl.

Go drink a Coke or two and let the engine cool until you can comfortably lay a hand on a cylinder head or exhaust pipe. Then restart the engine, select the left mag and run the engine up to between 1,000 and 1,500 rpm for two or three minutes. If that "bad" spark plug was really fouled, it won't fire at even this low power. Shut down the engine and immediately go out and carefully feel for the relatively cool cylinder head and exhaust pipe. If one cylinder feels lukewarm and the other jugs and their exhaust pipes are too hot to touch, obviously the bad plug (or some other problem) is in the cooler cylinder. To determine which plug, you or a mechanic can simply trace the ignition leads to the left mag.

(To avoid blistered fingers, put grease-pencil marks on each exhaust pipe, close to the cylinder head. The marks on the hot pipes will turn to ash, but the cold pipe will retain the grease mark.)

The first time I used this procedure was during a ferry flight of an old Beech 18. I had taken on a load of highly leaded military 115/145 avgas in the Azores, and the port engine ran slightly rough (very rough on one magneto) en route to the Portuguese Madeira Islands. The check pinpointed the culprit: a very lead-fouled spark plug. After replacing the plug, I continued on to Africa. I've used the procedure several times since then and, in addition to bad plugs, have been able to trace a broken ignition lead and a cracked mag distributor.

Flow Control

Let's finish up our discussion of engine checks with the fuel system. Most pilots dutifully draw a "checker" full of fuel from each drain cock during preflight inspection. Chances are, though, that there's *more* fuel in the line between the tank and the gascolator or low-point drain than can fit in that little plastic cup or tube. Don't count on the water displacing all of that fuel in the long, skinny line. You had better drain a good, large quantity of fuel occasionally, especially if your bird has been sitting out in the rain. (If the grass has grown up over the wings since the last time the bird was flown, better have the fuel system emptied and refilled with fresh fuel before flying.) Most checker tubes hold only two ounces of fluid. You'd have to fill one of them 64 times to drain one gallon of fuel. And what's that, close to two bucks?

Don't overlook any special procedures required or recommended for your fuel system. For example, there's an airworthiness directive on some Cessna high-wingers that outlines techniques to shake loose any water that might be trapped in their bladder tanks. And some of the old Piper low-wingers with four-tank systems require a *long* drainage period to ensure that the outboard cells shed all of their contaminating water through the long fuel lines to the gascolator. Better have a one-quart Mason jar handy.

Last item: those fuel tank vents. Sure, during an annual or 100-hour inspection, mechanics will probably check the external condition of vent hard lines and rubber hoses. But *don't* count on them to actually check the air flow through these lines. In some areas of the country, there are nasty little bugs that love to set up housekeeping in these lines. A lot of pilots cover their pitot tubes, but almost nobody protects those little vent tubes under the wings.

Vent Test

I would rather have a plugged pitot tube than a stuffed fuel vent. The airplane will still fly with no airspeed reading (and pilots should be able to cope with the loss of the airspeed indicator), but the engine will stop dead if the fuel tank isn't vented.

Your fuel cap may have a relief valve to open the tank to atmospheric pressure if the vent tube fails, but you don't want to count on it. Better to check the condition of the standard vent system, and there's an easy way to do this: Put a long piece of plastic tubing over the vent opening, remove the tank cap and blow gently into the tube while holding your ear close to the open tank port. If you don't hear a little air flow or if you feel resistance as you blow air into the tube, you may have a blocked vent.

And, while the fuel cap is off, check its seals *closely*. Water in the fuel could come from refueling from a contaminated source or from condensation; but it's much more likely to come from rainwater leaking though deteriorated seals in the filler cap.

Ground Power Check

I'd like to close this chapter with a different sort of test, one that will tell you, simply and directly, if your engine is healthy.

A long time ago, when most air-cooled engines were round (radials, that is), engine and airplane makers specified "field barometric power checks" for those with mechanical superchargers. The simple and useful test could be performed while running up the engine for the magneto and propeller checks.

To do it, the pilot would note the reading on the manifold pressure gauge before starting the engine and then, during run-up, adjust the throttle to get the same reading (field barometric pressure) and determine whether the appropriate propeller speed was being obtained. If, for example, the specified 29.8 inches of manifold pressure (MAP) at Miami did not produce the specified 2,000 rpm, *something was wrong*. Any deficiency in rpm was an indication that the engine probably had a sick cylinder or two, or some other problem.

Today, neither engine- nor airplane-makers provide ground check specifications. Engine manufacturers simply cannot, because of the varieties in installation of any particular engine or propeller model. And airplane builders *won't* because of their all-consuming concerns about product liability.

But you can develop *your own* ground power check procedure. There's one catch: You can't start unless you know your engine is running OK and that airplane performance is nominal. If you have doubts about your engine's health, you won't be able to rely on your baseline. But if you *know* your engine condition and airplane performance are OK, plan to conduct a quick check during the next run-up and pick your own figures of MAP versus rpm.

Let's suppose the manual for your "Bugcrusher" specifies 2,000 rpm for the mag and prop governor checks. However, the manual does not tell you to look for 23 to 24 inches of manifold pressure (MAP) at sea level (or about one inch less for each thousand feet of field elevation above sea level) at the specified 2,000 rpm. That doesn't prevent *you* from observing that your healthy engine requires 23.5 inches MAP to achieve 2,000 rpm for the mag check at Miami (elevation, 10 feet). If you are at Denver or Albuquerque (a mile, and more, higher), you will get 2,000 rpm with only about 18 to 20 inches of MAP.

For average, everyday use—especially if you don't roam much from sea level to mountain airports, or vice versa—just note the MAP needed for the mag or prop governor check. It should *not* change much from day to day. But if you should later find that you need three more inches MAP to get 2,000 rpm at the same field elevation, you might have weak cylinders or some other problem (even if the mag check was OK).

Got an airplane with a fixed-pitch propeller and no manifold pressure gauge? You can perform the same check just by using full throttle for a few seconds during the run-up. The Type Certificate Data Sheet and, maybe, the manual for your airplane will state maximum and minimum values for static rpm at takeoff power on the ground for the propeller you're using. With high density altitudes, the power output will be lower, but so will the load on the fixed-pitch propeller—so it will turn about the same rpm.

If you fly a multi-engine machine, don't be too surprised if there is a difference of one or two inches MAP between the two engines at the designated mag-check rpm. Most likely, the props are set at opposite ends of the low-pitch tolerance limits. Or, it could be that one prop is an inch shorter than the other due to repairs. If you should see a difference of five or six inches, though, there probably is something wrong in the engine that needs the extra manifold pressure to get the prescribed rpm.

Keep in mind that the ground power check procedures outlined above are *relative*. The MAP you note during the check has to be related to what you found when the engine was in good condition.

All you really have to know is what manifold pressure it takes to achieve mag check or prop governor check rpm at the approximate airport elevation. If someday you have to use several more inches to achieve that same check rpm, then maybe the task of supplying sufficient power to spin the prop to the magic number is falling on only a few of your cylinders. Other possibilities are problems with ignition, carburetion, air induction or exhaust. For sure, the information you get during the power check will be valuable to your mechanic.

One caution on the ground power check: Strong surface winds will affect test results considerably. A headwind will "windmill" the prop and let you achieve the test rpm with less MAP. Tailwind effect is just the opposite. If the wind is blowing over five knots, face the airplane crosswind.

The ground power check could save you from an early overhaul. It also could save you from an accident. An engine that suddenly goes weak on a power check might just be trying to warn you that it's close to quitting, completely.

A Little Knowledge

Years ago, pilots had to have an intimate understanding of the workings of their machines. Commercial pilots couldn't even take the right seat until they could recite such things as the thicknesses of their wing and fuselage skins cold.

Our equipment has become more reliable over the years, but you still have to have a little mechanical knowledge—at least enough to know when it's a good idea to cancel a flight because of a mechanical problem and to intelligently brief your mechanic about the problem.

Hopefully, we've gone a few big steps beyond the checklists here. But if you really want to know more about your engine and its related systems, I'd suggest the FAA's *Airframe and Powerplant Mechanics Powerplant Handbook*. It's a few dollars well spent.

Aging Engines

We'll close our discussion of piston engines with some words for those of us who fly behind high-time engines. There's absolutely nothing wrong with a high-time engine, provided it's been cared for and operated properly over its lifetime.

That proviso is the real catch. Most of us have to share the engine with others, or are operating an engine that we don't really know the history of. Problems can arise that are not expected.

Once again, here's Bill Kelly on how to keep tabs on the health of your older engine.

That Old Grey Mare....

So, maybe "Old Bessie" *is* getting a bit old and tired. But does that mean you shouldn't expect the engine to produce the power it could deliver when the airplane was fresh from the factory years ago?

First thought: The FAA would never allow an airplane/engine combination to be certificated if the takeoff or maximum-continuous power output dropped drastically with accumulated flight hours—especially not within the engine's recommended TBO (time between overhauls).

Although it's not in writing, your Lycoming or Continental *is* expected to put out its full rated power clear up to and beyond TBO—*if* you keep it in good condition, *if* you get the "accessories" (magnetos, injector servo or carburetor, exhaust pipes, etc.) overhauled or repaired when necessary, and *if* important things like mag timing and carburetor/injector settings are regularly checked and adjusted.

That big, heavy chunk of "basic engine"—the crankcase, crankshaft, cylinders, pistons, valves—*is* usually good for TBO or more with only routine maintenance and parts replacement.

Yes, I acknowledge that there are a few "problem" engines that may give you early internal distress. But even those infamous O-320-H2ADs in several years' worth of Cessna 172s have had better reports recently, thanks in large part to more owner and pilot care in servicing and in making "gentle" starts.

And, yes, there are some engines apparently more prone to cylinder head cracks, crankcase cracks, valve problems, etc., than some other engines. But a lot of the "problem engine" troubles can probably be attributed more to poor pilot procedures than to the engine, itself, (in particular, foul-ups such as "shock cooling" during low-power descents, high-rpm starts and excessive mixture leaning at high power settings).

For now, let's forget those so-called problem engines and stick to "aging" engines in older airplanes.

The Long Run

Sure, based on problems discovered during your flying or during required inspections, you may have to undergo an early "top overhaul." But, overall, the basic engine "power section" is a long-lived piece.

And during its well-maintained TBO life, it *is* going to continue to put out the power. Performance is *not* going to suffer just because of the hours amassed on the engine.

Consider what you would do with the family auto if at about 100,000 miles (about 2,000 hours at 50 mph), your tail pipes are blowing a lot of white smoke after start-up, your oil consumption has increased to one quart every 300 miles and the tail pipe is sooty. Well, it's only an auto; maybe you'll live with the problems for another 20,000 miles, then trade it in on a newer car.

I faced such a decision two years ago when my old GMC panel van got to be hard to start, produced a lot of smoke when it did start and used a lot of oil. But the power was still good. I decided to go the easy route, and after a complete valve and head job, I now have a clean-burning V-8.

You might have to do the same with your airplane engine, especially if you *have not operated the engine frequently* and/or if you haven't made regular and frequent oil changes. An engine that "sits" for weeks or months on end without lots of flying may get lots of corrosion and rust, and have a lot of sediment in the oil settle in bad places. You're almost sure to get scraping of metal against metal when you do start the engine for your very infrequent flights, because the lube oil has run off some of the critical wear areas.

Consider that truckers do *not* consider 100,000 miles on an engine much more than just a break-in. Those big semi's may well run a million miles or more on their big diesels or gasoline engines. But they *do* get regular maintenance, oil changes and needed parts replacement, and lots of regular, heavy-duty road miles.

The best bet for your aging airplane and engine is *frequent* flying!

Now, say that during your last annual inspection on "Big Boomer," your friendly A&P reported that two of your four or six cylinders showed less than 60/80 psi on the differential compression check. (That "60 over 80" reading means that for 80 psi of air introduced into the combustion chamber above the piston at a prescribed flow rate, the retained pressure was only 60 psi. Twenty pounds are leaking some-where—maybe between the piston and cylinder wall, or around the valves.)

Is that enough reason to pay for two new or overhauled cylinders? *Probably not!* Enough reason to pull the two offending cylinders for a valve and ring job? Again, *probably not!*

Listening for Leaks

You've got to consider *who* ran that differential compression check.

Is he or she well-qualified? Did he suggest that you go fly another five hours, then return with the engine still warm for a re-check? When he reported that cylinder number 3 showed only 50/80 psi on the differential check, did he "listen" at the exhaust pipe, induction air inlet and crankcase breather or oil-filler hole?

If he didn't, then you don't know *where* your supposed compression leak of 30 psi is coming from. You don't need a new cylinder if the problem is only poorly seating valves, maybe due to dirty valve seats or worn valve guides.

If it's a "blow-by" of the piston and rings, there should be a hiss audible through either the oil filler or crankcase oil breather. If it's a bad exhaust valve or valve seat, the leak should be audible near the appropriate exhaust pipe.

If air is leaking around an intake valve, there should be a hiss audible near the main air induction opening. (Be careful here. Don't stick your head within the prop arc to listen near the induction air filter. The prop might kick through under that 80 psi pressure. You might have to remove the intake pipe from the offending cylinder.)

The piston ring blow-by might go away with another few hours of flying and as you get some recent lubrication on the rings and cylinder walls (and, maybe, as the ring gaps rotate away from alignment with each other). If it's a bit of carbon on a valve seat, that also may go away with just a little more high-power operation. Your mechanic can check by "staking" the offending valve stems with a soft hammer (gently pounding the valve open, then closed to check for seating), as described in the FAA's A&P powerplant manual.

Now, if you're getting a 20/80 psi "static" reading on a cylinder or two, you *may* have a real problem. If you're getting 0/80 psi, you may have a disaster in the making—maybe a hole in a piston or a sticking valve.

Checking Compression

Let's talk for a while about that "differential compression" check.

The testing device, unique to airplane engines, introduces a calibrated volume of 80-psi air to an individual cylinder and measures the pressure that the cylinder contains. For this discussion, let's call this a "static" pressure test.

If this test is performed when the engine is cold and hasn't run for a few days, there's a good chance that the portion of the cylinders and rings on the upper side have lost their oil film. It's drained down via gravity, and you won't get a good cylinder/piston seal. Result: a blow-by leak of that 80 psi air into the crankcase. Best bet: *Go fly*. Then, after getting the engine hot, do another static check.

If "listening" to your static compression check indicates exhaust or intake leakage, especially in an older engine, there's a good chance that a bit of carbon has broken loose and is holding a valve slightly off its seat. Again, the best bet is to go run the engine. Run it hard and, preferably, in flight. (Or try that valve stem staking that we mentioned earlier.) Then go back for a re-check.

If your engine is an old, low-compression variety or even a modern turbocharged (and, thus, low-compression) engine, maybe you haven't been leaning it sufficiently for low-power operation, especially while taxiing. Maybe you are making your own carbon and other deposits.

Even a non-turbo, modern, high-compression engine—injected or carbureted—may be running so rich at idle that it generates its own internal carbon (and lead) contamination.

I remember a Piper twin that I worked on several years ago. I assisted the old-time mechanic in checking the right engine, which we would later use in checking AFM engine-out performance figures. Two of the six cylinders showed rather low compression on the static differential pressure test.

We flew a "hard" one-hour flight and re-checked. The results were still low, about 50/80 psi.

This engine was right at its TBO, and you might suspect that it was worn out and not producing its rated power. There was just a little blow-by audible in the oil filler hole when doing this static check. Reason enough to buy two new cylinders? No, not yet. Had there been a bad audible leak around exhaust or intake valves, maybe it would have been time for a "borescope" (inserting a thin, lighted, magnifying, flexible telescope through an open spark plug hole) *before* ordering those new or overhauled cylinder assemblies.

A borescope check might reveal a burned valve or cracked valve seat and save you the cost of an entire cylinder assembly.

But what my master mechanic did was pull out his old "dynamic" compression test gauge (similar to the one you can buy for $20 at the auto parts store).

'Dynamic' Testing

This one checks cylinder compression as the engine is turned at starter motor speed (with a spark plug removed from each cylinder to allow the fastest rotation speed) and with wide-open throttle (to allow maximum cylinder pressure). The powerplant manual calls this a "direct" compression tester.

It's important to keep the ignition turned off while doing this check. For safety, disconnect the high-tension leads from the plugs still in the engine. Even with one plug removed from each cylinder, the engine may still try to run if the *other* plugs fire and there's any air/gas mixture available. It won't run very fast, but enough to hurt you if you get in line with the propeller. And the open spark plug holes may blow a lot of flaming fuel if the remaining plugs fire.

What we found with this "dynamic/direct" compression test was that the two low cylinders had *good* dynamic compression! During that earlier static differential test, those two cylinders would hold only about 50 psi of the inserted 80 psi. But when the engine was turning, with its pistons pumping, the compression in all six cylinder was *almost equal*.

The A&P manual isn't too definitive about dynamic test results, stating only that any cylinder more than 15 psi lower than other cylinders is "suspect." My old Volkswagen "Bug" repair manual is a little more specific, stating that "actual test results are not as important as the difference between the readings." It goes on to say that "all readings should be from about 114-142 psi" (reasonable for a 7-8:1 compression ratio) "... a maximum difference of 28 psi between any two cylinders is acceptable ... greater differences indicate worn or broken rings, leaky or sticking valves, or a combination of all...."

Conclusion on our Piper twin? Well, yes, a well-worn engine with blow-by of the piston and rings when not rotating. But once turning and pumping, the combustion chamber pressures were satisfactory and all nearly the same. Thus, the engine *was* capable of putting out good power.

The engine was old and worn, and ready for overhaul. It was eating some oil. But it still had its power output available. Delaying the overhaul much longer would probably result in more cylinder wear and a higher eventual overhaul cost. But, for the time being, its normal power would be available for flying.

As a double-check, my mechanic checked the temperatures in each cylinder immediately after a high-power ground run. The temps reasonably correlated (they're never the same, due to differences in baffling and air flow), but there were no "cold" cylinders.

Our final check was airborne, in single-engine climb configuration—the most critical configuration. With the well-worn right engine "motating" and the relatively low-time left engine/prop shut down and feathered, we measured single-engine climb performance. Then we reversed the procedure. Results: No appreciable difference in rate of climb; thus, no real difference in horsepower output.

Hours of Power

What does all of the above mean to *you* and the well-worn engine in your Old Bessie?

Well, first: Total hours, alone, do *not* necessarily indicate the power capability of the engine, nor, necessarily, does a differential compression check.

Many *years* since the last engine overhaul and infrequent operation and oil/air filter changes may play a greater part in *lowering* power output and increasing internal wear.

Power also can ebb if you don't have regular checks on spark plugs, ignition harness, magneto timing and carb/injector settings.

For your Old Bessie, or even the "Thunderboomer II" that you are considering purchasing, *hours* on the tach are not usually an indication of engine *power output*. Those hours, along with regular oil analysis and tear-down of the oil filter during oil changes, probably give the best indication of engine *wear*.

Engine wear has lots to do with your overhaul cost and, maybe, with the *safety* of continued operation but, generally, little to do with engine power capability. In general, that old Lyc or Continental is good for within a percent or two of its rated power, even at TBO time.

Now, let's look at how you can check your engine's power output during your preflight run-up. *No*, a "mag check" tells you nothing about engine power output capability. Sure, a "bad" mag check will indicate some slight loss in power capability due to the lack of firing from a spark plug or two. And, of course, a check of your constant-speed prop governor (and a "feather check" of the props on a multiengine airplane) only inform you about the operating condition of the prop system.

What you need—and don't have—to check power output is a "torque meter" to measure the engine's "twist" at a particular manifold pressure (MAP) or throttle setting.

But we *do* have a form of torque indication available in any recip airplane: *the MAP at a given rpm.*

The propeller, whether constant-speed or fixed-pitch, acts as a torque source during the ground run-up checks. Even the constant-speed prop is going to be "fixed-pitch" (on the low-pitch blade angle stop) during these ground tests. Thus, it's possible to estimate overall engine condition *and power capability* just by checking prop rpm against a known MAP or throttle position constant.

Setting a Baseline

Unfortunately, the procedure isn't outlined in your AFM. Nor is it stated in the engine manufacturer's manual, since rpm vs. MAP will vary with the propeller installed and its low-pitch blade angle setting.

But, for Old Bessie, we can devise our own test, so long as we start with a known "good" engine to establish a baseline for the power check.

First, we need to know how good Bessie's engine is. We could go to the shop for an early annual, including a compression check and adjustment of ignition and carburetion.

Better yet, how about checking Bessie's climb and cruise performance against the figures in the AFM? Start out by thoroughly cleaning your propeller blades, front *and* back. Give the airplane a thorough washing and, maybe, a wax job (just like the manufacturer did before *its* performance tests). Get rid of any flaking paint, bug spots and bird doo.

Now check Section 5 of your AFM for the climb performance graph (full-power and "clean"). Note the desired IAS for the weight at which you will be flying. Check the AFM, also, for allowed leaning in the climb. Call your FSS and check the winds aloft; find the average wind direction up to about 7,000-10,000 feet AGL.

We are going to perform *two* climbs of about five minutes' duration each in opposite directions and try to get our headings nearly crosswind to minimize wind shear effects.

Ask the FSS briefer about reported turbulence; there's no point in gathering useless data in turbulent conditions.

Make up a data sheet with columns for *time, pressure altitude* (set your altimeter to 29.92 for this), *OAT* and *rpm*. Plan to take altitude and OAT readings every 60 seconds for about five minutes of continuous climb while flying right *on* the prescribed IAS and on a constant heading. No need to start these climbs at real low altitude; 2,000 feet AGL would be a good starting place and, hopefully, above most low-level turbulence.

Your first climb attempt is going to be a short one, just long enough to get the trim set for the desired climb IAS and to eyeball the needed nose-up pitch attitude.

Then, you'll descend to at least 500 feet below the starting altitude (2,000 feet) and slow to climb airspeed. Come in smoothly with the allowed maximum power—be it maximum-continuous power (MCP), full-throttle or "takeoff" power—while smoothly raising the nose and pegging climb IAS.

Start your stopwatch as you pass through the starting altitude (2,000 feet), record OAT and rpm, and *hold your airspeed constant*, right on the prescribed Vy. Take readings every 60 seconds.

Obviously, assistance *is* needed. Your copilot or flight engineer can record the data while you fly the constant IAS and heading (and call out exact altitude on his one-minute "marks").

Cool the engine gently after this first climb, then descend for a repeat—on a reciprocal heading to cancel wind effects. After the second climb, clean up (probably by just closing the cowl flaps) and get ready for two or three full-power "cruise" runs.

The first cruise run will be up high at about the peak of your climb, another halfway down to the climb starting altitude, and a final max-power run near the climb start point. Record power settings, IAS, altitude and OAT for each run—*and hold that constant altitude* for one minute before taking final readings.

Why *max-power* "cruise"? Because that's easier to set than an exact 75 percent. Achieving "percent MCP" cruise power counts on extremely exact rpm and MAP settings, and a variation of MAP with actual density altitude. Besides, we're interested in max power output for these checks. And, by using max power, we're probably going to need a full-rich mixture (unless the engine is running rough from an over-rich condition) and, thus, won't get into the variations in power by inaccurate leaning.

These flight tests will probably require about a one-hour flight. You might want to refuel immediately so that you can check total fuel burned and, thus, be able to make weight corrections, if needed, to your climb data.

Matching the Book

"Data reduction" is fairly easy since we only want a rough comparison against the AFM charts/graphs.

Let's say that between the two climb tests, you averaged 4,000 feet of altitude gain in five minutes. That's an average of 800 fpm. What was the "mid-altitude" of the averaged climbs, and what was the OAT at that altitude? Check your copilot's data sheet, determine "average" density altitude, then check this data against the AFM.

Let's say your average weight, considering fuel burned, was 2,000 pounds. If your AFM only states climb for max gross weight (and if you were within about 10 percent of that), you can correct your rate of climb (R/C) data to max weight by a strict weight ratio: R/C heavy = R/C light x (weight light/weight heavy).

Whoa! What's this? You averaged only 800 fpm in the climbs, but, for your weight and density altitude, the AFM shows 880 fpm? Old Bessie is down 10 percent in climb from what's stated in the AFM. At first look, you might guess that Bessie's engine has lost more than 20 of its 200-plus rated sea level horsepower.

No. If at a gross weight of 2,000 pounds and at your average density altitude, the AFM shows an 880-fpm climb, that's only 53 *climb* horsepower. Remember: R/C = (*excess* thrust horsepower times 33,000) divided by weight. (One horsepower equals 33,000 ft/lb per minute.) Excess horsepower is what's left over after powering your airplane *through* its drag *at* its climb speed of, say, 90 mph.

Now, taking your flight-data result of an 800-fpm climb and transposing that formula to THP excess = (R/C x weight)/33,000, we find that you were using 48 horses in the climb. That's a loss of only five horsepower from the AFM climb data (53 horses). For a, say, 250-horsepower engine, that's a "loss" of only two percent of rated power. And that's well within "data-scatter" possibilities.

You probably didn't fly the climb test as smoothly as the practiced company test pilot. And maybe your mixture was a little rich or the mag timing a little retarded.

Dirty and Draggy

So, overall climb test results: Old Bessie's engine is OK and we *can* proceed to put together a pre-takeoff ground power check based on this data.

But, first, let's check that full-power cruise data we gathered. Your

AFM probably has a chart or graph showing true airspeed (TAS) at various altitudes and power settings. Using your recorded OATs, correct your indicated altitudes for each run to density altitudes. Correct your IAS values for position error, then for density altitude, to get TAS.

Compare these to the TAS values shown in the AFM for full-power cruise. Don't be too surprised to find Bessie slower than the "book." Speed data isn't generally FAA-approved and may have evolved through a lot of optimism and computer-massaging.

Also consider that high-speed cruise performance is more a function of the *airframe* than the engine. A dirty airplane with lots of added radio antennas, poorly fitting landing gear doors, leaking cabin doors/ windows, etc., has *more* to do with loss of cruise performance than does loss of engine power. But, for our purposes, it was just another check.

If you find a *big* loss of cruise performance from what the AFM shows, *don't* immediately blame it on the aging of Bessie's engine, especially if the climb data was reasonable.

The first thing I would do is have the local repair station run a leak check of the static and pitot systems; it's *highly* likely that there are problems in your instrument pressure systems. Also, ask them to check the accuracy of the airspeed indicator if they have a "master" IAS gauge on their leak-checker (otherwise, they will have to remove the instrument and send it out somewhere for a bench check).

A combination of very low climb rate and much reduced full-power cruise *could* be an indication of greatly reduced engine power. But, from my experience, it's just as likely that you have a bad pitot/static system or a bad IAS indicator. You may have actually been flying faster than Vy in the climbs and faster than the indicated high-power cruise. Check first for a pitot system leak.

Ground Power Check

For now, let's accept our observed 800 fpm climb rate as reasonable assurance that Bessie's engine is OK and get on with devising that pre-takeoff ground power check.

Back when many airplanes had supercharged, radial recip engines, it was usual to have a "field-barometric pressure power check" included in the preflight run-up checklist.

"Field barometric pressure" was what the MAP gauge indicated *before* starting the engine. In the warm-up area, while doing the mag and prop checks, you would set the throttle (with the prop lever at full-low-pitch/high-rpm) to get the same MAP reading. Then you'd check the tachometer. Depending on the engine/prop combination, you would expect to read a constant—say, 2,000 rpm, plus or minus 50 rpm—on the tachometer, regardless of field elevation.

At Miami, field barometric pressure might have been 30 inches Hg. At Denver, maybe 25 inches. Setting the appropriate field barometric pressure, anywhere, during the run-up should have given that 2,000 rpm. If 30 inches at Miami only gave 1,750 rpm and if it took 33 inches MAP to get 2,000 rpm, you knew *something was wrong with the engine*, like a dead cylinder or two, so do *not* fly!

It's a little more difficult these days. Most of us don't fly mechanically supercharged or turbocharged airplanes and cannot achieve field barometric pressure on the MAP gauge with the engine running. Also, most of us don't want to use that much power in a dirty run-up area, especially in a "trike" airplane that may get a lot of prop erosion. Finally, none of our AFMs include such a check.

That's why we're going to devise our own check—and without even adding another step to the published run-up procedures.

Let's first consider Old Bessie, with its MAP gauge and constant-speed prop. The AFM calls for a mag check at 2,200 rpm. On your next flight, after checking mag rpm drop, note the MAP gauge reading.

Let's say it's about 23 inches and you're near sea level. A month or a year from now, you should still read about 23 inches MAP at 2,200 rpm when you're near sea level.

Density Effects

If you make a cross-country to Denver (elevation, about 5,000 feet), expect to achieve that same 2,200 rpm with about five inches *less* MAP (you lose about one inch of pressure per 1,000 feet of elevation above sea level).

However, you may have to *lean* the mixture slightly (toward best-power) to get an accurate check, especially if Bessie is an unsophisticated, normally aspirated type. When the engine is running too rich, the MAP reading for the 2,200 rpm will be *high*. Don't linger with the engine leaned; it will tend to get hot quickly. Be extremely careful of leaning a turbocharged engine (leaning probably isn't needed, anyway, if your turbo and carburetion are adjusted properly).

And, remember, this check is run with the "blue knob" (prop rpm control) full-forward. The actual prop rpm will be lower than what you have selected; thus, the prop blades will be on the low-pitch blade angle stops. In effect, you have a fixed-pitch propeller and, thus, a "torque meter" which we can use to check rpm versus an input MAP.

But suppose you are flying "Little Betsy," with a fixed-pitch prop and no MAP gauge. Not to worry, we can still perform a similar check and get a valid indication of power capability before lift-off.

Only, with Betsy, we are going to run the check at full throttle at the very start of the takeoff run. We can't do the check at mag-check rpm because we have no MAP gauge for reference. *But* full-throttle is also a good reference point.

Rather than "beat" the engine and prop with full throttle in the run-up area, we'll just make a point to check "almost-static" rpm before we exceed about 10 mph at the beginning of the takeoff roll, just after we reach full-forward on the throttle.

If Betsy indicates about 2,350 rpm near-static at Miami, then she should indicate just about the same, with full throttle, at Denver. (Once again, at Denver, you may have to lean to get closer to best-power mixture.) If, one day, Betsy only shows 2,000 rpm at full-throttle as you start your takeoff roll, *you had better abort* and taxi to the repair hangar. You are *missing* something—like, maybe, a whole cylinder worth of power.

Also, remember that Betsy's takeoff check has to be performed before you get much airspeed (about 10 mph, max). Checking at lift-off or initial climb speed is no good. The prop will be "unloaded"—i.e., "windmilling"—because of the higher forward airspeed and, thus, show a higher rpm.

If you want to check Betsy against the FAA's "book," find Betsy's TCDS (type certificate data sheet). It will usually show a full-throttle "static rpm" figure. (The TCDS is probably available on microfiche at your local repair station.)

Another related item: Nobody ever checks this on *twins*, but it's worth the time while doing the power checks to compare the observed MAPs. There shouldn't be much difference—one or two inches, maybe. But, five or six inches? *No!*

Time Won't Tell

Let's wind up this discussions with a few final thoughts.

First, engine *power* generally is *not* simply a function of how long the engine has been in service, especially if it is still within TBO. Power is *mostly* a function of good maintenance and parts replacement when required.

Likewise, power is *not* a direct function of that "static" differential compression check.

Second, you *can* run your own ground power check, as described above. You just need to have derived a good baseline on Bessie's or Betsy's engines when they were known to be in good running condition.

Lastly, as I've been told by experienced mechanics and by airplane and engine manufacturers' reps, total hours since new or since overhaul do *not* really reflect an engine's power-production capability.

On the other hand, lots of *years* with relatively infrequent flying and servicing may well lead to internal problems and, thus, possibly to low power output.

One easy way you can help your engine's power and longevity is to provide clean oil. Frequent oil changes are essential. The oil should be changed *at least* every six calendar months, every 25 hours of service if you don't have an oil filter or every 50 hours if you have a full-flow oil filter.

Remember, an aging airplane (with an aging engine) that is well-maintained and frequently flown is likely *better* than that 20-year-old "cream puff" you've seen advertised with only 500 total hours on the original airframe and engine.

Turboprops

Most of the pilots reading this book fly piston-powered aircraft. But there are a fortunate few who
either already do, or are considering, the step up to
turbine power.

Turboprops are a real double-edged sword. They offer lots of advantages,
like eye-opening performance and extremely high reliability. The drawback,
however, is cost. Turbines are thirsty and incredibly expensive to both
purchase and overhaul. (Believe it or not, however, it's possible to operate some
turboprops for not much more than the cost of some high-end piston twins. We
recently spoke to an MU-2 owner who stepped up from a Cessna 340. He
provided his cost figures, and on a trip-for-trip basis the operating and reserve
cost is remarkably close.)

This last chapter on powerplants was written by contributor Bill Kelly.

Turbine Basics

Once a pilot earns a multiengine rating, he or she can skip from a Twin
Comanche or Cessna 310 into a Cheyenne, King Air or Conquest
without going through any additional FAA-mandated training or
testing.

That's right, unlike the check-outs required for those new to
taildraggers or "complex" aircraft, the FAA does not require any
special certification when a pilot transitions from a piston twin to a
turboprop. (However, for a manufacturer or entrepreneur who sets out
to modify a recip-powered aircraft with turboprop engines, the FAA's
testing and paperwork requirements are formidable.)

The price of a turboprop aircraft, even an older one, is too high for
my personal flying needs. But if I were in a business that needed its own

air transportation, the benefits of operating a turbine-powered propeller airplane would have to be considered. In addition to the few new ones available, there are many bargains out there in the used aircraft marketplace. A knowledgeable aviation consultant just might convince you that a used Cheyenne, Conquest, Turbo Commander or King Air would be a better deal than a used recip-engine version of almost the same airplane.

There are also a few single-engine turboprop conversions, in addition to the very few new turboprop singles. Even Maule has an Allison-powered version of its standard STOL airplane. Several turboprop modifications have been approved for larger Cessna singles and Beech Bonanzas.

Many agricultural operators are switching to turboprop conversions of their older Ag-Cats, Thrushes and Air Tractors, because the old recip R-985s and R-1340s are in short supply and operating and overhaul costs (and lubricating oil consumption) have made the old radials less attractive as a powerplant.

So, assuming that at least some of you readers may some day transition to turboprop airplanes or at least have a chance to ride as copilot, let's touch briefly on some of the benefits and problems of turbine power.

We'll focus on the most common general aviation turboprop engines: the Garrett TPE-331 series, Pratt & Whitney Canada's PT6A and the Allison 250s. (Keep in mind that the Garrett is a slightly different breed of cat. It's a "fixed-shaft" engine, with the basic engine and propeller turbines fixed to the same drive shaft. The PT6A and Allison have a "split-shaft" arrangement, with a separate shaft for the propeller turbine from the shaft that rotates the basic engine compressor and its turbine stages.)

Intake, Exhaust

There are always questions about how air is directed through a small turboprop engine. Both the PT6A and the Allison powerplants have a "scoop" in front. Why, then, does the PT6A take in air at the rear of the engine but exhaust the gases at the front? Why does the Allison take air in right behind the propeller but exhaust it up front, also?

One might see these designs and conclude, wrongly, that the Garrett 331 must be lots more efficient because it sucks air in up front and blows it out the back, creating lots of jet thrust.

Well, first, forget jet thrust as any significant power factor at the relatively low airspeeds at which we'd be operating with these engines. Garrett ducts the exhaust out the back because it's a fixed-shaft design.

The hot gases do not have to be fed into a separate propeller power turbine that's way up front.

The PT6As and Allisons have to reverse the flow to get the final power surge—that little bit that's left over to drive the propeller turbine—up to the *front* of the engine where the turbines and reduction gear are located. And, if the designer has done a decent job, there is very little energy left in the exhaust gases. Almost all of the "ergs" were intentionally extracted in the turbine stages, to drive the gas generator section *plus* the propeller.

Lightweights

Among the chief advantages of any turboprop engine is that it provides more sea-level power per pound than a recip with a similar horsepower rating. There's lots of power in a lightweight package.

For example, the basic engine weight of a 700-horsepower Garrett is approximately 335 pounds; a 285-horsepower Continental IO-520 piston engine weighs about 100 pounds *more*. And, since the turboprop engine doesn't require external cooling air, except for its oil radiator, cooling drag is reduced and there's a much less "draggy" cowling.

The cooling is done *internally*. About 75 percent of air ingested through the compressor section is for cooling, and only about 25 percent of the inlet air combines with fuel for combustion. But the cooling air is still mixed with combusted air to provide energy to the turbine wheels that drive the compressor section and the propeller gearing. Little is wasted. Even the relatively low-temperature, low-velocity exhaust gases are usually directed somewhat rearward to provide a little "jet" thrust.

Thus, you can expect increased efficiency while flying an airplane with turbine power, because the installation is aerodynamically "cleaner." And you will probably have better useful-load capacity, just because the engine weighs less.

But, along with the lighter engine weight goes a c.g. problem in airframes initially designed for piston power but developed into turboprops. The manufacturer might have to stick the engine(s) much farther ahead of the firewall to keep loaded c.g. within limits. A typical tack is to locate the battery (probably a larger one) just behind the engine and ahead of the firewall.

At Altitude

Do *not* expect improved high-altitude performance just because you are flying a turboprop. Don't confuse "turboprop" with "turbosupercharged." All turbine engines are akin to naturally aspirated (non-supercharged) recip engines in that maximum available power drops almost as a direct function of increased altitude.

The usual attack on this lack of altitude performance is to install a turboprop engine of, say, 500 horsepower but "flat-rate" it to 300-400 horsepower for takeoff and/or max continuous operation. (Also, keep in mind that added power generally disrupts the airplane's pitch stability. You usually cannot shove 700 horsepower into an airplane that was certificated by the FAA for 300 horses.)

Although power will drop as you climb to higher altitudes, you *can* expect increased engine efficiency, in terms of specific fuel consumption (expressed as pounds of fuel consumed per horsepower per hour). Decreased SFC plus the increased true airspeed at higher altitudes make it advantageous to climb well above the turbulence and low-level weather. You will get much better "miles-per-gallon" at medium altitudes where you can still get adequate cruise power.

As you climb, you keep advancing the "power lever" (not throttle, although they seem to do almost the same thing) to stay at the flat-rated 300 or 400 horsepower until you run into other engine limits, such as compressor/turbine rpm or turbine temperature.

Of course, as you climb with a PT6A or Allison and keep advancing the power lever, both basic engine rpm (usually termed "Ng" for gas generator rpm but sometimes called "N1" to differentiate it from "N2" or "Np" for prop rpm) and engine temperature will climb. (As we'll discuss shortly, the fixed-shaft Garrett TPE-331 maintains rpm at or near 100 percent, but the indicated temperature will still climb as altitude is increased.)

Those "hot-section" temperature limits may be in the form of EGT or TOT (exhaust gas temperature or turbine outlet temperature, measured *after* all turbine stages), TIT (turbine inlet temperature, measured right after the hot gases leave the burner section) or ITT (inter-turbine temperature, measured between turbine stages).

For any given high-horsepower operation, expect that the temperature (EGT/TOT, TIT or ITT) will climb as altitude is increased at a constant power. On a warm or hot day, you may run into temperature limits at a rather low altitude (maybe even on takeoff) and be unable to maintain high horsepower to higher altitudes.

Also, the compressor section will have to work harder with the decreased inlet air density. Where on a "standard" day your PT6A or Allison might be able to achieve flat-rated takeoff horsepower at only 95 percent of rated compressor rpm, it may require nearly 100 percent of this rated rpm on a hot day. (Most small engines can be operated to 101-101.5 percent of "nominal" maximum rpm.)

So, don't expect standard-day turboprop performance on those warm or hot days. You may still be able to get sea-level power for low-altitude takeoff, but the power will begin to drop rapidly as you climb and as you adhere to the rpm and temperature limits.

An airplane modified with a relatively small turboprop engine rated at, say, 420 shaft horsepower may only be so-rated for a standard day (59 F at sea level). Do *not* expect to be able to achieve 420 shp on a summer day in Denver. Your power capability will be greatly reduced by the high density altitude, and you will *have to* modulate your use of the power lever to keep engine temperature within limits. Gas generator speed (Ng or N1) will be kept within limits by the fuel control governor, but the temperature may already be past the redline before you get to sea-level rated power.

Burn and Grind

On many of the turboprop engines, *not very much is regulated or governed.* On the PT6A and Allison 250, only the basic gas generator section (the compressor plus the compressor-driving turbine) rpm (Ng or N1) is governed. As mentioned earlier, this is done by the fuel control governor. And propeller speed is, of course, kept within limits by a standard prop governor.

But, *you*, the pilot, are the "governor" of engine temperature (EGT/TOT, TIT or ITT) and engine torque. (Torque is equivalent to power output at constant prop rpm. It's *almost* the same as manifold pressure in a recip, in that you control it with the "go" handle—the throttle or power lever.)

You can easily burn up the engine by exceeding temperature limits. You can also grind up the engine by exceeding power or torque limits.

Any of these temperature limits can easily be exceeded by excessive forward positioning of the power lever.

A special note is needed here to differentiate the Garrett TPE-331s in later factory-built airplanes, including some Turbo Commanders and Mitsubishi MU-2s, Conquest IIs and the Cheyenne 400. These engines *are* protected by electronic monitoring to limit both engine temperature and torque. The electronic "big brother" even monitors and controls the engine start—providing ignition and fuel at the proper time, and terminating starter motor operation at the proper rpm. The electronic limiting *is* good, but the pilot still has to *monitor* the engine gauges. Earlier Garrett models, especially as retrofitted on previously recip-powered airplanes, may be missing the automatic limiting controls.

On many of the small turboprop engines (Pratt & Whitney Canada PT6As and Allison 250s), the power lever *only* sets the governing for the basic engine fuel control and, thus, basic or gas generator section rpm (Ng, N1)—usually, something over 30,000 rpm.

On the fixed-shaft Garrett TPE-331 series, prop rpm is always directly related to basic engine rpm by the reduction gear ratio. It is usually relatively high, even during taxi, as compared to the PT6A or Allison 250. A small reduction in engine/prop rpm is usually allowed for cruise, as well as a lower "ground idle" rpm for taxi on some models. But, basically, the Garrett TPE-331 is a 100-percent-rpm engine, all the time.

Design Departures

The PWC PT6A and Allison 250 series are "free power turbine" engines—the propeller is driven by a separate turbine through reduction gearing. The prop is not on the same shaft as the basic engine turbine and compressor. Thus, these engines can be started with the props in "feather," and prop rpm will be relatively low while taxiing. The result is lower taxi noise than with Garretts.

In flight, the PT6As and Allisons usually allow a wide range of cruise rpm, as do comparable recips. The props on most of the PT6As can be feathered in flight or on the ground, with the basic engine still running at idle on the power lever. You can't do that with a Garrett; the basic engine compressors and turbines would grind to a halt. You can't do that with most Allison installations, either, since feathering also cuts off fuel supply to the engine.

Advantages, disadvantages? Depends on what you consider most important. The fixed-shaft Garrett is certainly of simpler construction—it's all on one shaft. And the two compressors are "centrifugal-flow," only, without the multi-piece, expensive "axial-flow" stages found on the PT6A and Allison. But, especially on the older, smaller Garretts, your taxi rpm and noise may be a little higher. Once in flight and with 100 percent rpm set (approximately 2,000 prop rpm), you will always have that same prop and basic engine rpm, no matter what the power, and there won't be a spool-up delay, waiting for the prop and compressor section to accelerate to max rpm.

The free power turbine design of the PWC and Allison engines allows you to select desired prop governing rpm, regardless of basic engine rpm. But, during lower power output—say, on landing approach, the basic engine rpm will drop, and so may the prop rpm. Spool-up time probably will be a little longer than with a fixed-shaft engine.

Are these differences significant? Probably not. *All* of these turbo-prop engines exhibit excellent acceleration characteristics. You may have read a little about long spool-up times on some monstrous airliner fanjet engines of 20,000, 40,000 or 60,000 pounds thrust. Don't worry about it on any of the small turboprops.

Most of the "difference" is in design philosophy and growth potential. And *all* of these three basic GA turboprops have *grown* considerably since the original model. Most of the growth has come through increased air flow, with better and/or bigger compressors, plus better turbines to drive the compressors. A good bit of the development has been via better metal components with higher temperature tolerances. Thus, the engine can run at higher internal temperatures and develop more power for the compressor turbine and propeller turbine stages. (Sort of like installing high-compression pistons in your old recip.)

Over-torque, Over-temp

It bears repeating that power output (engine torque) and engine temperature (EGT/TOT, ITT or TIT) are purely functions of the pilot's setting of the power lever, except for the electronically controlled Garretts.

There is *no governing* of temperature on most of the turboprop installations. You, as pilot, can *over-torque* or *over-temp* just by advancing the power lever too far forward, too quickly. Engine damage will be done quickly. You won't be warned by a slow rise in cylinder head temperature or by illumination of an overboost light.

Turboprop engine temperature, especially, is critical. These engines will probably always be operated close to their EGT/TOT, ITT or TIT limits. You *have* to operate them there to get the desired power output. But you do *not dare* to exceed those limits. If you do, serious and very expensive damage will occur to the "hot-section" components: combustion chamber, rotating turbine blades and stationary turbine inlet guide vanes. We might equate severe over-temp damage to the damage you can get in a recip from preignition or detonation. In either case, metal will melt and burn. But in the turboprop engine, it's steel, not aluminum pistons and cylinder heads, that will melt.

Slight but continual over-temp operation will probably erode turbine inlet guide vanes, start cracks in the burner can and maybe allow rotating turbine blades to stretch until they start to rub the outer casing.

The situation is similar to operating your turbocharged recip with an excessively lean mixture at high power and doing valve and seat damage. But repairing an "over-temped" turboprop engine is *much* more expensive than a burned-up recip.

Small turboprop engines require hot-section inspections (burner and turbine assemblies) about every 1,500 hours. They are equivalent to "top overhauls" of recip engines. However, even minor hot section heat damage is likely to cost the equivalent of a new or overhauled recip engine. (Sort of like sending your recip in for overhaul and finding that the crankcase, crankshaft, all cylinders and the camshaft are beyond repairable limits, and you have to buy all new parts.)

Starting Strategies

Probably the greatest potential for damaging a turboprop engine exists during starting. And most problems can be attributed to pilot error. You *must* have a good battery or APU (auxiliary power unit) before doing a "light-off."

Until that compressor and turbine assembly gets up to vicinity of 45-50 percent of rated rpm, it is *not* "self-sustaining." It must have starter motor power to assist in engine acceleration. Without sufficient starter assist, the fuel control will continue to feed fuel, trying to accelerate the engine. Without the necessary additional air flow provided by increased rpm of the compressor, internal temperatures will climb.

Sure, you can get by on a warm day starting your old recip on a weak battery. If it fires, it will run. Better not try this with a turboprop engine. It probably gets hotter during starting than at any other time. You *have* to have a good electric power source. You cannot jump-start your turboprop engine off a pair of car batteries, either. A typical APU requirement is 800 amperes at 28 volts DC. That means that the airplane battery, itself, is fairly massive (and expensive, maybe even a nickel cadmium battery—Nicad) so that it is capable of "unassisted" starts.

You not only have to watch indicated starting temperature (EGT/TOT, ITT or TIT), you also have to watch rpm acceleration. You don't dare to let that rpm stagnate at, say, 30 percent rpm. If you do allow the rpm to hang up, internal temperatures of *non-instrumented* parts will rise rapidly.

A caution here: Several turboprops have a "momentary" starter motor switch in the cockpit. You have to *hold* the switch in the "on" position until reaching the minimum starter motor cut-off rpm, which usually is around 50 percent of max-rated rpm. If you let go of that switch early, something inside *is* going to burn up. And maybe long before your EGT/TOT, ITT or TIT gauge shows excessive heating.

I remember when, many years ago, a bad batch of JP-5 jet fuel was pumped aboard our aircraft carrier from a tanker. Later tests showed excessive entrained water and, worse, lots of bugs—bacteria that grew like the moss on rocks in a moving stream of fresh water. Neither the ship's nor the airplanes' filtration systems could remove all of these contaminants. As a result, minute amounts accumulated in the engine fuel flow dividers, just ahead of the burner section fuel nozzles. The upper flow dividers would stick closed, probably due to "heat soak" effects after the previous engine shut-down, and not pass fuel to their assigned nozzles during the next start.

Before the problem was isolated, several J65 turbojet engines were burned to a crisp during start. The pilots never received any indication of a problem on their EGTs. The only cockpit indication was a stagnation of the rpm increase during start, followed almost immediately by a "cut" signal from the plane captain (crew chief) after he saw big sparks coming out of the tailpipe. The fireworks were burning pieces of turbine inlet guide vanes and rotating turbine blades. (All of the starting fuel flow was going through only a few of the lower injector nozzles, resulting in a big, hot flame that acted as a cutting torch.)

Watch the Gauges

Similar bad things can happen to a small turboprop engine if you make a bad start—if you don't watch for a steady rpm increase and that the temperatures stay below the limits.

As mentioned earlier, you have to have a good battery and/or an APU (also called a ground power unit, GPU). Your starter motor has to be good, too. You must closely monitor the engine instruments during start, particularly the tachometer and temperature gauge. You have to be ready to *immediately* cut off fuel flow. This is accomplished by retarding the "condition lever" or "engine manual fuel lever," which is similar to pulling the mixture control in a recip to the "idle/cut-off" position.

The pilot has to closely adhere to the published starting procedures. Do *not* open the engine fuel flow control until at or above the stated "minimum light-off" rpm. You have to ensure that ignition is provided before or at the same time as fuel is introduced. Some installations have an "ignition-on" advisory light (although it usually indicates that there is power to the ignition unit, not necessarily that there is any "spark"). Other installations only allow you to listen for the "pop, pop, pop" of the high-tension igniter plugs. All turboprop AFMs instruct that if there is no light-off within several seconds of fuel introduction, *the start must be terminated* by cutting off fuel flow.

I once saw a pilot burn off a horizontal stabilizer deice boot on a brand new Cheyenne. He had not energized the ignition system switches before shoving the condition lever ahead to get fuel flow to the burner section. After many seconds of waiting for ignition, he finally realized his error and then turned on the igniters. BOOM and WHOOSH! Lots of unburned fuel was still in the engine, and when he finally engaged the spark plugs, it came out all at once as a long plume of burning fuel. The 20-foot tongue of flame singed the nacelle paint, then melted the deice boot way back on the tail. He was lucky he didn't damage the engine, too.

Later, the same pilot tried starting both engines at the same time from the airplane's single Nicad battery. Again, completely contrary to the AFM. But this time, he was a little smarter concerning PT6As and terminated both starts when rpm stagnated from lack of sufficient electrical power. Again, he's lucky—no engine damage.

If you've ridden aboard a turboprop commuter recently, you may have wondered why the pilot started the right engine first, maybe even before everyone was strapped in, and then revved up that engine for a minute or so before cranking the other engine.

Maybe he was only trying to get the air conditioner on line, but more likely he was recharging the battery after the first start so that it had enough power to start the other engine. He might have been doing a "cross-start," using battery power plus generator output from the running engine to crank the other starter motor.

Rather than the rather anemic starter motor and separate low-amperage alternator found on most recip airplanes, most turboprops have a single, combined DC starter/generator. It's all in one big, expensive chunk. As a starter motor, it absorbs tremendous electric power and provides high torque over a wide range of rpm.

Typically, it operates as a starter until the engine is accelerated to about 50 percent of its rated rpm, although at decreasing torque as rpm builds. When you turn *off* the starter function and engage the generator function, it's typically capable of at least 200 amperes' output.

Another word of caution here: Generator output is likely to be at a maximum immediately after a battery-only engine start. The generator has to recharge the airplane battery, which was exhausted by that single engine start. It's not unusual to see a generator output of 150 amps right after starting a turboprop engine. Those "amps" are a lot of horsepower and can drag down engine rpm (and raise the EGT/TOT, ITT or TIT) in some cases if the engine isn't accelerated above its minimum ground idle rpm *before* engaging the "GEN" function.

Read, re-read, memorize and follow the AFM starting procedures!

That may seem like a lot of words on starting, but that's where most of the severe damage is done. I remember one young ferry pilot who managed to do $20,000 of internal engine damage by not following the proper start procedure. He turned off the starter motor too soon and then didn't turn off the fuel soon enough when Ng stagnated way below idle rpm.

Even the smallest of the GA turboprop engines costs almost $200,000 new. The price is not much less for one that's been used and overhauled. You might get two to three times as much use between overhauls than you would get from a recip engine of similar power. But a turboprop engine requires a lot of tender loving care to achieve its 3,000- to 5,000-hour TBO.

Reverse and Beta

One item that is sure to be new to pilots who transition from piston to turboprop airplanes is the provision for the use of reverse thrust. Most of the small turboprop installations allow for reverse thrust operation—on the ground, only, of course. Some airplanes have a lock-out mechanism to prevent use of reverse or "beta" range until there is weight on the wheels. Not necessarily so for single-engine applications; there may be only a "ramp" on the power lever quadrant or a "trigger" on the power lever to prevent inadvertent reverse thrust or beta application.

The "beta" bit is widely misunderstood. Beta generally is a range near flat pitch, when the propeller blades are between forward pitch and reverse pitch. Usually, it's selected with the power lever after idle power has already been set. In beta, the pilot usually directly controls prop blade angle with the power lever and the basic engine is running at idle power (except for the Garretts, which stay near 100 percent rpm).

With the fixed-shaft Garrett in a single-engine STOL or cropduster installation, you may be able to get just a little beta at very low airspeed while airborne with the power lever slightly ahead of the idle stop. It provides for a little bit of drag on final approach. But, generally, beta is a no-no while airborne.

Beta typically is a means to reduce excessive thrust during taxi. It is not reverse thrust at low airspeed. Except for that little bit of built-in allowable flight beta on a Garrett STOL or cropduster installation, beta could be a *lot* of reverse thrust at flight airspeeds. Don't *ever* try to override the beta/reverse lock-out device. Going to reverse thrust while airborne doesn't only provide a sudden large increase in drag, it might also result in a complete loss of air flow over the tail surfaces. And that could mean a complete, sudden loss of all aerodynamic control and a *hard* pitch down or up.

Another consideration, especially when flying a single-engine taildragger, is *not* to suddenly ram in full reverse right after touchdown. Have that tail wheel firmly on the ground and be steering straight before you *gently* apply reverse. That application of reverse thrust is probably going to kill all air flow over the rudder and maybe greatly reduce your directional control during roll-out.

Air Restart

Most airborne turboprop engine failures are due either to a control mistake made by the pilot or to fuel exhaustion. Certification regulations don't allow you to "starve" the engine of fuel still remaining in the tanks. Usually, *all* available fuel has to reach the engine through a single fuel tank selection. There is no tank-switching to keep lateral trim balanced.

There's a good reason for this. Once an engine is "flamed-out," an entire new starting sequence is required to get it going again. If you run a tank dry on your recip, it will probably roar to life again as soon as you switch tanks (plus reduce the throttle and advance the mixture, maybe turn on the electric boost pump).

Not so with a turboprop engine. You will have to turn on the ignition again, reset almost all control levers to their starting positions, then crank the engine with the starter motor to minimum starting rpm. If it's a fixed-shaft Garrett, you won't need the starter motor, but you may have to engage the propeller unfeathering pump to get the prop back to low pitch and high windmill rpm before you dare to introduce ignition and fuel.

The ignition system normally is used only during initial start-up, though most installations provide "constant ignition" or so-called "air-start ignition" to keep the plugs firing continuously when flying in very heavy rain, icing conditions or turbulence. This is a very high-energy spark source, and it doesn't have lots of longevity. Don't use it when you don't need it. Once the engine is running, it doesn't need spark anymore (although some AFMs may call for constant ignition during takeoff).

Another subject: "bleed air extraction." A typical installation may use high pressure, high-temperature bleed air from the engine compressor section for engine anti-icing, cockpit instrument pressurization and cabin pressurization and air-conditioning. But energy doesn't come for free. If you bleed-off engine air, the engine will have to work harder to provide the demanded power to the propeller. The more the bleed, the higher the engine rpm and temperature for any given propeller power.

The same consideration goes for operating with very high generator loads. Amperage is horsepower extracted from engine output. You can't keep adding electrical load without also adding stress to the engine. There usually is an AFM section on "load-shedding" to prevent overtaxing the remaining generator after the other generator (or engine) fails on a twin.

Remember, both high electric and bleed air loads *reduce* the power capability of the basic turboprop engine.

Fuel and Oil

A turboprop engine should *not* use anything like the one quart of oil every eight hours or so that your recip uses. It certainly should not drip oil after a prolonged period of inactivity. The exhaust stacks should *never* be oily.

But you *do* need to check oil quantity. On some models, the oil must be checked shortly *after* shutdown. You cannot let the engine sit for two days and expect an accurate reading on the dipstick, because the oil may have drained into lower parts of the engine.

You must adhere closely to the requirements of the AFM. Don't mix oil types or brands, unless there are provisions in the manual for doing so. Carry an extra two quarts of your own brand at all times.

Most turboprop engines were designed to use jet fuel primarily, although they can be operated on avgas for a small number of hours between overhauls. Some special installations (in cropdusters, primarily) may be allowed to run on diesel fuel.

Some AFMs specify the need for additives (such as "Prist") with each fill-up to combat fuel icing and microbial growth which could cause fuel flow problems. Remember, jet fuel is primarily kerosene, and it can hold lots of water (and water-borne bugs) in solution. And that entrained water could freeze into tiny filter-clogging ice particles when the fuel gets real cold.

Most turboprop engines designed for high-altitude flight include an oil-to-fuel heat exchanger to make sure that only liquid fuel gets to the engine and its filters.

One last point on fuel: When you do your weight and balance calculations, remember that jet fuel weighs an average of 6.7 pounds per gallon, versus the usual 6.0 lbs/gal of avgas. Remember, too, that if you spill kerosene on your hands while draining the tanks, filters, gascolators, etc., the smell is going to stay with you forever unless you wash it off immediately. It's not as dangerous as the possible lead poisoning from avgas, but it is much longer-lasting. Once it gets on your clothes, it does not wash out quickly. (I've got an old military Nomex flight suit that still smells like JP eight years after my last ferry flight of a Twin Otter.)

Maintenance Tips

Some words of caution are in order for those who like to perform their own preventive maintenance: The fuel system in a turboprop installation is akin to that of an injected diesel engine. Turbine fuel is directed through atomizing nozzles into a very high-pressure part of the engine: the combustion chamber.

Very high fuel pressure is needed. It is measured in *hundreds* (rather than dozens) of pounds per square inch. This is no place to mess with "owner/operator preventive maintenance" replacement of fuel lines. Let a professional do the work.

Some caution also applies to engine rigging. Sure, knowledgeable owners sometimes try to sneak by (illegally) adjusting the propeller governors on old recips if max rpm is a little low or high. And, now and then, some will adjust a push-pull cable end if the mixture doesn't quite reach full-rich at the carburetor or if the throttle push-pull cable doesn't quite reach the "full-open" stop.

Don't mess with *any* adjustments ahead of the firewall on a turbo-prop engine! There's a good chance that "basic-engine" fuel control rigging is also tied into propeller control rigging and, maybe, into some engine bleed air control rigging to the fuel control, as well.

It takes a real pro, preferably one who has graduated from a "factory school," to make *any* adjustments in the front end.

Manual Throttle

With a PT6A installed in a "Normal" category single-engine airplane, you might get an additional "emergency" or "manual throttle." Depending on the engine and its fuel control design, power output could be very sensitive to contamination and/or failure of the engine fuel control. This might not be such a serious concern in a twin turboprop, since the affected engine will probably only drop to approximately idle power. But it would still be the equivalent of a "dead" engine in terms of propeller drag, since the prop will be windmilling without any usable driving power and create lots of drag.

But, for some of single-engine installations, the manual throttle provides a "faucet" control of fuel flow to the engine. It completely overrides the basic engine fuel control and provides the pilot with direct and instant control of fuel to the burner nozzles.

Be careful with this control if you have one. (Cessna Caravans and Navy T-34Cs have this feature on their PT6As.) It doesn't have any limiting on maximum accelerating or minimum decelerating fuel flow. You could over-temp, stall the compressor or cause a flame-out if you don't use this control very gently.

Another feature provided on almost all installations is "overspeed governing." In addition to the basic max rpm governing (usually 101-101.5 percent of basic engine max rpm) provided by the prop governor and/or fuel control basic governor, there will probably be another circuit which is capable of cutting back on engine fuel flow if engine rpm exceeds by several percent its normal limits.

Typical max overspeed is 103-105 percent of that rated 30,000-plus rpm, and the overspeed governor is designed to preclude ever exceeding that maximum rpm. Some installations require an "every-flight" check of the overspeed governor, others only when rigging work has been done on the fuel control, etc. Consider that the overspeed limit is a *structural* limit, mostly for the engine. *Maybe* those turbine blades will stay attached to 110 percent rpm, maybe not. But once you have gone beyond the allowed limits, structural damage may have been done and a blade could fail in the not-too-distant future. Better read the engine manufacturer's manual on allowed overspeed (as well as allowed over-temp) operation.

Remember that DC-10 engine failure which resulted in the crash-landing in Sioux City, Iowa. You do not want rotating parts to depart your engine at supersonic speed. So, watch the tachometer and perform the overspeed governor checks as required.

Airspeed Limits

One item that causes a lot of confusion, especially when considering conversions from recip to turboprop power, is "maximum allowed airspeed."

Let's say that you paid the bucks to have your piston-powered airplane converted via an STC (supplemental type certificate) to a turboprop. The recip airplane had a Vne of 180 mph, and the yellow arc on the airspeed indicator went from 150 to 180 mph. But now, your expensive conversion has an IAS redline at 150 mph and *no* yellow arc.

Sorry, guy, that's the consequence of FAR 23 turbine engine regulations. Your airplane became the equivalent of a "jet," and you have to comply with the regulations that were really meant only for the first civilian jet airplanes (Sabreliners, etc.). No more Vne at 180 mph. You are stuck with a "Vmo" (max operating airspeed) near the equivalent of the old "Vno" (max structural cruising speed), which was probably the top of the original green arc on the IAS indicator.

Vmo replaces Vne during a turboprop conversion, unless the STC holder has done a complete new structural substantiation for maximum gust loads clear to the original Vne.

This doesn't make much sense after you've just spent kilobucks to install a better engine and get a cleaner installation that will allow more speed. But that's the law. Though the airplane probably can and will go much faster than before, it's *not allowed* to go any faster than the old Vc or Vno (top of the original green arc). Your airplane has become a jet, as far as the FARs are concerned, even though there's still a propeller up front.

Good, Not Foolproof

We haven't covered *everything* in this primer, but we have touched on some of the more critical considerations for turboprop operation. Most critical is the pilot's knowledge of the installation and how deeply he or she has delved into the AFM, especially the limitations section and normal procedures.

It's a good idea, too, to read the engine manufacturer's installation manual, pilot tips, etc.

Contrary to what you could get away with in operating your old, familiar recip, you have to know the engine limits *cold*. And you have to *memorize* the entire starting procedures. You do *not* have time during engine start to slowly read and follow, one by one, the steps listed in an abbreviated checklist. Things happen too fast.

One final thought: When you fly a turboprop, you fly the latest technology for power output from a small package.

Be it a Garrett, PWC or Allison engine, they are all *good*, and they are constantly being improved and upgraded in power and longevity. Overall reliability probably exceeds that of any "piston-slapper." But *you* will have to be good. Turboprop engines are *not* foolproof. They are more demanding of pilot proficiency than the recips.

• Section Three •

Fuel
Systems

The
Fuel Supply

Y*our engine may be in peak condition, but it'll still die on you if it's not fed. This second section deals with fuel, from the tanks to the carburetor. First up is a look at the whole system from Bill Kelly.*

Fuel System Ins and Outs

That old Lycoming or Continental engine in your airplane will probably run forever so long as you give it the needed fuel, oil, spark and air, along with the required inspection, maintenance, repair and overhaul.

But, too often, the "fuel" portion of the power equation only gets attention from the firewall, forward (gascolator, fuel pumps, carburetor, injector servo, injector nozzles, etc.). Nobody worries much about the fuel tanks, themselves.

Unless they are leaking expensive fuel onto the ramp or there's a service bulletin or AD note concerning wrinkles in bladder cells, water entrapment or some other problem, why worry about the fuel tanks?

Almost nobody worries about the caps on their fuel tanks. But we should. They're probably the biggest culprit when it comes to crashes caused by water-contaminated fuel.

Inspecting the seals on your fuel caps should be a part of each and every preflight inspection, as well as included in every 100-hour and annual inspection. But, even visual inspection of the seals is no absolute guarantee that the caps won't leak water into the tanks.

A quick check of the airplanes on the local ramp showed that about a quarter had pitot tube covers but none had covers over their fuel caps.

Just a little blowing rain or a couple of inches of snow around the fuel cap, and you are almost sure to get water in the fuel tank—water that can stop your engine cold.

Two power losses on takeoff caused by water contamination (which escaped sumping on preflight) prompted one pilot, Norm Smith, to develop removable "rain covers" for flush-type fuel caps. The caps are available for $18.95 a pair from Smith at Aero-Trim, 1130 102nd St., Bay Harbor, Fla. 33154. As I've mentioned previously, an old coffee cup and some duct tape will suffice for most other types of caps, albeit not very elegantly.

But, there's more to fuel caps than just their tendency to leak rainwater into the tanks. Some are designed to also serve either as primary or backup vents for the fuel tanks.

Your aircraft flight manual (AFM) may *not* tell you that your fuel caps are vented. So, you'd better not replace those fuel caps with anything but the specific item called for in the airplane's parts manual.

For example, in a Cessna P210N, primary venting is accomplished by an air line to the top of each fuel tank (see the accompanying illustration). But, each fuel cap also contains a "vacuum-operated" vent to allow air to enter the tank in case the primary vent becomes blocked.

Of course, that "vacuum" feature had better work properly, or you could lose fuel flow if the primary vent becomes blocked.

Venting Requirements

FAR 23.975 states, "Each fuel tank must be vented from the top part of the expansion space...." FAR 23.969 states, "Each fuel tank must have an expansion space of not less than two percent of the tank capacity, unless the tank vent discharges clear of the airplane...."

Other parts of FAR 23 (and the older CAR 3 small-airplane certification rules) require that vent outlets be located so as to minimize chances of blockage by ice or other foreign matter, that vents be constructed to prevent fuel siphoning and that vent lines be installed in such a manner that there are no "undrainable areas" where "moisture" can accumulate.

Also, tanks with interconnected outlets (as in single-engine airplanes with a "both" position on the tank-selector valve) must also have an interconnected vent system to assure equal vent pressures and, hopefully, equal fuel usage from both tanks.

As you can see, the venting system gets a lot of attention in the regs, and for good reason. Just let the vent system become blocked, and you are in for some serious problems—like engine stoppage.

My old two-cycle lawn mower engine had a plastic, screw-on cap with a "vacuum-operated" vent. The flapper-valve vent closed tightly when the engine wasn't running (to prevent a full tank from leaking) but allowed air to enter as fuel was used. Just a little inhaled dust was enough to jam the valve and stop venting of the expansion space above the fuel level. Result: engine stoppage after about five minutes of lawn cutting. Fix: occasional cleaning of the flapper valve.

You might get the same result (a slow reduction in flow to the engine) if the vent becomes blocked in your high-wing, gravity-feed fuel system.

But, what if your airplane (high-wing or low-wing) has a fuel pump between the tank and the engine? You will still get a stoppage of fuel flow, but maybe not until you have "pumped" sufficient fuel out of the tank to cause a considerable "vacuum" within the tank—i.e., a big difference between tank internal pressure and the pressure of the air outside the tank. Maybe, enough pressure differential to cause a structural failure of the tank, itself!

The situation may not be so bad initially if your fuel "tanks" are flexible rubber bladders.

If a bladder vent becomes blocked, there may be a continuation of fuel feed for quite a while. Just like one of those "burpless" baby feeding bottles, the bladder may collapse slowly while allowing fuel to flow without an increasing air space above the fuel level.

The trouble is, that bladder is probably only attached, within its wing cavity, on the top side. It will collapse from the bottom upwards, probably lifting your fuel-level gauge float with it, and, maybe, also trying to lift the tank outlet tubes.

It's likely that you will get erroneously high fuel quantity readings and an unexpected loss of power. You could even get a failure of the bladder, itself, or the outlet tubing—and a sudden disastrous internal fuel leak.

Yes, your vent system *is* important. But, you have no cockpit gauges to warn of venting problems! And nobody *ever* bothers to provide a protective cover for their external fuel vent outlets.

There are all sorts of insects out there looking for low-cost housing. Bugs of all sizes. Bugs to fit any hose or tube internal diameter. Many of these pests like to reside in the suburbs or way out in the country—with a long crawl to their front door. They may build their nests deep inside your fuel vent lines, way out of your sight during preflight inspection.

There's probably a small fortune to be made by the entrepreneur who designs a variety of "vent plug" protective covers, complete with long red banners to catch the attention of a pilot who may be slumbering through his or her preflight.

Overkill on fuel vent safety? Maybe. But, ask the Aztec pilot who lost his left engine and barely made it back for a safe landing while nursing a dying right engine. Both inboard tank vent openings were plugged with mud dauber nests, and the left rubber fuel bladder had collapsed.

Vent Checks

While waiting for good vent tube plugs to come along, what can you, as a pilot, do to ensure your venting system operates properly?

Here are a few caveats and suggested procedures which should be performed regularly, though not necessarily every time you fly:

1. Do *not* shove coat-hanger or safety wire up your external vent tube. You might damage an internal check valve or punch a hole in flexible tubing.

2. Immediately after engine shutdown, open each fuel cap *slowly*, holding your ear close, and listen for any sound of air "hissing" *into* the fuel tank. If your vents are clear, there should *not* be any of that. (However, you may hear air hissing *out* of the tank if your vent system has anti-siphon check valves.)

3. Occasionally, connect a long piece of rubber or vinyl tubing to your external vent outlet and lead it to the fuel cap. Open the cap and gently blow into the tube. You should be able to hear or feel the air flowing through the vent and into the tank. Check each tank and each vent opening.

Remember, that vent system is supposed to ventilate the air/vapor expansion space above the fuel level, so that air may enter the tank as fuel is used. But, as some of you have probably seen, there are a few production airplanes out there that can "siphon" considerable fuel onto the ramp when the tanks are full.

According to FAR 23, that shouldn't happen, except when it's caused by thermal expansion of the fuel or when the airplane is parked on a ramp with more than a one-percent slope.

That's for production airplanes. I still remember the problems we had with a kitbuilt airplane that had fuel tankage running almost the full span of each wing leading edge. This airplane had no wing dihedral. With a full fuel load, the vent openings in each wing were well below the fuel level. The fuel caps, way outboard on the wings, weren't vented.

During a ground test, fuel flow to the gascolator was gradually but excessively reduced as the first 10 gallons of fuel were drained to the engine feed line. Reason: Vent air couldn't enter the wing tanks when they were full; so, flow slowed as the tanks gradually "pulled a vacuum."

Fuel didn't "siphon" overboard because the vent lines ran clear inboard to the fuselage, then upwards in a big loop, before connecting to the under-belly vent outlet.

Trying real hard, with a lot of lung pressure, you could blow bubbles through that vent outlet into the full-tank fuel. But, you couldn't count on that kind of vent pressure in flight. Vent air should go into a vacant space *above* the fuel and should not require a lot of ram pressure.

Sure, this is probably not a problem with factory-built airplanes. But, watch it with your kit airplane. That vent has to be just as good as the fuel outlet line from the tank to the engine.

Selector Secrets

Some of you Cherokee drivers may have wondered why your fuel selector has only "left, right, off" positions, instead of the "left, both, right, off" selections of a Cessna 172.

Why not a "both" position in the low-winger? Well, it's another part of the certification regs. The fuel system has to be designed so that it won't suck air from a tank that's low on fuel while also connected to another tank that still contains fuel.

So, in your Cherokee, you aren't allowed a "both" position because if, for example, the right tank outlet became unported (due probably to low fuel or unbalanced flight), the engine pump would rather suck air than the remaining fuel in the left tank.

That's not a problem, usually, in a high-winger with gravity flow from the wing tanks to the gascolator. Even if the right tank empties first, gravity fuel head pressure from the left tank will keep the right tank feed line partially filled, and the engine won't suck air.

That problem kitplane mentioned earlier had only a "both" selector position for the wing tanks. We ended up with a separate vent for the isolated center wing section sump area, where the two tanks joined, and had to drill small venting holes in the filler caps.

So, again, watch it with your homebuilts. Too many of the designers and builders have not read FAR 23. Vent problems are *serious* problems!

A similar plastic homebuilt, which did *not* have a center section sump area (somewhat isolated by wing rib dividers, and anti-crossflow tubes from each wing tank), crashed following fuel starvation. The approximately 20 gallons of remaining fuel had sloshed into one wing in unbalanced flight and left the engine sucking air from the center section supply tube.

There *is* some reason behind the voluminous FARs and CARs that cover airplane certification. But, remember, your factory-built isn't any better than either of the above-mentioned kitbuilts if all parts of the fuel system aren't working properly!

Collapsed Cell

Here's a problem that I experienced recently in an old PA-30 Twin Comanche. It was a fuel system "failure" precipitated by a right, inboard (main) fuel tank cap system that wasn't in good shape.

I had noticed during preflight that the door which covers this fuel cap compartment had a rather weak camlock fastener. It took only a light twist to open the door. Also, the "thermos-bottle" tank cap was slightly loose in its filler neck, even with the locking arm lever in the "locked" position.

These old thermos caps are dandy when they fit properly. Lift the locking lever, and the rubber seal shrinks to a smaller diameter to allow the cap to be removed for refueling. Shove the locking lever down, and the rubber seal is expanded to a larger diameter to, supposedly, grip the filler neck tightly.

Some of them are adjustable to allow a tighter "grip" when locked. Those on the PA-30 are adjustable, and we should have adjusted this particular cap before the flight. We also should have installed a new lock on the door covering the cap compartment.

It was a test flight, to check some new "speed mods." I was sitting in the right front seat, taking data and flying some of the test points. At the conclusion of a high-speed dive test, I happened to look out at the right wing, inboard of the nacelle. *Wow!* A tremendous gush of light-blue fuel!

The filler door was open, and the fuel cap was missing. Fuel was flowing overboard like water out of an opened fire hydrant.

Yes, the door had come open. Then, the loose fuel cap had departed, since the door wasn't there to hold it in position. Piper had designed the parts properly, but they hadn't counted on dumb pilots who would fly with both a defective door and a loose fuel cap.

Contrary to what you might think, the fuel wasn't really being sucked out by the low-pressure air running over the top of the wing. No, it was being pushed out by a collapsing rubber fuel bladder cell. That low pressure atop the wing allowed ambient pressure around the bladder to push the rubber cell upward and force the fuel out through the open cap.

We immediately slowed the airplane and positioned the fuel selector for the right engine to the auxiliary tank, while heading for the downwind leg. As airspeed decreased, the overboard fuel flow also dropped. I could look almost directly down into the fuel tank filler neck. What I saw was the *bottom* of the rubber tank jammed against the bottom of the filler neck.

The bladder had collapsed. The gauge read almost 3/4 quantity remaining, but the tank was nearly empty.

Had this flight been made on a dark night, in IFR weather or single-pilot, the problem might not have been noticed. Believing what the fuel gauges were showing, we might have lost power from the right engine at a critical moment on landing approach.

Another note on fuel bladders: As mentioned earlier, they are usually held in place only on the upper surface with snaps or lace attachments to the upper wing skin. The bottom of the cell is free to rise, or the sides to move inward, if there is a big imbalance between air pressure inside the bladder and the ambient pressure in the cavity around the tank.

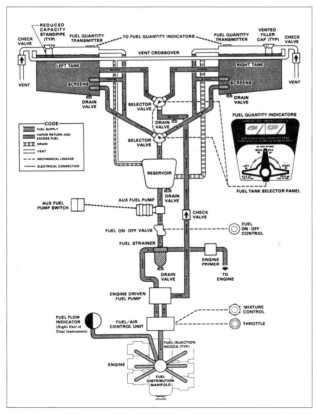

Typical GA fuel system, this one from a Cessna 210. In this system, vents in the caps back up the primary vents.

You *have to* have good venting, and you *have to* keep the fuel caps in place. The bottom of the bladder *has* to stay in place against the bottom of its cavity in the wing, or your fuel system is in *big* trouble.

Strainer Specs

FAR 23.977 specifies that "there must be a fuel strainer for the fuel tank outlet or for the booster pump ... [of] 8 to 16 meshes per inch...." That's similar to the mesh on a window screen.

This strainer is supposed to keep "big pieces" of contamination in the fuel from getting into the engine. There may well be a much finer filtering device downstream of this screen.

The reg is rather specific about the size of this strainer screen: "The clear area of ... the strainer must be at least five times the area of the outlet line."

In other words, this is *not* simply a dime-size flat screen such as you might find in a water supply line to your home laundry machine. This strainer may take the form of a long "finger strainer" inside the fuel tank; but, in this case, it must be accessible for inspection and cleaning.

Frequent inspection of the fuel strainer is important, especially if you do your own autogas refueling from five-gallon cans. It is also important if your airplane has integral "wet-wing" tanks, with a lot of rubbery sealant around the seams, or if the leading-edge tanks in your old Cherokee have ever been "sloshed" internally with sealant to stop leaks.

It doesn't take much contamination with 1/16th-inch-diameter "big pieces" (of peeled tank sealant, for instance) to block this fuel screen.

So, when you drain your gascolator, don't just look for water. Look for sediment, also. If there is a lot of dirt, have your mechanic drop the bowl and clean it, as well as the screen. When he's done with the gascolator, *you* check to be sure that the bowl is square in its housing and that the retaining nut is properly tightened and safetied.

Keep Caps On

Several years ago, a friend had to make an engine-out forced landing in his ancient homebuilt.

He had been doing some welding work and fabric replacement on the steel-tube fuselage frame. He had drained the fuel tank, which is ahead of the instrument panel, just behind the firewall. He then blow-dried the inside of the tank and left the fuel cap off for several days for additional ventilation while he completed the fuselage repairs.

His steel fuel tank was similar to others still out there today and like some homebuilt fuselage "header" tanks. The tank tapered down to a pointed sump area at the bottom, and the fuel line was at the very bottom of this sump, with *no* finger screen.

This setup was good for getting every last drop of fuel, but also was effective for having the engine inhale every last bit of crud from the tank. A better design would have the fuel outlet slightly *above* the bottom of the sump, and the bottom of the sump would have a drain fitting.

Just a few flights after completing the fuselage repairs on this homebuilt, the engine quit. Good pasture landing, and no damage. No fuel flow from the gascolator drain, even with the tank almost full. The pilot removed the main fuel line running from the tank bottom to the gascolator—and blew out a great big Florida bug.

Moral: Don't leave your fuel tank uncapped. You might get killed by a cockroach.

Valve Variables

The selector and shut-off valves in your fuel system are directly in the line between the fuel tank and the engine. If a valve should jam, you might not be able to select another tank or shut off fuel flow in an emergency.

Many valves have a prescribed internal lubrication requirement. Check the service manual for your airplane and make sure this gets done.

In many airplanes, especially multiengine airplanes, the selector handle is in the cockpit, but it remotely operates valves in the wing roots via pushrod or cable linkages. In some airplanes (the Piper Aerostar, for one), the selector activates an electric motor which, in turn, operates the valve (lose your electrical system, and you can't switch tanks).

At least during annual inspection, somebody should check that each valve *completely* follows position changes of the cockpit control handle. A partially open selector valve may not provide sufficient fuel flow for high-power operation.

It's a good idea for pilots to get in the habit of running the engine(s) on *each* of the available tank selections while taxiing out for run-up. But, do *not* select another tank just before moving onto the runway. Make sure you're running on the "takeoff" tank(s) at least by the time you get into position for the engine run-up.

And, don't wait until you're on the downwind leg to select your "landing" tank. Make that switch while you're still up high, with plenty of time to re-select in case the engine quits.

FAR 23.955(e) requires that "it must be possible ... to regain full power and fuel pressure in not more than 10 seconds" (in a single-engine airplane, 20 seconds in a twin) after running a tank dry.

But, don't count on that!

I once ran a ferry tank dry in an A36 Bonanza while overhead "Podunk Airport" at 2,500 feet AGL. Even with an immediate switch to a main tank and energizing the boost pump, I didn't get the engine back again until rolling out on the runway after a dead-stick (but prop-windmilling) landing.

In some airplanes, you can get a big slug of air into the fuel lines and fuel pumps that will be hard to clear. The electric boost pump in Continental fuel-injection systems might change your situation from dead engine due to fuel starvation to dead engine due to over-rich mixture.

Do your fuel tank switches up high!

Alert for Leaks

Fuel lines don't get much attention, especially those aft of the firewall. Usually, they are almost built into the airframe—hard to inspect and hard to replace.

They frequently reside under floorboards and behind fiberglass insulation in side panels—potentially very corrosion-prone areas. You probably can't get to the whole length of each fuel line, even during the best of annual inspections.

So, you, as pilot-in-command, had best be alert for the first signs of airframe fuel line problems. At the first whiff of fuel fumes in the cockpit or the first sighting of a drop of fuel on the belly, *go see your mechanic!*

There's been a recent rash of corroded airframe fuel lines. Usually, the problem starts as a tiny pinhole leak. But, that's just shortly before the whole line is ready to break.

Remember, a single teaspoon of gasoline in the belly or wing is more powerful than the same teaspoonful of plastic explosive.

Aeroquip recently sent me its Service Bulletins AA135 and AA91, on flexible fuel lines. Most likely, these hoses will be forward of the firewall, but they may also be prefabricated hoses that *you*, as the pilot or owner, are allowed to replace under the "preventive maintenance" provisions of FAR 43, Appendix A.

Aeroquip SB AA91 covers such problems as kinks and twists in the hoses, as well as brittle rubber hoses, seeping end fittings, etc. These are problems that *you* might precipitate by installing your own hoses or using hose of unknown origin or vintage.

Don't mess with this kind of "preventive" work, yourself. But, you *can* do the inspection for the possible problem areas.

Bulletin AA135 is interesting. Aeroquip is concerned with premature aging and failure of its 601-type rubber hoses, and deduces that the problem is mostly due to the use of "low-lead aviation gasoline" (100LL).

Reading between the lines, I deduce that they are probably also concerned with the use of no-lead auto fuels in these rubber lines. Their recommended fix is to replace, with Teflon hose, any 601 rubber hose that has been installed for two years or more.

For further information, contact Aeroquip Aerospace Group in Jackson, Mich., 517-787-8121.

Gauging Gauges

Let's conclude this discussion of fuel systems with just a few recommendations on fuel gauging systems:

1. The best "gauge" is eyeballing the fuel level in a full tank.

2. Next best is a dipstick reading of a partial fuel load. Unfortunately, there aren't many calibrated dipsticks out there, and, on many airplanes, you can't even see the fuel level when the tanks are half full.

3. Don't trust *any* fuel gauge system completely. You can calibrate your own gauges by carefully comparing cockpit fuel gauge readings with quantities added during top-offs. If you have a "totalizer," so much the better for comparing fuel-added to fuel-used. If a particular gauge is way off, make a placard reading, for example, "5 gallons (or 1/4 tank) remaining when gauge reads 1/2."

4. At least once every two years, drain the tank completely. Then, add the AFM-stated "unusable" fuel and check for a zero reading on the gauge.

Keep in mind that your airplane probably doesn't go through full tanks of fuel as often as your automobile. The tanks in your airplane are likely to contain a lot of stale and, maybe, dirty gasoline. Your tank caps are exposed to the weather and are much more likely than your auto fuel caps to leak water.

Your airplane engine runs at very high power output for a good bit of its life, and it must have access to a full flow of clean fuel. You can't just pull off to the shoulder of the road when the engine quits due to a fuel problem.

Fuel-related engine failure is a big problem, and one that is fairly easily avoided. Just because your fuel system is simple does not mean you can ignore it. Mismanagement happens in airplanes with even the simplest of systems, as does contamination and mechanical failure.

Here's Brian Jacobson with some guidelines on avoiding engine failure, with a particular emphasis on fuel.

Fuel-Related Power Loss

Modern technology has produced some wonderful tools that we use in our daily lives, but one thing it hasn't given us is an engine that burns air as its sole fuel. Yet, each year, many pilots try to make their aircraft engines run on air.

It is not that we don't know better. Our flight instructors taught us from the very beginning how to ensure that adequate supplies of fuel are aboard our aircraft and how to be certain there is no contamination. This is so crucial to the safe conduct of a flight that it has to be uppermost in our minds as we conduct ourselves from preflight to touchdown.

Unfortunately, too many pilots, high- and low-time alike, ignore the basics. Either they fail to set personal limitations regarding fuel or just set them aside, hoping the impossible can somehow be achieved.

Recently, I read a report about a student pilot who landed at an airport with his fuel tanks nearly empty. The airport operator did not sell fuel to transient aircraft, and the employee on duty refused the fueling request. The student took off again, apparently without consulting his instructor or anyone else. A few minutes later, his engine quit. He escaped injury in the ensuing crash landing, but his airplane was substantially damaged. The owner of the operation that denied the fueling request stated that he would have authorized it because of the near-empty condition of the student's fuel tanks. Unfortunately, the owner was not at the airport when the student was there, looking for fuel.

Knowingly taking off with no fuel in the tanks is tantamount to playing Russian roulette with a fully loaded revolver. It's easy to think you can make it to the next airport that appears on the chart, but the odds are solidly against you.

In another recent case, a pilot took off from a California airport with the tanks in his A36 Bonanza nearly empty. His engine quit shortly after takeoff. The pilot turned back toward the airport but landed short of the runway. He was seriously injured.

Takeoff Minimums

Some airplanes have requirements that the fuel tanks not be below a certain level before takeoff. This assures that fuel will be available at the pickup points in the tanks in the event the airplane has to make sudden turns or maneuvers.

Fuel sloshing around inside the tanks can cause these points to be uncovered and result in the loss of engine power as air replaces the fuel in the lines. This phenomenon is called *unporting.*

A pilot should have thorough knowledge of the fuel system in each type of airplane he or she flies. He also should, based on that knowledge, have a minimum fuel requirement for takeoff and another absolute minimum fuel requirement in flight.

In other words, if the winds are a lot stronger than forecast or if weather conditions or ATC requirements have put you far off your time estimates, don't keep trucking along, hoping to make it to your destination. You don't want to put yourself in the position of having to hope someone hears your ELT and will come to find you.

Before you reach your minimum in-flight fuel requirement, have a plan for landing at an en route airport and refilling the tanks.

Fuel gauges in most light aircraft are notoriously unreliable. If you are basing your decisions solely on the gauges, you are in trouble from the very start. How often have we heard the story of a pilot who fails to visually check fuel quantity, only to have the engine quit at some point before he expected to run out of fuel? The excuse is usually something like: "According to the gauges, I still had plenty of fuel left."

Fuel quantity in high-wing airplanes generally is harder to verify than in low-wingers. It is necessary to get a ladder and climb up high enough to remove the cap and peer into the tank.

Another method, the one I use on my Cessna 172, is a plastic tube called the "Fuelhawk." Mine is calibrated for the 172, but they are available for other types of aircraft, also. The markings on the tube give an accurate reading in gallons when the person conducting the pre-flight inserts the tube into the tank, covers its open top with a finger and pulls the tube back out of the tank.

What You See...

Sometimes, just looking inside a tank can be misleading. For instance, with a Piper Cherokee I once owned, I could only be sure of how much fuel was aboard if I could see that the tanks were full or if the fuel level was at the tabs. With both tanks topped, I had 50 gallons. At the tabs, I had 36 gallons. After that, it was just guesswork. Safety of flight should never be left to guesswork.

Recently, I flew as a safety pilot for a friend while he caught up on his instrument currency. His airplane is a Beech Musketeer, and, with the fuel tanks full, the gauges read only half-full. When I saw that we were taxiing out with what appeared to be half tanks, I asked him how much fuel he had. He told me he had just topped the tanks and that the gauges never read correctly.

He had spent much time and money trying to fix them, but nothing worked. So, he did the smart thing. He figured out how much fuel he burns per hour at different altitudes. He uses those figures and his watch as a fuel gauge.

Fuel cannot be taken for granted. Once, a pilot left his twin-engine airplane at an airport in Mexico overnight. He came back the next day and took off, only to have his engines promptly lose power. After the off-airport landing, no fuel was found in the tanks. Someone had stolen the fuel he had purchased the day before. Apparently, the pilot did not visually check the tanks, and if he was relying on the gauge indications, obviously, the gauges weren't working properly.

In another case, an Air Canada Boeing 767 ran dry a few years ago while up in the flight levels. It turned out the captain was an avid soaring enthusiast and was skilled enough to land the airplane, with minor damage, at a closed airport. There were no injuries to those aboard.

The recently delivered aircraft was having problems with its electronic fuel tabulation system. The fueler who did the conversion from gallons to liters, using an approved alternative system, made a major error in his calculation. The crew did not "stick" the tanks themselves, which is akin to a general aviation pilot not visually checking his fuel level.

Starving the Engines

Exhausting the fuel supply is only one reason an engine or engines might quit from a lack of fuel. The NTSB has documented many cases of engine failure due to other fuel-related causes.

A good example is a Bonanza pilot who had the cabin door pop open while cruising along at 5,500 feet over Oklahoma. He slid from the left seat over to the right seat to close the door and, apparently, inadvertently shut off the fuel selector in the process. The airplane suddenly became very quiet and was damaged when it hit a fence during the resulting forced landing.

The first thing to check should your engine quit for any reason is the fuel supply and whether it is making it to the engine or not. If you have a fuel pressure gauge, look at that. If there is no pressure indication, you may have emptied a tank or placed the selector in the wrong position.

Once, years ago, I was flying a charter in a Cessna 310 up the coast of Maine at 7,500 feet on a beautiful fall day. In the right seat was my lone passenger, who happened to be a student pilot. Apparently, the meeting I was taking him to was important for his business, because he was uneasy throughout the trip. Directly over the Portland airport, the right engine quit.

I looked at the fuel flow gauge and determined that the engine was not getting fuel. Meanwhile, my passenger just about jumped through the roof of the airplane. I told him to relax. While I was looking down at the fuel selectors, I explained to him that we were right over the Portland airport, so there was no reason to panic.

Then, I saw the reason for the power loss. My passenger, in his jittery condition, had placed his left foot on the fuel selector and moved it just enough to shut off the fuel. I pulled the throttle back a bit and reached down and turned the fuel selector back on. The engine came back to life immediately.

I explained to him what had happened, and he apologized and settled down for the rest of the flight. He learned a lesson that day that I am sure he has not forgotten.

Carburetor Ice

Another cause of fuel starvation is carburetor icing. On my Continental-powered 172, I have to be alert for it. Those engines are prone to carburetor icing, and any time I detect the slightest drop in rpm, I pull on the carb heat, which clears it right away.

Pilots who don't recognize the onset of carburetor icing are involved in many accidents and incidents. The first indication will be a loss of rpm in an airplane with a fixed-pitch propeller, or a drop in manifold pressure if you have an aircraft with a constant-speed propeller.

When carb ice starts to form, you may notice that you are pushing in on the throttle to maintain the selected rpm or manifold pressure. You may do that without thinking anything is wrong at first, but if the tach or MP gauge continues to show a loss, pull the carb heat control on.

You should see a slight drop in rpm or MP as the mixture is enriched, then an increase. How much you have adjusted the throttle will determine how much of a recovery there is. You will need to pull the throttle right back to its normal position once the heat does its work and the engine recovers.

If you are flying along fat, dumb and happy in conditions conducive to carb icing and, suddenly, the engine starts coughing and wheezing, pull the carb heat out right away. If you are lucky, you may catch it in time.

If the engine does not recover, leave the carburetor heat on while you look for a place to land. On some engines, there is enough residual heat at low rpm that, depending on how much time you have before making the unscheduled landing, the icing problem may clear up enough for sufficient power to be generated to continue flying. The more power the engine puts out, the more carb heat will be available.

Danger Zone

For carburetor icing to form, you do not necessarily have to be in visible moisture. Humid air can cause problems if the outside air temperature is in the right range.

As air gets colder, it usually becomes drier. That reduces the chances of encountering carb icing. At air temperatures of 14 degrees Fahrenheit (minus 10 Celsius) or lower, any moisture suspended in the air will be frozen. Carburetor heat should not be used. It is possible to induce carburetor icing by heating those frozen particles so they get through the carburetor inlet only to freeze again on the internal throttle plate.

Also, due to the venturi effect inside the carburetor as air passes through, the temperature drops. If the outside air temperature is in a range near, but above, freezing, remember that it is still possible to encounter carburetor icing.

My first airplane was an Alon Aircoupe that had a 90-horsepower Continental engine. During my first winter as a private pilot, I would go out and do touch and goes often. It was disturbing when I would push the throttle in and the engine would choke and sputter before coming up to speed.

My mechanic suggested that an overhaul of the carburetor was necessary, and he did the job to the tune of a couple hundred dollars. Alas, I was one surprised pilot when the next time I flew the airplane, the same condition existed. There was much head-scratching and hair-pulling over that until the A&P called Continental and learned that the air was so dense in the winter that it changed the fuel/air mixture to the point where the engine couldn't handle sudden changes. I learned to leave the carburetor heat on until I had the throttle in and the engine was producing power. That was an expensive lesson, even in those days.

Water Hazards

Water in the fuel supply can turn your day sour rapidly. There are at least three ways in which fuel can become contaminated with water.

First, be wary of an airplane that has been idle for a long time. The amount of moisture suspended in the air varies from day to day, and, with temperature changes, water condenses inside fuel tanks. This is why we drain some fuel out of each tank and the fuel strainers before flying. The longer an airplane sits without someone taking samples from the fuel drains, the greater are the chances that water will accumulate.

Another way to get water in the fuel system is to refuel while it is raining. The heavier it is raining while the refueling is being conducted, the more water will get in the tank if there is no effort made to keep the water out.

Finally, there could be water in the fuel that is being pumped into your tanks. If there's a leak in the vendor's underground tanks, they could, without knowing it, deliver contaminated fuel to your airplane. There's also the possibility that, if the vendor doesn't sell much fuel and the level of fuel in the storage tank is low for a long period, condensation could cause the fuel to become laced with water.

There have been many cases in which pilots drained tanks until they got what they thought was pure fuel, only to have the engine quit on takeoff from water contamination. Sometimes, it can take a while for water to settle to the low points in the fuel tanks. Draining tanks immediately after fueling will not always guarantee that you have all the water out of the system.

When circumstances demand that you fly an airplane that you suspect might have water or other contaminants in the fuel, have an A&P ensure that the airplane is in flyable condition. The mechanic can check the entire fuel system and make sure he drains or flushes any contaminants present.

Mechanical Glitches

Most accidents and incidents following loss of power are the results of pilots who do not pay enough attention to their fuel systems. Occasionally, though, mechanical and maintenance problems cause engines to quit.

In one incident, a pilot was landing in a crosswind and, apparently, let the airplane drift to the right side of the runway. When he applied power to go around, the engine did not respond. The airplane wound up in a swamp next to the runway. Investigators found that the idle speed was adjusted so low that it was not sufficient to maintain engine operation.

Another accident happened when a pilot switched tanks, only to have the engine quit. He switched back to the other tank and continued his flight, thinking he had enough fuel in that one tank to get to his destination. He didn't. The airplane received extensive damage when he landed in a field short of his destination. The reason the engine wouldn't run when the tanks were switched was that a fuel vent was blocked with insects and debris.

In another incident, a pilot suffered burn injuries and a rented Cessna 172 was destroyed when he tried to start the engine. Maintenance personnel had removed the carburetor and failed to cap the fuel line.

There was no placard in the aircraft indicating the aircraft was not airworthy, and the employee who gave the pilot the key to the 172 apparently wasn't aware of the situation, either. The pilot said he did a complete preflight but didn't notice that the lower cowl was attached with only two screws. When he tried to start the aircraft, the engine was doused with fuel.

We all know that an adequate supply of good, clean fuel of the proper grade is necessary for safety of flight. Why, then, do so many of us make the mistakes we have just discussed? Get-home-itis? The feeling that "nothing is going to go wrong"? The "I can handle it" syndrome? Or, "Aw, it's just a little water"?

When your engine becomes silent because there either is no fuel left in the tanks or none is getting to the engine, wishing you had done something differently will be of absolutely no help at all.

Induction
Icing

I nduction icing affects both IFR and VFR pilots, and, like water in the fuel, can bring a perfectly healthy airplane down.

First let's talk a bit about the phenomenon, itself, and how it works. Later on in the chapter we'll describe an aircraft accessory that can help you deal with it effectively.

Here's ATP Wally Miller to talk about the perils of carb ice.

A Persistent Threat

Not many of us like to curl up with a volume of NTSB accident reports on a cold winter's night. But maybe we should. Accident reports can provide valuable lessons—sometimes as much as from what they *don't* say as from what they do.

Take engine failure, for instance. Though it's a major cause of general aviation accidents, all too often the probable cause of a power loss cannot be determined.

Consider the following excerpt from one accident report: "The pilot was on a local flight in his homebuilt, two-thirds-scale P-51 Mustang. During the initial climb, the engine sputtered and quit.... Post-accident inspection failed to reveal any evidence to explain the reported engine failure."

Another report, on a Beech 35 Bonanza, reads: "The pilot said that shortly after takeoff, the engine failed. He had already retracted the landing gear.... Post-accident investigation failed to determine the cause of the engine failure."

Yet another, on an AT-137 Air Tractor agplane, noted that "after lift-off, the aircraft sustained a partial loss of engine power." The report went on to say that the pilot "dumped his chemical load as the aircraft descended. He maneuvered the aircraft to avoid several obstacles, but the left gear eventually separated after the aircraft landed in soft dirt.

"A post-accident examination of the aircraft and the failed engine failed to account for the reported partial loss of engine power; the disassembly of the engine did not reveal any preimpact malfunction."

And so it goes. There are scores of "undetermined" engine-failure accidents and incidents each year. Several reports go a step further than the ones just cited, however. They contain statements such as, "Examination of carburetor icing probability curves revealed that weather conditions were favorable to the formation of icing."

When I first read that description, I could not recall ever seeing an "official" carburetor icing probability chart. I set out to find one. During two weeks of looking at government and commercially published sources in my library, the files—and elsewhere—there was no chart to be found.

I called the FAA, the NTSB and other groups. I talked to people in both field and staff offices. Their consensus was that there is no official carburetor icing probability chart published by the FAA, probably because engine icing characteristics vary to a small degree among different aircraft.

Characteristics of different models of the same aircraft may even show slight differences. They don't appear to be significant, however.

Since that initial, fruitless search, I have found two different charts. One is published by England's Civil Aviation Authority. The other is in an aircraft icing pamphlet published by the AOPA Air Safety Foundation. It is adapted from a chart prepared by Canada's Ministry of Transport (see the accompanying illustration). Although the charts vary slightly, the ominous message they convey is the same: Carburetor icing will get you when you least expect it!

Out of Sight

Most thinking pilots hit the books at least once each year to bone up on "icing." Most often, though, our concern is about *structural* icing.

Even a half inch or less of rime ice is easy to spot on the leading edge of a wing. It scares most pilots because its meaning is clear. The airfoil is beginning to distort. And, usually, the build-up on the tail is even worse.

The thought of structural icing sends shivers down the spines of those who have had a good dose of it and lived to tell their tales. Its dangers are obvious to anyone who cares to look at the relatively high fatality rate in structural icing-related accidents.

The "rules" on structural ice are pretty clear. Most pilots know them. Smart pilots avoid icing conditions like the plague if their aircraft aren't properly equipped. They have well-planned courses of action in mind if and when they run into conditions which jeopardize safe flight. They know what they are doing. They think ahead of the situation and the airplane.

Still, airplanes literally fall out of the sky every year because of the increased weight and inability to overcome the aerodynamic inefficiency of ice-distorted airfoils. Structural ice is such a serious flight hazard, in fact, that a separate section of the area forecast is devoted to it.

But, when did you ever get a forecast of *carburetor* icing? What charts and weather reports pinpoint areas in which the risk of carburetor icing is high? Could you put your finger on any legend that describes levels of carburetor icing severity?

If your experience is similar to mine, the answer to all of these questions is, "Say again?"

That's too bad, because icing in carburetors kills people just as surely as structural ice does. A very tragic difference between structural and carburetor icing, however, is that experts say carburetor ice can occur at temperatures up to 100 F—on days when there isn't a cloud in the sky.

Unfortunately, the rush to bone up on icing seems to come only as winter approaches, and most of the emphasis is on structural icing. Other hazards, including induction system icing, are too often shortcut or overlooked altogether. They shouldn't be. Here's a case in point:

A Long Ten Seconds

It was a beautiful afternoon. There wasn't a cloud in the sky. You could see forever. The sun was bright, and the temperature at takeoff was 76 degrees.

We had methodically familiarized ourselves with the small airfield. A survey from the air before entering the traffic pattern to land had shown the field to be completely surrounded by trees. We had noticed that immediately after taking off from Runway 28, the closest suitable landing area was about 30 degrees left of the departure path and a minute and a half away. Prior to that, nothing but trees.

Numerous instructional sessions before that flight had taught us there was nowhere to "take it in" if we got into trouble right after takeoff—a typical situation in many areas.

The student pilot in the left seat of the Cessna 172 had been distracted by helicopters in the pattern and had missed an item on the "before landing" checklist: carburetor heat. Not a typical performance for him.

He was good at details and seldom missed a checklist item. Normally, I would have mentioned it immediately. But, this time, I delayed. (After all, the temperature *was* 76 degrees.)

After touching down on the 3,000-foot runway, I "took" the aircraft and executed a touch-and-go to give him a short break. He had been working hard and doing well. Just before lift-off, I asked, "What did you forget on that last pattern?" I could almost see the instant-replay camera running in his head.

The initial climb-out progressed smoothly for the first hundred feet, but it was slowly becoming apparent that we had a problem. Something was drastically wrong—bad-feeling-in-the-pit-of-the-stomach wrong. The engine sounded "flat," and the airplane seemed to "hang up" at 200 feet AGL and 73 knots. It wouldn't climb or accelerate. The throttle was full forward. Outside, it was a mild, sunlit, beautiful day. Inside, we weren't having much fun.

Since our first training flight together, I had emphasized the proper use of carburetor heat, especially during descent and landing. I had stressed immediate use of carburetor heat at any hint of an engine problem close to the ground. I instinctively reached for the carburetor heat lever and pulled it full-out.

My concentration on positive, straight-ahead aircraft control and maintenance of flying speed was intense. Mentally, I prepared to make the eight-knot transition to best glide speed should the engine totally quit—a tough thing to do when you're only 200 feet above the treetops. But, there was literally nowhere else to go.

As I was just about to slow to best glide speed, the rpm and airspeed both started to increase. Carburetor heat had saved the day. It was the longest 10 seconds I have spent in quite a while.

"Same Difference"

To understand what happened, let's examine an accident that occurred in Illinois. A Cessna 182 was climbing after taking off for a sport parachute drop. The engine quit, and the pilot instructed his four parachutist/passengers to assume the crash-landing position.

The pilot made a good landing, and there were no injuries. But, the nose gear was damaged when it dug into the sod. If the aircraft had *not* been damaged, we might never have known about this accident. The cause was blockage of the carburetor venturi ... by a piece of duct tape.

The same thing happens to many other airplanes every year—with one exception. The culprit is ice, instead of duct tape. But the effect is identical: The airplane loses power and stops flying. As a good old boy once said, "Same difference."

Recent accident reports indicate a continuing lack of understanding about carburetor icing—what causes it, what to look for ahead of time, how it can be detected in the early stages, what to do about it (and how to do it) if it occurs, and what *not* to do.

Forewarned, Forearmed

Carburetor icing probability charts need to be posted in every FBO and flight school. Simply being aware that it can happen when least expected is half the battle.

The old adage that "flying is hours and hours of boredom punctuated by brief moments of stark terror" would be funny if it wasn't occasionally true. If you have experienced carburetor icing, you know what I mean. If you haven't, be aware that you can prevent it almost 100 percent of the time. But, you have to know what you're doing.

If you are a flight school owner or a flight instructor, ask yourself this question: Where is the nearest carburetor icing probability chart posted? "Out of sight, out of mind" is another adage that comes to mind. Absence fosters lack of awareness.

Just promoting a healthy consciousness of carburetor ice is a good place to begin. Accident reports help to illustrate the need for that awareness. Consider this excerpt from the NTSB report on a crash that occurred in Creve Coeur, Mo.: "The pilot reported that shortly after takeoff, after attaining an altitude of about 100 feet, the engine began losing power. An emergency landing was made in an adjacent corn field, where the aircraft was substantially damaged.

"The temperature and dew point were 81 and 50 degrees, respectively," the report continued. "According to icing probability charts, conditions were conducive to carburetor icing." Perhaps, availability of a probability chart could have created an awareness that icing was possible—even on a day like the one described in this report.

Among other reports on accidents caused by carburetor ice, the following temperature/dew point combinations are disclosed: Tecumseh, Mich.—83/69; Santa Paula, Calif.—60/40; San Juan, Puerto Rico—78/69.

"Clear and a Million"

Suffice it to say that this silent killer can be present when it is least expected. Though much less obvious than structural icing, carburetor icing is potentially much more dangerous because of its insidious, "stealthy" nature.

The weather doesn't have to be "clear and a million" to get us on the alert for carburetor icing. Recently, I was flying with a instrument-instructor (CFII) candidate. We entered the clouds climbing through 400 feet and were still in them when we leveled off at 2,000 feet.

It was one of those days when you can feel the moisture-soaked air. Water was dripping from the trailing edges of the Cessna 172's wing struts. The cockpit felt "sticky." The airspeed was jumping between 90 and 100 knots. It was a solid-IFR day, with just enough turbulence to challenge complacency. The temperature was in the 70s. Carburetor icing probability charts show that *serious icing* is possible *at any power setting* on a day like that. I kept a close eye on the tachometer.

We followed the controller's vectors toward the outer marker for an ILS approach. He advised that we would be going through "a small area of rain" in about 30 seconds.

I quickened my scan to check the airspeed and tachometer more often than usual. I wanted to catch those first subtle indications of the onset of carburetor ice.

My mind wandered back to that touch-and-go months earlier when carburetor heat saved the day. I wondered how many other pilots had been lucky enough to fly out of a situation like that and how many emergency landings had been made, with no damage or injury, due to iced-up carbs.

My reverie was disturbed by a noticeable increase in turbulence and rain on the windshield. About that time, the rpm started subtly but noticeably to decrease. I reached for the carburetor heat control.

Forewarned *really* is forearmed. It is fortunate that I had checked the probability chart before going to the airplane and was extra alert for carb icing.

View from the Cockpit

Prompt recognition requires keen awareness of the probability of icing and alertness for its initial indications.

With constant-speed propellers, steady deterioration of manifold pressure at a constant throttle setting will probably be the first indication. The rpm will remain constant.

With variable-speed, fixed-pitch propellers, rpm will start to drop off and will be accompanied by airspeed reduction if not caught early.

Airplanes with exhaust gas temperature (EGT) gauges provide additional early warning of impending trouble—even before engine power reduction is apparent. EGT will start to decrease with the onset of carburetor ice.

In the absence of any action by the pilot, ice will build up in the carburetor until it effectively strangles the engine. Loss of airspeed will ensue from the progressive decline of engine power. It may even be necessary to retrim the airplane to maintain altitude.

Engine backfiring or complete power loss are the eventual outcomes of carb ice.

Even though preparation and thought are essential to prevention, carburetor icing can still reach out and grab us just about anytime. If it does, get the carburetor heat full-on ASAP. Leave it full-on until things return to normal and you're sure they're going to stay that way. Follow the rules, know what you're doing, and use the airplane checklist.

There are plenty of icing hazards to go around—*all* year round. Carburetor icing is just one of the hazards. Before your next exposure, it might pay to get into the books and develop a plan of action to keep you out of trouble. Just remember that carburetor ice can happen when we often least expect it. Be aware.

We mentioned up top that there are gadgets that can help you deal with carb ice. No, it's not the carb heat or alternate air door. It's a carburetor ice detector.

In the case of one of these devices that's really a misnomer, because it's actually just a thermometer that has a probe strategically placed in the carburetor throat. When it says the temperature is correct for icing, you apply heat. Simple, and it works.

Another system uses a photocell, while a third uses electrical conductivity to actually sense the presence of ice.

Of the three, one is no longer made. We include a description here because it did work, and many examples are still flying.

Carb Ice Detectors

Not long ago, a pilot related to us an experience he had with that old bugaboo, carburetor ice, while cruising over mountains in a Cessna 150. The elusive hazard caught him by surprise, but a Flight Service specialist's suggestion that he try carb heat saved the day.

As the pilot recalled, it hadn't occurred to him that carb ice might be the problem. After all, he was at a high power setting and, like most pilots, had been taught that ice is most unlikely in such a situation. He said the heart-stopping experience of having his engine go quiet unexpectedly made him a true believer—that the threat of carb ice should never be taken lightly.

One way a pilot can arm himself against the threat is to equip his aircraft with a carb ice detector. In this report, we'll review how carb ice forms and take a look at several devices on the market that can alert pilots to the hazard.

No Easy Solution

The need for a means of detecting ice in the induction system has been evident for as long as ice has been frosting the insides of carburetors. Engineers who have undertaken the task have had to come up with solutions to two basic problems: first, how to get to where the trouble actually starts; and second, exactly what to measure. The answers to these problems aren't quite as obvious as they might seem at first glance.

Induction ice is formed when air moving through the intake system is cooled below the dew point, allowing moisture to condense. The moisture contacts the metal parts of the system and, if they're cold enough, freezes on them. Ice can form remarkably quickly. FAA tests found that under certain conditions it takes only a few seconds for ice to form.

For condensation to occur, induction air has to be sufficiently moist, and there has to be a mechanism to cool the air. The cooling mechanism in a carbureted engine exists in the carburetor, itself. Pressure is lowered as the air passes through the venturi, and this causes a corresponding drop in temperature. The lower pressure also pulls fuel into the carb and causes it to vaporize. Fuel vaporization lowers the temperature even more. The difference in the temperatures of the outside air and that inside the carb can be as much as 70 degrees Fahrenheit.

Trouble Spot

The refrigeration effect is greatest where the pressure drop and fuel vaporization take place, just downstream of the venturi in the vicinity of the throttle plate. That doesn't mean ice can't form elsewhere in the system—there is, for example, another pressure drop downstream of the throttle plate. But the most likely location is near the throttle plate.

So, it would seem that installation of an ice detector would be as simple as drilling a hole into the side of the carb somewhere between the venturi and the throttle plate and sticking a sensor probe into it. While that's true as far as it goes, it doesn't tell the whole story.

In the early 1980s, FAA conducted an induction icing study in which a borescope was placed inside an operating carburetor, which was then caused to ice. The resulting photos showed that ice tends to form first not on the walls of the carb or in the venturi, but on the throttle plate.

Good Measure

So, just how does one go about determining the presence of ice inside a working carburetor? There are as many different methods of finding ice as there are detectors.

The simplest way is, in fact, not to measure the ice, itself, but the conditions conducive to its formation. A temperature probe, called a thermocouple, is installed in such a way that it can read the temperature inside the carburetor. Theoretically, if carb air temperature is kept out of a particular range, no ice will form.

While this approach has the virtue of being able to detect the likelihood of carb ice before it actually forms, it suffers one serious drawback. As with most exhaust gas temperature gauges and cylinder head temperature gauges, the temperature is measured at only one point, which may not be the coldest spot in the carburetor.

Tests have shown that the location of the carb's coldest point varies, depending on throttle setting, and it's possible to get ice even if the temperature at the probe's location is well above freezing. Also, cold temperatures don't necessarily guarantee the formation of ice; there must be sufficient moisture present as well. Simply measuring temperature can lead to false results.

Beams and Wires

Rather than measuring temperature to predict icing, other systems are designed to detect ice, itself. Two methods are used—one electrical, the other, optical.

The optical method uses a light source and photocell inside the carburetor. If ice interrupts the light beam traveling from one to the other, a warning is triggered.

The electrical method relies on ice grounding a wire and completing a warning circuit.

The drawback to these systems is that, by definition, they provide no advance warning. They let the pilot know that ice, or at least frost, is already there. In the vast majority of cases, there will be plenty of time to deal with the ice. However, the FAA carb ice study observed power losses in as little as 30 seconds from the start of ice formation.

The electrical and optical systems also share the drawback of being mounted in a fixed location. The ice may not cooperate—it might form where the detector can't sense its presence (see photo). By the time the detector sounds off, there may already be a chunk of the stuff sticking to some other, nearby part of the carb, about to shut it down.

What's Available

There are two carb ice detection/warning systems available from established manufacturers, and a third was once available on a custom-order basis. Each uses a different method of operation. They are the

Richter temperature probe, the ARP ice detector and the Shivers ice detector. While you can no longer buy a new Shivers detector, an airplane you fly may well have one installed.

The most common and oldest is the Richter system. According to the company, it's been in service since 1956 and nearly 58,000 have been installed. Much of the popularity is probably due to the fact that the system was offered as optional equipment by Cessna on new aircraft.

The Richter system consists of a temperature probe, wiring harness and gauge marked in degrees Celsius. There's a yellow arc on the gauge, indicating a caution zone that should be avoided.

Richter Probe

The probe is installed in a pre-existing hole in the side of the carburetor just upstream of the throttle plate, opposite the idle jet. The hole originally was drilled by the carb manufacturer to install the idle jet, then tapped and fitted with a threaded plug.

The Richter probe fits the threads, so installing the system is as simple as removing the plug, screwing in the probe, routing the wiring harness and installing the gauge in the panel.

According to the company, it should take no more than an hour to an hour and a half to install the system; a mechanic familiar with the installation can do it in about 30 minutes.

The systems are STC'd for a wide variety of carbureted airplanes. Richter gauges are sold by Mid-Continent Aviation, at (800) 821-1212.

ARP Detector

The ARP ice detector, while quite similar in installation to the Richter probe, is a different device entirely. It uses the photoelectric principle described above.

The system has been around since the early '60s, and there are about 3,000 in service, according to inventor and ARP company owner Al Puccinelli. It's been offered as optional equipment by Piper. The probe is much like that used in the Richter system; in fact, it is installed in the same hole. The ARP system also comprises a cockpit-mounted unit with a sensitivity control, a warning light and a loud horn. The cockpit unit is available as either a separate "black box" or in a panel-mounted configuration.

Installation is much the same as for the Richter system, and the time involved is comparable, Puccinelli said, though he did add that the time is considerably greater for some airplanes because of the difficulty in getting at the carburetor. In any case, he noted, installation time should not exceed three or four hours.

On Guard

Use of the ARP system is different from the Richter temperature gauge in that it does not need to be monitored. At engine start, the sensitivity control (for brightness of the light source) is turned so that the warning is on the verge of going off—much like the way a radio squelch knob is used. Anything that gets in the way of the light beam sets the detector off. According to Puccinelli, the detector is so sensitive that merely flying through a cloud can set it off. Of course, the sensitivity can be adjusted to suppress false positive readings.

Unlike the Richter system, ARP's carb-ice detector is STC'd for installation on a carburetor, rather than on individual aircraft. The certification applies to all aircraft equipped with Marvel-Schebler carburetors, which equates to the vast majority of the general aviation fleet.

The ARP detector is available from ARP Industries, 36 Bay Drive East, Huntington, N.Y. 11743. The phone number is (516) 427-1585.

Shivers System

The Shivers carb-ice detector uses the electrical detection principle. Ice buildup bridges the gap between a wire mounted just off the surface of the throttle plate and the plate, itself, thus completing a circuit and causing needle movement in a cockpit-mounted gauge. Like the Richter probe, the gauge must be monitored occasionally.

The big difference between the Shivers detector and the others is the location of its sensor. Shivers puts it on the downstream side of the throttle plate, just about where FAA tests determined that icing tends to show up first.

Panacea?

While any of these systems can help avoid a carb-ice-induced loss of power, none is perfect. Naturally, the makers of each of the detectors defend their own designs, but all three have limitations and characteristics that are important to be aware of.

Makers of the Richter and ARP probes claim they are placed right where ice starts to form in the carburetor. FAA studies of these devices, however, have shown otherwise.

Differing positions of the throttle plate have a profound effect on the air flow inside the carburetor, and any one mounting location is not necessarily ideal for all possible conditions. Indeed, the FAA carb icing studies found that the lowest temperatures in the carb are at the throttle plate, not near the wall of the carb. The photo above, taken during these tests, clearly shows a significant ice accumulation on the throttle plate, yet the detector probe mounted in the side of the carb is ice-free.

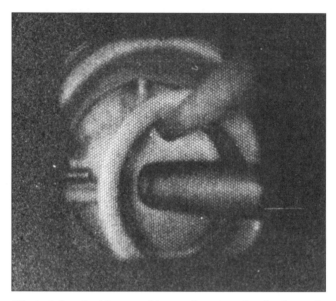

Photo taken inside a working carburetor clearly shows ice accumulation on the throttle plate. Ice detector probe (small projection at left) remains clear of ice.

False Positives

Both the ARP and Shivers systems can produce false positive results. The ARP system's high sensitivity can lead to the pilot mistrusting the Lastly, the Richter probe doesn't actually detect ice at all. It merely reports on one of the conditions necessary to produce icing: temperature. Moisture is also needed. Without enough water vapor, it won't matter what the temperature inside the carb is—ice won't form. In fact, the face of the gauge tells the pilot: "Keep the needle out of the yellow arc during possible icing conditions." Of course, "possible icing conditions" are very poorly defined.

Still a Good Idea

However, none of these drawbacks should be considered a fatal flaw, in our opinion.

Rather, they're limitations that can easily be dealt with if the pilot is aware of them. Any one of these systems, properly used, can help keep the pilot airborne and his engine free of ice. Even if they're not perfect, they're far better than the alternative of guessing when the engine might quit.

• Section Four •

Instruments and Avionics

The Electrical System

T his section deals with the items on the panel and the
systems that drive them: electrical, vacuum, avionics and gyros.

Our focus here, once again, is on coping with and avoiding failures, and
alerting you to what's important and what's not.

First up, John Conrad takes an inside look at your electrical system.

Untangling the Electrical System

Many pilots are content not to probe the mysteries of electricity. The
electrical diagrams that appear in the aircraft owner's manual remain
little more than passing curiosities. If the proper thing lights up when
the switch is thrown, then all is well.

But what happens if the proper thing *doesn't* light up when the
switch is thrown?

What happens when the engine won't start on a cold and lonely
ramp in the middle of the night? What happens when smoke fills the
cockpit while you are in IFR conditions?

At times like these, it is essential that the pilot thoroughly understand the aircraft's electrical system so that he or she can take corrective
action.

Many pilots who shy away from the electrical system believe it to be
dangerous. Certainly, it is powerful. Not one of us could continuously
pull the engine through by hand at the same speed it can be spun by the
electrical starter. But powerful doesn't necessarily mean dangerous.

The electrical system is potentially "dangerous" only if it is not
understood by the pilot. To better understand the electrical system,
let's examine each element separately.

Battery Basics

The battery most often used in aircraft is a plastic box containing lead grid plates immersed in a solution of 10 percent sulfuric acid and 90 percent water.

A battery is, in effect, an electrical storage tank.

When an electrical current is run through the battery, the water is broken down into its base elements—hydrogen and oxygen. The hydrogen eventually passes out into the air during the charging process. The oxygen attacks one set of the battery's plates and turns them first into lead oxide and then into peroxide.

In charging the battery, electrical energy is turned into chemical energy. When we want to use that energy, we connect an appliance, such as the aircraft starter motor, to the battery with two wires. The charge stored in the battery then flows through the starter motor and releases its energy.

Though it may not be important to understand the exact chemical reaction that occurs, it is important to remember that while being charged, an aircraft battery gives off hydrogen, a very explosive gas— as witnessed in the spectacular demise of the Hindenburg zeppelin.

An aircraft battery has to be treated with respect. Every effort should be made to keep sparks or open flames away from it.

Should you smell a sulfurous, acrid smell in flight, shut off the alternator immediately. You may be smelling the chemical byproducts of a battery that is being overcharged.

Also, remember that the water in a discharged battery can easily freeze. In the wintertime, it is important to be sure the aircraft battery is fully charged before shutting down the engine.

Don't taxi around the airport with all your lights and radios on and then pull the mixture as you roll into the chocks. The battery will be less than fully charged, and a good hard freeze will put you out of business. A good practice is to let the engine run a few minutes in the tie-down with all the accessories turned off so that the alternator can "top-off" the battery before shutdown. (Your engine and turbocharger will profit from this cool-down time, too.)

In order for the battery to perform its electrochemical magic, the plates must be completely immersed in solution. Every hundred hours of engine operation—or at least every six months—the caps should be removed and water should be added to fill the cells up to the indicator ring. Failure to do this reduces the effectiveness and life of the battery.

Whether you service your battery with distilled or tap water is a matter of choice. I've always used just plain old tap water. It's more convenient, but it does introduce trace elements such as iron, sodium, calcium and fluoride into the chemical reaction that goes on inside the battery.

Alternator

The alternator takes mechanical energy from the engine and converts it into electrical energy.

To do this, a small amount of current must be supplied to the alternator field from the battery. If the battery is stone dead, the alternator will not begin charging when the engine is hand-started.

So, if there isn't enough power to click the master switch solenoid, you had better plan on charging the battery before flight if you want to use any of the aircraft's electrical accessories.

It is important to know the location of the alternator and the method by which it is driven.

Modern aircraft cowlings tend to hide the alternator from all but the most aggressive preflight inspection. So, unless you know where to look and exactly what to look for, you're liable to miss it.

Some alternators are belt-driven off a large pulley right behind the propeller. There may be only a very small section of belt visible to the pilot. Nevertheless, it is important to be sure that this belt is very tight and not twisted before each flight. You should be able to move the belt only about a quarter of an inch.

Some alternators are belt-driven off a pulley on an accessory case on the back of the engine. If you have one of them, check that belt every chance you get. Should it break at cruise rpm, not only will you lose your electrical supply, but the belt could be thrown and wreak havoc on other components in the engine compartment.

The alternator, itself, should be checked occasionally for loose fittings or wires which look like they have been hot. Any discoloration of the insulation should be checked out by your mechanic.

Wiring and Circuits

Electrical energy is carried from the alternator to the battery and from the battery to the aircraft accessories through stranded metal wires.

Electricity flows well through metal. To operate an appliance, such as the landing gear motor, one metal wire has to be run from the positive pole of the battery to the motor, another from the motor back to the negative pole of the battery. Electrical energy flows out of the battery, through the wire to the motor and through the other wire back to the battery.

If the wires were bare and made contact with each other, electricity would flow directly from one wire to the other and bypass the motor.

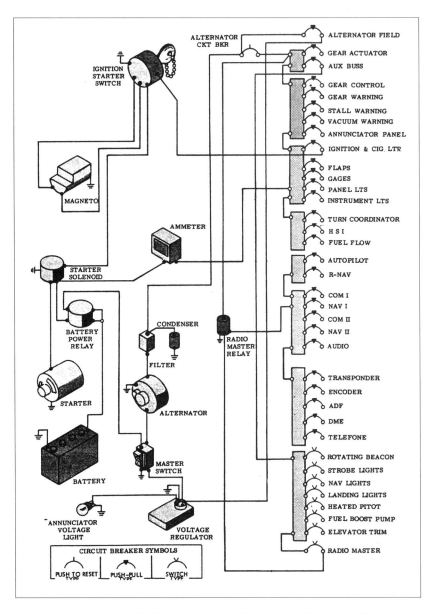

Some manufacturers offer clear and detailed electrical diagrams. Shown here is one from Mooney. On the panel, itself, the breakers are all clearly marked with their amp ratings, which can serve as a quick guide to shedding load in an emergency.

This is called a short circuit. To keep this from happening, the wires are covered with one or more coats of plastic insulation. So long as the insulation remains in place, a short circuit can't happen.

In addition to wires, metal portions of an aircraft's structure can be used to conduct electricity. In almost all aircraft, the negative pole of the battery is connected to the fuselage. Therefore, to run the landing gear motor, electricity flows through one wire from the positive terminal on the battery to the motor and returns to the negative pole through another wire connected to the fuselage at some convenient place. It may even be connected inside the motor. In any case, the "return path" is via the aircraft's metal fuselage.

Of course, in old wooden airplanes and new composite designs, two wires are required because neither wood nor fiberglass is a good conductor of electricity.

Check for Chafing

There are numerous advantages to using the fuselage as a conductor, such as saving weight and expense. But there is one disadvantage. Every exposed metal part on the aircraft becomes an uninsulated wire.

A short circuit can occur any place the aircraft fuselage chafes the insulation of a "positive" wire.

Sometime soon, crawl under the panel and take a look at the miles of wiring up there. Have someone move the controls through their full travel and be sure that no wires are rubbing anywhere. There's the potential for fire any place a wire rubs on a moving part.

Though most airplanes are built with all the wires safely bundled away, the ravages of time and mechanics take their toll. Sometimes the wires just sag over the years and end up touching the control linkages. Or tie-wraps become brittle and break, allowing a wire bundle to drop. Often, the addition of new radios requires cables to be rerouted.

It's a good idea to take a peek under the panel every few months to be sure there is no chafing.

Switches

Switches are nothing more than devices that allow us to open or close a circuit.

Normally, the switch handle moves a piece of metal that breaks or completes the circuit. Some switches use a small electrical circuit to operate another, large switch. The aircraft master switch, for example, is really two switches—a small one located in the panel and a great big one located near the battery. When the pilot closes the small switch at the panel, the current runs to an electromagnet which closes the big switch.

The "click" you hear when you turn on the little master switch is the real master switch closing somewhere else in the airplane. The starter motor and the avionics master switches are hooked up the same way. These types of switches are called solenoids.

Some switches are a little more complicated. The landing gear switch, for example, is often wired to close a circuit in either position. When we throw the switch to the "up" position, current flows from the switch to a wire which powers the landing gear motor in the direction that will raise the gear. When we put the handle in the "down" position, the current flows through a different wire that makes the motor run in the other direction and lower the gear.

Circuit Breakers

A circuit breaker does just what its name implies. It is nothing more than an automatic switch which breaks a circuit if the electrical demand becomes too great.

A circuit breaker is rated for the amount of electricity it can handle. For example, a landing light requiring 10 amps could be connected to a 15-amp circuit breaker. If for some reason the landing light drew more than 15 amps, the breaker would stop the flow of electricity to the light.

Likewise, a transponder drawing only three amps would be connected to a five-amp circuit breaker. Substituting a 15-amp circuit breaker wouldn't affect the transponder; but if something went wrong inside of the old squawk box, it probably would have to glow as hot and as bright as a landing light before the oversize circuit breaker would pop.

The ratings posted on circuit breakers can be used as rough guidelines for load-shedding, should the alternator fail and the pilot be faced with the need for strict rationing of the juice remaining in the battery.

Putting it Together

As you might have already guessed, *amperage* is a measure of electrical current, volume or flow.

Two other terms vital to a discussion of electrical circuits are *voltage* and *wattage*. Voltage is a measure of electrical potential, or pressure. Wattage is an expression of power, or the effect of voltage and amperage.

Related mathematically: Wattage is the product of voltage multiplied by amperage.

Applying a bit of first-year algebra, we can turn the equation around to figure voltage when the other two items are known. For example, a

120-watt light bulb would require one amp of current if that current was supplied at 120 volts.

If the voltage, or electrical pressure, of the system is reduced to 12 volts, electricity would have to flow at 10 amps to light the same bulb. This shows that the lower the voltage, the greater the current required to do a given amount of work.

The size of the wires used to carry electrical current is related to the volume of the current. The higher the current (amperage), the bigger the wire we need to carry it.

Therefore, if we can increase voltage (thereby reducing amperage), we can use a smaller wire to supply current to the appliance. That is just what most general aviation aircraft manufacturers did when they switched from 12-volt to 24-volt systems. They switched because smaller wires, switches and circuit breakers are cheaper and lighter.

Bearing the Load

One last factor we need to consider is electrical load. Everything we hook into an electrical circuit, from the wires to the accessories, has some resistance.

The wires, themselves, provide very little resistance. If we hooked a wire directly from one battery terminal to the other, the current flow would be so great because of the lack of resistance that the wire would become red-hot. But if we broke the wire in the middle and connected a light bulb, resistance of the bulb would reduce the current flow to a point at which the wires wouldn't even get hot.

So long as the wires are large enough to carry the current to the load, everything is fine. If we hooked our light bulb up with very fine wire, which couldn't handle the load, the wire would get hot and burn out. That is why the starter motor in your airplane has a great big wire hooked up to it, while the little light bulb that powers the compass light has a very fine wire. The starter motor requires much more current than the compass light.

Smoke in the Cockpit

Now let's consider a few situations that would require application of our newly acquired electrical knowledge.

Say we detect a faint odor of smoke from burning plastic. We look around and notice that the transponder is not working and its circuit breaker has popped. Should we reset the circuit breaker?

In this case, I would say no. The smoke obviously came from somewhere, probably the transponder. To shoot the juice to the transponder again would do more damage to the unit. Obviously, whatever went wrong in the squawk box caused it to draw more current than the circuit breaker could handle. The circuit breaker did its job and opened the circuit. No further action is necessary.

What if the circuit breaker just popped and there was no odor or visible smoke? In this case, it's possible the CB may have just vibrated out. One attempt to reset the CB might be in order. But don't keep resetting a circuit breaker that keeps popping out.

Let's consider a more difficult situation. You switch on the landing light and soon thereafter note a strong smell of burning plastic and wires. The landing light is working properly and the circuit breaker hasn't popped. But things are getting hot. What should you do?

It's probable in this case that you wouldn't remember that you had just turned on the landing light. I think most of us would turn off the master switch and land in the dark.

But the problem might have been caused by a loose connection on the landing light switch. As the connection became looser, less and less of the wire remained in contact with the switch—so the effective "size" of the wire had gradually been reduced to the point at which it became very hot. The circuit breaker would not have popped because the light never drew over 15 amps.

Setting a Standard

Situations like this are very difficult to diagnose. The pilot needs a standard procedure which will allow him to identify and isolate the problem.

The first step is to turn off the master switch and let things cool down. Don't worry about ATC if you are IFR. Take care of the airplane first. The instant your "blip" drops off the radar screen and you stop responding to their calls, they'll get the hint.

The next step is to turn off everything that has its own switch. Turn off all the lights, the avionics master switch and each radio. Pull all the circuit breakers that can be pulled by hand.

When this is done, allow a couple of minutes for the smoke to clear and for your nerves to settle down. Then turn on just the "battery" portion of the master switch. Wait a while and then begin to restore circuits one at a time.

As soon as you have determined that you have minimum lighting and avionics capability, switch on the alternator. Obviously, whenever the smoke starts up again you have found the problem.

Fumbling in the Dark

There is no substitute for a thorough knowledge and understanding of your particular airplane's electrical system.

It would be difficult to read the owner's manual in the dark. You might have to go by memory. You should know the answers to some important questions that may arise during a flight.

For instance, if your airplane has an avionics master switch, is there a backup switch that can be used in the event that the solenoid fails? Will that backup switch supply power to the avionics even if the master switch is off?

Do the landing gear lights actually indicate the position of the landing gear, or the position of microswitches far removed from the gear?

What exactly does the "press-to-test" button on the annunciator panel do? If a microswitch were to fail, would you get a gear-down indication or a gear-up indication?

Will the landing gear warning horn blow if you carry a lot of power on final approach? Will putting the gear handle in the "down" position silence the gear warning horn regardless of the true position of the gear?

Can the electric flaps be retracted without electrical power? Is a split-flap condition possible?

If you need to use an auxiliary power source to start your engine, should you do it with the master switch off or on?

You should know the answers to all of these questions. But as a neophyte aircraft electrician you may not. It might be a good idea to spend a few quiet evenings digging the answers out of your owner's manual.

The next time you prepare for a flight review or an instrument competency check, reread the sections pertaining to the electrical system and then ask questions of the flight instructor. You're paying the bill. You might as well learn something. If your instructor doesn't know, or if you're unsatisfied with his answers, seek out a mechanic.

As pilot-in-command, you owe it to yourself and your passengers to be knowledgeable about the general aspects of electrical systems, as well as your own airplane's peculiarities.

Your Avionics

I nstruments may be what makes flight in IMC possible, but without your avionics, it's not feasible. Keeping everything working is often frustrating, and almost always expensive.

We once owned a Mooney that had a full-bore King IFR stack with RNAV, and all the bells and whistles, including a radar altimeter and flight director coupled to a Century IV autopilot. It was great when everything was working, but seen as a whole it was so complex that at any given moment something was on the fritz...the RNAV display kept burning out, and the flight director wouldn't do a coupled approach. Even so, one of our editors did all his IFR training and got his rating in that airplane, usually with only one reliable nav radio. A test of patience, to be sure.

So, while not as absolutely critical as keeping the engine running, making sure your avionics are happy is nevertheless very important to the IFR pilot. And, when things do fail, it's important to get the right information to the radio shop to ensure that the repair is done quickly and correctly. (We never did find out why the FD wouldn't couple, by the way.)

Caring for your Avionics

Modern technology has so permeated our lives that we cannot imagine working or playing without it. Our flying is no different. It wasn't so very long ago that most pilots were perfectly satisfied with a few basic instruments.

Times have changed. Many of us now fly with enough avionics equipment and instruments to keep an airline pilot happy. Often, we don't even know how to take advantage of all the bells and whistles.

These technological wonders have contributed to the significant improvement of aviation's safety record. But we have become so used to having all of this equipment working properly that when something malfunctions, our safety margin may suffer.

Early in our aviation careers, we learn, one way or another, that the black boxes we've come to depend upon can act up in embarrassing and, sometimes, potentially hazardous ways.

If you're an aircraft owner, you know that correcting avionics problems can be extraordinarily expensive. As a pilot, you know the troublesome units can, at least, become a small handicap or, at their worst, present a difficult circumstance.

When you encounter a problem with your avionics equipment, there are several steps that you, as the pilot, should take prior to reporting the problem to your avionics shop.

In some cases, you may find the problem to be a simple switch position, while in others, you'll be helping the technician to isolate the difficulty so that repair time is minimized.

Regardless, taking the few steps that follow can save money and help make sure the problem is corrected properly. And, it could prevent you from encountering a situation such as follows:

It was well after work hours when a local avionics repairman was called out to the airport by an irate pilot claiming that all of the money he'd paid for repair of his radio was a waste.

On the dark ramp, the pilot railed at the technician until, to the pilot's embarrassment, he was shown that the squelch and volume knobs were turned full up, causing the annoying static. Meekly, the pilot got in the airplane and left.

Environmental Factors

The environment in which our avionics operate is the biggest contributor to their premature demise. Heat and vibration are the most common culprits. Others include the corrosive nature of the atmosphere, voltage spikes, poor installation, extreme cold and water damage.

The easiest problem to deal with is overheating. Heat comes from two sources: the sun and the equipment, itself. Among the ways to minimize the effects of solar heating are to shelter the aircraft when not in use in a hangar or covered tie-down, or to utilize sunshades to keep the cockpit cool. Another way is to cool the avionics before starting by either opening the cockpit or avionics bay or by turning on an auxiliary fan.

The easiest way to cool operating equipment is with adequate air flow, if necessary from an auxiliary cooling fan. A properly installed auxiliary fan will more than pay for itself in reduced equipment failures.

Vibration can be dealt with by either reducing the source or, when possible, by better isolating the equipment. Having your propeller(s) or rotor dynamically balanced can significantly reduce vibration and contribute to longer avionics and instrument life.

Voltage spikes can be prevented by using an avionics master switch to isolate the equipment during engine start and shutdown.

Switches and Knobs

Cockpits with even a minimal amount of avionics are pretty complex. As pilots, we are faced with a great array of switches, knobs, gauges, displays, etc., which makes it incredibly easy to overlook something.

Therefore, we need to recognize that in our combined roles as pilots, meteorologists, navigators, load masters, observers and flight engineers, we're pretty busy and that we need to take the time to assess our *own* performance before blaming the equipment or the technician.

So, the absolute first step when encountering an avionics problem is to re-check the switches and knobs on *all* your radio gear before declaring a problem. This is especially true for seldom-used switches you typically don't move during a flight.

Perhaps, someone bumped the panel while getting in, or, maybe, the airplane just came out of maintenance and a switch had been positioned differently for a check. Maybe your headset cord is partially pulled from the socket. If it's a rented airplane, the last pilot might be in the practice of pulling circuit breakers after flying.

It's a good idea to check every switch—using a checklist, if possible—to make sure the equipment *is* the problem before calling your avionics specialist. It is rather costly, to say nothing of embarrassing, to have an avionics specialist find a misplaced switch for you.

Also, it's a good idea to consult the equipment manual before declaring a problem. (Several years ago, I spent a couple of months with a useless loran receiver because I failed to re-initialize the unit, as required. It was quite embarrassing to have the manufacturer tell me the page I should have read.)

If it *is* an equipment problem, it's important to give your avionics technician a good assessment of what's going on. Simply taxiing in and saying, "The ADF doesn't work; fix it," might cause the technician to spend a long time narrowing things down. And, a problem that's intermittent may not show up when the airplane is sitting on the ramp.

Let's face it, most problems with our radios don't occur during a tight instrument approach. Most are discovered while cruising in VFR skies, when there's time to nail down what the problem is and under what plugged in, unplug one and see if that improves reception.

Check for side tone in your headphones (can you hear your own voice?). Listen for a "click" when you press the transmit button. If one comm is working, ask ATC whether they are receiving a carrier from the other when you try to transmit. (The carrier manifests itself in most radios as a background hum. In fact, it is actually a "lack of noise.") Voice modulates over this carrier. A carrier without voice narrows the tech's search.

Weak transmissions are often caused by improper mike technique. Boom mikes must actually touch your lip to be effective. Hand mikes should be held close to your mouth. Speak clearly and do not whisper. Improper technique can cause ATC to report difficulty in hearing you even when everything is working right.

On the ground, check that the antennas are clean. An antenna covered with grime can significantly impede radio performance.

Some other things to check: Does adjusting or turning off the squelch have an effect? Is there any background noise from the engine electrical system when you listen to the blank spots between ATIS announcements? Does changing power settings have an effect? Is noise apparent all the time or only when receiving? Is the noise a buzz or a squeal? Does the position or operation of the flaps, gear or other equipment have an effect?

Navigation Problems

Problems with nav radios and indicators commonly involve total failure, inaccurate indications or scalloping.

Check the other nav receiver, if you have one, to see whether it also is affected. If an indicator isn't responding, check if the failure is in all modes (VOR, LOC, GS) or only one. Check for normal audio, proper TO-FROM indications and warning flag operation.

Ensure that you have tuned the radio correctly. Try another VOR. Identify which needle (or needles) is off (VOR, LOC, GS or all). Will the OBS knob still center the needle? Are the errors always of the same amount, or do they vary? Record the amount of error in degrees or dots.

If the needle is scalloping (swinging back and forth like a windshield wiper), try another VOR. Compare navs if you have two. Observe if both CDIs exhibit the same problem. Check for stable indications in other modes (LOC, GS). Perform a 360-degree check and see if the needles stay centered while you make a tight turn.

ADF malfunctions usually appear as either an unsteady or sluggish needle, or one that won't point to the station. Thunderstorms might cause an unsteady indication. After the usual radio checks, verify that the audio is OK in both the ADF and antenna positions. Check the ADF with all other electrical systems shut down. If the needle is steady or responds properly, or if the audio is better, turn on each system until you find the one that causes a problem.

Transponder problems usually involve either incorrect altitude readout in Mode C or transmission of the wrong code. Check whether the light illuminates during ground interrogations and when you ident. Be aware that ATC allows a variance of 300 feet in reported altitude. So, first, double-check that the barometric setting is correct. Record the errors between what you set and what ATC receives. After checking for the usual radio problems, try operating it only in Mode A.

For incorrect codes, it is very important to identify the exact problem. With ATC's cooperation, try different codes throughout the range. Check whether the problem is always in the same "window" or digit. Is it always off the same amount, or does it seem to occur randomly? Is the altitude readout sent correctly even if the code is not? Try turning off other avionics. Interference from DME is common.

Distance-measuring equipment usually fails by providing incorrect information. Early units are notoriously inaccurate. After checking for those same radio problems, make sure the DME is tuned (or channeled) to a station and not on "hold." Take note of whether both ground speed and distance are in error. Check whether the error is consistent or not. Once again, try turning off other avionics and see if operation improves. DME is particularly susceptible to interference from the transponder.

Autopilot Dilemmas

The most complicated system for a technician to troubleshoot is the autopilot. But, according to our experts, upwards of 90 percent of all autopilot problems are pilot-induced.

Lots of them could be avoided if we would just read our manuals and supplements, and perform the preflight checks.

The cause of a problem that is not pilot-induced should be isolated. If you don't do it, the technician will have to fly the aircraft or go flying with you. A typical autopilot can have 20 or more components, any of which can cause a problem.

The autopilot manual may provide some tips on troubleshooting. Be aware that loose rigging and other related problems can make it impossible for any autopilot to do its job well. Archie Trammell suggests that you should switch off the autopilot first and hand-fly the aircraft. He notes, "Don't expect a simple autopilot to fly it any smoother than you can." Basic checks include verifying servo action by moving the heading bug and watching the yoke move. Also, check that the autotrim will take the load off the controls.

Autopilots often fail to hold altitude or heading. When this happens, write down the axis—pitch (altitude) or roll (heading)—and the selected mode or modes. If the autopilot is causing oscillations in pitch or roll, the technician will need to know the "period" (the time it takes to complete a single oscillation). Note if the oscillation damps out over time, continues unabated or gets worse. Try to quantify the amount of movement in feet or degrees.

Also make note of the aircraft's load and balance, and the approximate fuel state. (Is the fuel load unbalanced?) Be sure to record how the instruments react vis-a-vis what the aircraft is doing. Do they lead or follow, or are they in phase? Does the position of the gear or flaps affect the problem?

Finally, determine if the problem can be related to high or low speed, climb, cruise, descent or approach.

Pinpointing a Problem

Here are a few things to look for when you have a sick black box:

Determine if the problem occurs during precipitation and/or in dusty conditions. The movement of these particles across the skin of the aircraft can set up static charges. Rain can leak into seams of the fuselage, and ice can adhere to antenna surfaces, causing problems.

Temperature may be an important factor. Did the radio go on the blink after baking all day in the summer sun or becoming cold-soaked on a frosty ramp in January? Did the problem occur immediately after you turned the radio on, or after it warmed up? What was the cabin temperature? The outside air temperature (being fed through the cooling duct)?

Flight conditions also should be noted. Were you in turbulence when the problem occurred? Were you climbing, descending or in a tight turn? Did you have an unusually hard landing or operate from a rough strip? Were you flying in moist or salt-laden air (near the ocean or large lake area)?

Your technician also may want to know about any unusual electrical system indications. Did the high-voltage light illuminate? What was the ammeter or voltage meter reading? Were you near or in thunderstorms (lightning) or experience St. Elmo's fire? Did any other equipment act up before, during or after the problem occurred? Did you accidentally turn off or on any other switches? Was your strobe light on?

Questions, Questions

In addition, your technician will want to know what you tried and observed while operating the equipment. Here are some of the questions you should be prepared to answer:

1. If there's a duplicate of the equipment (i.e., another transponder or nav-comm of the same make and model), was it working properly?

2. Did you experiment with any related equipment to see if indications normalized? For example, did the nav radio operate properly after being uncoupled from the autopilot? Did the transponder work when the altitude mode was turned off? (The combinations are endless. Try all you can think of, even some you think are too remote to be possible.)

3. If the component is tied to a speaker/headset combination, did you try using only one or the other? Did you try your spare microphone?

4. Did you check other frequencies and/or switch positions to see if the problem is restricted to certain areas?

5. Did you check the knobs and switches for looseness (by moving them back and forth)? Was there any grinding or scraping when you moved them through their full travel?

6. Have you been using the unit, and had it worked properly in the past? A problem that suddenly happens may be quite different than one that occurs when a seldom-used item malfunctions after being fired up for the first time in a long time.

7. If the problem was static, did you try switching magnetos on the ground to see what happened? This could disclose poor shielding of a mag or ignition lead. Also, seeing the problem clear after turning the alternator off and on may indicate bad diodes in the alternator.

Peekaboo Problems

By far, the most difficult problem is the one that shows itself only once in awhile. The previous notes will greatly help the technician diagnose an intermittent problem. However, the best way to solve the problem is to catch it in the act.

So, if you're on the ramp getting ready to go and the problem rears its ugly head, shut down and run for the radio shop. Don't bang on the panel and get things going again. Given the opportunity, a technician can gain a lot from seeing your equipment when it's out to lunch.

At many airports, of course, the nearest avionics shop isn't just across the field. It may be on the other side of the state. In such cases, there are a few things you can try, yourself, to narrow down where the problem lies. This may include switching the trays of identical radios.

However, don't try "fixing it yourself" *without first consulting an avionics technician* by phone or otherwise.

The release mechanisms on radios vary a lot, and you can do

hundreds of dollars worth of damage by not removing and reinstalling the equipment properly. So, consult your technician, first, so he or she can instruct you in the proper procedure.

Also, if you perform any maintenance on your radios, be sure you get the advice of someone who is knowledgeable about follow-up procedures. Perhaps, your avionics shop can recommend someone they've dealt with in your area to provide assistance. After all, you don't want your avionics repair to be less than perfect ... or go up in smoke.

Preventive Maintenance

Although we all know that avionics problems will eventually occur, there are a few things that can be done to make your visits to the avionics shop less frequent.

Here are a few tips on keeping your black boxes in good working order:

1. Turn on *all* of your equipment, even if you're not using it. When you turn on your avionics, they are warmed by the energy going through them and will be rid of any accumulated moisture that eventually could cause corrosion or dirt problems.

Even by operating equipment in the "standby" mode, you will get the circuits energized to get rid of the moisture. For a nearly negligible energy penalty, you'll be preventing serious problems in the future.

2. Have your equipment removed periodically for cleaning and testing. Dust and corrosion are constantly at work within cases and around connections. By occasionally having the items cleaned and tested by qualified people, you'll be assuring top performance.

If you leave your airplane outdoors or operate it where dirt and dust are commonplace, you should have your equipment serviced more frequently.

3. Don't use excessive force when pressing buttons and switching frequencies. (Once, feeling lighthearted, I jabbed my transponder ident button a little too lightheartedly and found myself with a $60 repair bill.)

4. Periodically switch through all the frequencies on the equipment. This will allow the contactors to rub against one another, decreasing the incidence of corrosion on contact surfaces. This will also help clear accumulated dirt from the contacts between your equipment checkups.

5. If you are planning to fly at night, check the back-lighting of the radios for proper operation. Light bulbs can burn out, and the wrong time to discover this is when you're trying to dial in a VOR by moonlight. (While checking the lighting, also check to see if your flashlight is still aboard and has good batteries.)

6. Don't turn on your avionics until *after* your engine is running. Conversely, turn them off *prior* to shutting down. This will help eliminate voltage spikes from the charging system during these transient periods.

In many cases, your avionics stack is the most expensive part of your aircraft. With preventive maintenance and good operating technique, your avionics equipment will give you many years of satisfactory service.

When trouble does occur, your preliminary efforts may mean the difference between a quick, economical fix or frustrating returns to the shop with impressive repair bills.

When something fails in flight, you are not likely to remember all these items. So, you might want to make some notes to carry aboard the aircraft. It is important while troubleshooting to *write down* the results of each test. This will save you a great deal of time, trouble and money. More importantly, you will get back in the air with all your equipment fixed and working properly. And that's a plus for safety.

Vacuum Systems

If we had to label the systems in an IFR-capable aircraft in importance, after the powerplant and its supporting fuel system we'd have to say the gyros and their supporting vacuum (or pressure) system.

While we're trained to handle partial-panel situations, make no mistake: gyro failure is a very serious thing in hard IMC.

We've devoted much of this book to keeping the engine healthy and running, but the fact is that it's a marvel of ruggedness compared to the vacuum systems, and, worse, when the vacuum system goes it usually does so without warning.

Avoiding Gyro Failure

One of the great pleasures a pilot experiences during instrument training is the relief that comes *after* a session of partial-panel work. When the heading and attitude indicators are finally uncovered, instrument flying seems so easy compared with the struggle of maintaining control using only needle, ball and airspeed.

It's human nature to avoid unpleasant experiences, and few pilots make the effort to stay sharp on partial-panel procedures after earning their instrument ratings. Few, if any, VFR pilots seek out partial-panel training, even though the skills would come in handy should the gyro instruments spool down while flying at night or on a hazy day.

Unfortunately, we're putting a lot of faith in one of the most fragile systems aboard our aircraft. The record shows that the pneumatic—vacuum or pressure—system can give up the ghost at any time, and there's no way of anticipating just when. About 50 outright failures are reported each year (see the accompanying article), and it is likely that many more go unreported.

Paradoxically, accidents following pneumatic system failures are relatively rare—only about two a year. But they are lethal. NTSB's records for the years 1983 through 1988 include 12 such accidents. Only one did not involve fatalities.

(That no one was killed in that accident is a miracle. It involved an 850-hour pilot whose Cessna 182 lost both its vacuum pump *and* electrical system during an IFR flight, knocking out the turn coordinator as well as the attitude and heading indicators. He lost control several times but managed at one point to recover from a spin. The 182 eventually descended below the clouds, and the pilot made a successful emergency landing.)

The record shows, too, that in addition to a dangerous dependence on our pneumatic systems, our faith in ancillary and redundant systems may be misguided. Though the chances of a simultaneous failure of the pneumatic and electrical systems in any aircraft must be astronomical, the Skylane pilot was among several aviators who experienced the double whammy—the others with tragic results. (Elsewhere in this issue, Tom Lusch describes how to use the ADF to survive with *less* than a partial panel.)

Oil to Dust

Knowing the limitations of a pneumatic system begins with a thorough understanding of how the system works. Unfortunately, there have been no real advances in pneumatic system design in over 30 years. Some critics even suggest that today's carbon-core dry air pumps represent a few steps backward. Originally, gyro instruments were driven by air collected and accelerated by externally mounted ventures. The next step was "wet" pumps with metal innards cooled and lubricated by engine oil. They were reliable but had to have air/oil separators to clean the air flow. These devices were problematic, often creating an unsightly mess on the belly of the aircraft.

The dry air pumps aboard most aircraft built since 1970 are air-cooled and lubricated by carbon dust. If you were to crack open an aluminum housing on one of these pumps, you'd find a mechanism that looks and functions much like a paddle wheel on a Mississippi riverboat. The hub, or rotor is spun by a plastic shaft sunk into the engine's accessory pad. One of the pump manufacturers, Airborne, has stuck with carbon rotors. The other, Sigma-Tek, has switched to an aluminum rotor to lessen damage during shipment.

Slots in the rotors house thin carbon vanes. The slots in Airborne pumps are slanted to the right or left, to accommodate either clockwise or counterclockwise rotation. (When ordering an Airborne pump, you have to specify the model number that will work on your accessory pad.) The slots in Sigma-Tek's "bidirectional" pumps are oriented perpendicular to the bore; therefore, the rotor can be spun in either direction.

As the rotor spins, centrifugal force pushes the vanes outward until their heads brush up against the inner bore of the housing. As the vanes scrape past the intake port, air is drawn into the chambers between the vanes, compressed and then expelled through the discharge port.

As the vanes wear, some of the carbon dust remains within the housing; the rest is expelled through the discharge port and, hopefully, trapped by an in-line filter.

Plumbing

Most general aviation aircraft have vacuum systems, which means the gyros are plumbed to the intake side of the pump and, thus, are spun by air flowing into the pump. Some aircraft have pressure systems, blowing air into the gyros and, if so equipped, into the deice boots and cabin door seals. Still others (the Cessna 414, for example) use vacuum to spin the gyros, pressure to inflate boots and door seals.

Generally, vacuum pumps have higher internal compression ratios and, therefore, work harder—and hotter—than pressure pumps. Pressure pumps, on the other hand, are harder on the gyros, because they force relatively hot air into the instruments.

Typically, a pneumatic system failure is precipitated when one or more of the carbon vanes splinter and jam the rotor, which then cracks or shatters. The plastic shaft running from the pump into the accessory pad then breaks under the load, isolating the jammed pump from the engine.

Too often, analysis of a pneumatic system failure ends right there—with a broken pump. In many cases, the culprit isn't the pump. There's something else amiss in the system: a clogged filter, a leaking hose or fitting, a gummed-up valve. Heat is the biggest killer of dry air pumps, and problems elsewhere in the system can cause a pump to work harder—and hotter—than it should and break prematurely.

Troubleshooting

Good maintenance by a sharp mechanic can go a long way to extend the life of a dry air pump. A common mistake made by many mechanics, though, is to solve a pilot's complaint of a lower-than-normal reading on the aircraft's vacuum gauge by simply cranking up the pump's regulator.

The catch is that the vacuum gauge is plumbed into the system near the gyros and doesn't provide a reliable indication of how hard the pump is working. There may be a leak, a collapsed hose or a clogged filter between the gyros and the pump. A proper response to a low vacuum reading is to check pressure *at the pump* to see if it's being subjected to an excessive load. A pressure check is also a good idea during annual or 100-hour inspections to provide an indication of the pneumatic system's health.

About two-thirds of the service difficulty reports filed on pneumatic systems during the past eight years involved pump failures; the remainder cited problems with jammed check and flow valves, damaged hoses, contaminated filters and inoperative vacuum/pressure gauges.

According to Airborne, a big problem in aircraft with deice systems is the lack of a filter between the dry air pump and the valve that controls the flow of air into the boots. The valves are lubricated with oil, which turns into a sludge when contaminated with carbon particles from the pump. Sticking valves can make a dry air pump work very hard, so periodic cleaning is a good idea, as is frequent replacement of filters and inspection of the condition of all hoses and fittings.

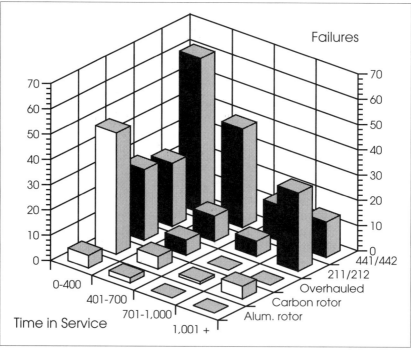

Service history of vacuum pumps. White bars are Sigma-Tek, black are Airborne.

How Long Will Your Pump Last?

Dry air pumps begin to wear out the moment they are first used, but determining when they should be replaced is a matter of guesswork. Manufacturers are loath to establish mean time between failures (MTBFs) because of the myriad variables of installation, maintenance and operation that can play a role in pump failure. The manufacturers, Airborne and Sigma-Tek, unofficially point to the service-hour specifications in their pump warranties as rough guidelines for replacement.

The service-hour specs otherwise hold very little meaning to most owners of general aviation aircraft. For instance, Airborne warrants its light-duty 211/212-series pumps for 1,000 hours or one year after installation. A typical lightplane owner would be hard-pressed to meet the service-hour spec before the calendar year runs out; but Airborne presents the 1,000-hour figure as a good time for replacement of light-duty pumps in aircraft flown IFR.

Similarly, the warranties on Airborne's medium-duty 241/242-series pumps (designed to run *two* sets of gyros) and its heavy-duty 441/441-series pumps (deice boots and door seals, as well as gyros) are both one year or 400 hours. Here, Airborne hedges its bet by saying an owner should get 700 hours out of these pumps unless there's a problem somewhere in the pneumatic system.

The other manufacturer, Sigma-Tek, now produces only the aluminum-rotor light-duty IU128005 pump, which has a three-year/700-hour warranty. Replacement is recommended at 700 hours. Sigma-Tek no longer makes carbon-rotor pumps, which had a one-year/1,000-hour warranty.

But it appears that using the service-hour spec from the warranty as a replacement guide may not be all that realistic. A review of nearly 500 service difficulty reports (SDRs) submitted from 1984 through May 1990 indicates that a disturbing number of dry air pumps fail some time between first engine start after installation to 400 hours in service.

Several reports gave a clear thumbs-down to the use of overhauled Airborne dry air pumps. For example, a Chieftain owner reported that four overhauled pumps failed within 20 hours of service. Another report said three overhauled pumps were tried in an Aerostar 601P but none was able to produce enough pressure to inflate the door seal; a switch back to factory-new pumps solved the problem.

Judging from service difficulty reports, setting up a realistic replacement schedule for dry air pumps isn't a task that can be achieved with any degree of confidence. Our recommendation is to use the manufacturer's recommendation as a guideline but to fully expect that the pump will fail at just about any time. Good maintenance will do much to put off the inevitable, but the poor service history reflected by recent SDRs indicates that installation of a backup system in any aircraft flown on instruments or at night is indispensable.

Tilted Horizon

Studies of instrument scanning patterns have shown that pilots spend nearly three-fourths of their time gazing at the attitude indicator. Unless you have one of Sigma-Tek's new indicators, which have gyro warning flags, or take in the vacuum/pressure gauge regularly in your scan (improbable due to the typical banishment of these gauges to the far corners of the panel), a pneumatic system failure will take some time to detect.

It could take up to 10 minutes for the gyros in the attitude and heading indicators to spool down, and the first indication that something's amiss is conflicting information being provided by the instruments—for instance, a discrepancy between the attitude indicator and the electrically driven turn coordinator.

Once a failure has been verified, it's a good idea to cover the instruments with suction-cup pads, business cards, sticky note paper—whatever's handy—to eliminate them from your field of view, so you won't by reflex react to what they're showing. Before your next flight, re-read the supplemental information on your autopilot; if it uses the air-driven gyros, rather than the electric gyro in the turn coordinator, to sense roll and pitch, you'll have to shut it off.

Declare an Emergency?

Now, it's time to get some help. The accident record indicates that the more a pilot dawdles on partial panel, the more the odds are stacked against a safe conclusion of the flight. In one case, a 1,500-hour commercial pilot reported that he lost the gyro instruments in his Comanche 260 but declined the controller's hint that he might want to declare an emergency and land. He pressed on even after the controller advised that the aircraft was off course and losing altitude. The course and altitude deviations continued, and the pilot radioed, "I'm in trouble," shortly before the wings and tail separated from the Comanche.

Another pilot pressed on and was doing just fine on partial panel...until his Bonanza began picking up ice.

Pneumatic system failure in IMC is just cause, in our opinion, to consider declaring an emergency and getting as much help from ATC as you can. If you're receiving radar services, at the very least ask ATC for "no-gyro" handling to get you to the nearest area with VMC or to an airport where a surveillance approach can be conducted.

No-gyro service eliminates much of the workload involved in using the turn coordinator and magnetic compass to maintain course. Instead of issuing headings, the controller, watching the aircraft on radar, will simply tell a pilot when to begin a standard-rate turn (and in which direction to turn) and when to stop the turn. During a surveillance (ASR) approach, it will be up to the pilot to comply with altitude instructions and to make all turns on the final approach course at half-standard rate. Don't be concerned if you don't have the published procedures for the ASR approach; in a pinch, the controller will relay the vital information.

Conclusions

The system that provides air flow to the attitude and heading indicators, deice boots and door seals is one of the most fragile in any aircraft. The accident and service records suggest several steps that pilots and aircraft owners can take to manage the risks of pneumatic system failure.

• Become familiar with the system in your aircraft and make a timetable for maintenance and replacement.

• Be especially careful after a new dry air pump is installed. If a system problem has gone undetected and unsolved, chances are the new pump will fail posthaste. It's a good idea to fly only VFR for the first five or 10 hours.

• Check the system carefully during preflight. Listen for unusual noises as the gyros erect or a howling sound that might be the death knell of an ailing pump. If gauge pressure is lower than normal, have your mechanic check pressure at the pump to see what's going on.

• Do gentle S-turns while taxiing to check the instruments for proper movement.

• Don't take off at night or into IMC if something's not functioning properly. This may seem rather basic, but three of the 11 fatal accidents involved pilots who launched with passengers into adverse conditions *knowing* their pneumatic systems weren't working.

• Even if you're flying a twin or a single with two pumps, be prepared for *complete* system failure at any time. That means periodic refreshment of partial-panel skills.

• No matter how sharp you are in partial panel work, don't press on if you lose the gyros in IMC. Get as much help as possible from ATC and head for VMC or an airport where you can shoot a no-gyro ASR approach.

• Consider equipping your aircraft with backup equipment. There's plenty on the market, including failure-warning devices, backup pneumatic systems and electrically driven "peanut" attitude indicators.

Pitot/Static Systems

O ne of the things we learn in instrument training is how to interpret conflicting indications from the basic instruments. Depending on exactly what's wrong, those indications can be downright baffling.

The key to reacting appropriately in the event of failure is understanding what is happening and why. Unless you have a clear picture of just how the VSI, altimeter and airspeed indicator are hooked up, and how they interact with one another when something goes wrong, you could find yourself in big trouble.

Pressure Plumbing

Picture yourself as pilot in command of an airplane that has just entered the clouds after departing IFR from an unfamiliar airport. You note that the airspeed is about 20 knots above normal climb speed, so you increase pitch. But, soon, the airspeed is way too high again, so you add some more pitch. You glance at the attitude indicator and see that it is indicating 10 degrees too high, but you can't remember if you aligned the little airplane symbol with the horizon line prior to takeoff. The airspeed is once again quite high, so you increase pitch even more. Now, the attitude indicator shows that the nose of the airplane is 20 degrees above the horizon, but the altimeter isn't moving up at all and the vertical speed indicator is showing that you're in level flight.

What's wrong? Which instruments are telling the truth, and which are lying?

If you haven't been able to analyze this problem, you would probably die in the stall/spin accident that is imminent. A thorough review of the pitot-static system is in order.

Actually, there is no *pitot-static system*. The term is a misnomer that has caused much confusion. There is a pitot tube, which is connected by a pipe to the airspeed indicator. Then, there is a static port, which is connected to a pipe that branches out to the airspeed indicator, altimeter and vertical speed indicator. To refer to this accumulation of plumbing as the pitot-static system because it is all attached to the airspeed indicator makes no more sense than referring to the "fuel-electrical system" because the hardware from both is attached to the engine. The pitot tube and the static port are two different things and perform separate functions. At no point are they connected, not even in installations where the static port is built into the pitot tube.

Airspeed Indicator

The pitot tube protrudes into the relative wind created by the airplane's progress through the air. It transmits ram air pressure to the airspeed indicator, where the pressure is mechanically translated into a display of airspeed.

If there is a leak in the tubing between the airspeed indicator and the pitot tube, less pressure will be transmitted to the instrument and the airspeed indication will be erroneously low. If that tubing should become disconnected, *no* pressure will be transmitted and the indicated airspeed will be zero. The airspeed indicator also will read zero, in certain cases, if the pitot tube become blocked.

Inside the airspeed indicator, there is a tiny brass bellows called an aneroid. The aneroid is connected to the needle on the face of the airspeed indicator by a series of levers and gears. Ram air from the pitot tube causes the aneroid to expand and move the little levers and gears which, in turn, move the needles on the display.

If the pitot tube is completely blocked, the air pressure in the instrument is trapped. If the airplane continues to climb, as it did in our example, the aneroid in the airspeed indicator is moved into lower air

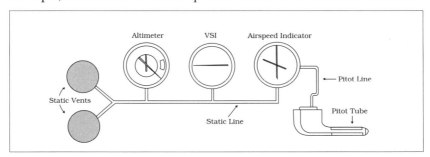

While the three instruments are all interconnected, the line from the pitot tube goes only to the airspeed indicator.

pressure at higher altitude. The trapped air in the instrument expands, and the airspeed indicator reads higher than it did before. If we raise the nose to slow the airspeed, the airplane climbs higher and the bogus airspeed indicates higher, even though the airplane may be desperately near stalling.

You may also have noticed in the previous example that the altimeter and vertical speed indicator (VSI) weren't indicating a climb. That's because, by the time the pilot scanned these instruments, the airplane had already been slowed to the point that it couldn't climb. It was on the back side of the power curve.

Signs of Blockage

So, what is the indication of a blocked pitot tube or line?

It depends. If the blockage is complete and airtight, the airspeed indication will remain the same as it was when the blockage occurred. If the airplane then climbs or descends, the airspeed indicator will act like an altimeter. It will indicate a higher airspeed as you climb and a lower airspeed as you descend. If there is a small leak in the system, or if the pitot tube drain hole isn't plugged by the blockage, the airspeed will just gently go down to zero.

(If the vagaries of this instrument leave you feeling a little insecure, that's good. The airspeed indicator deserves a watchful eye.)

But, remember, there is one other item in the aircraft that will indicate airspeed: trim. In conventional production airplanes, the trim establishes an aerodynamic relationship between the wing and the empennage. When trimmed for a specific airspeed, the airplane will try to maintain that airspeed. If the pilot raises the nose of the aircraft and slows down, as soon as he or she releases control pressure, the nose of the airplane will drop in an attempt to regain aerodynamic balance.

Similarly, if the nose is forced down and airspeed increases, the nose of the airplane will lift when the controls are released, because the airplane is trimmed for a slower airspeed.

Therefore, if power is left constant, whenever you change the trim of an aircraft, you change the airspeed. If you change the trim, and the airspeed doesn't change, the airspeed indicator is in error. Likewise, if you change pitch by holding pressure on the controls, the airspeed should change accordingly. If you add back pressure, the airspeed indicator should show a slower airspeed in a matter of seconds. If it gives any other indication, the instrument is suspect.

Plugged Ports

Signs of blockages in the static system are more subtle but often more dangerous.

Line service people sometimes play a hand in plugging static ports, albeit inadvertently. While attending to your pride and joy, they might rub a glob of Johnson's finest carnauba into the opening or inject a couple of tablespoons of wash water.

Wax or some other obstruction in the static port is easy to diagnose. If, after takeoff, you notice that objects on the ground are getting smaller but the altimeter indicates that you are still sitting on the runway, something is obviously amiss. A pull on the alternate static source selector will solve the problem, if you remember where it is and how to use it.

A little bit of water in the tubing between the static port and the instruments can be far more insidious than a simple blockage. If the water is in liquid form—that is, if the tubing where the water is concentrated is above freezing temperature—the water will move back and forth with changes in barometric pressure. As the pressure decreases (during climb, for instance), the water flows along the tube toward the static port. The pressure on both sides of the moving obstruction remains the same. When the airplane descends (and barometric pressure increases), the water moves back toward the low point, and no one is the wiser. Even a static system test will not reveal the presence of this water.

A far more insidious static line blockage occurs when water in the tube freezes in level flight. When the static source is blocked in level flight, the airplane can begin a gradual descent without the pilot even knowing it. The barometric altimeter, the encoding altimeter and the altitude pick-off for the autopilot are all hooked up to the same pipe. Should that pipe become blocked, the autopilot will think the airplane is flying level, the controller will think the airplane is maintaining its assigned altitude, and you will think everything is hunky-dory, even though the airplane is gradually descending. (If the airplane is descending at 200 feet per minute, it will be below the highest obstacle along the airway in 10 minutes—half that time if the airway isn't over mountainous terrain.)

A good rule of thumb pertaining to the alternate air source is: When in doubt, pull it out. In other words, any time you suspect a blockage, open the alternate air source and see what happens. It doesn't cost a thing, and it could solve your problem.

A pilot needs to know how each instrument will behave when either the pitot tube or static source is blocked. Once this information is understood, diagnosis of in-flight instrument problems becomes much easier.

• Section Five •

Airframe Systems

Pressurization
and Oxygen

F or an IFR pilot, high altitude is a wonderful thing. If your airplane has enough performance, you can often fly above the weather while your normally aspirated colleagues are slogging along through the murk.

Turbocharging lets the airplane get up high, but to take advantage of it the pilot needs a boost, too, in the form of either oxygen or pressurization.

Of the two, pressurization is far more comfortable for both pilot and passengers. No cannulas or nosebags to deal with.

The drawback, of course, is complexity. Sealing a cabin and pumping it up above ambient pressure, then controlling that environment, is no trivial task. First we'll look at pressurization systems. Later in the chapter we'll look at oxygen and hypoxia.

The Pressure's On

One of the possibilities that pilots operating in the flight levels need to consider is the unexpected loss of cabin pressure. Such an occurrence, while not common, is not altogether unheard of, either.

A search of NASA's Aviation Safety Reporting System for the period 1986 through 1992 turned up 553 reports of cabin depressurization incidents. No doubt, there were many others not reported.

There are various reasons why the pressurization system in an aircraft can fail. In this chapter, we'll review how pressurization systems work and take a look at emergency descents following a decompression.

Pressurization systems come in a variety of designs, but they all work in the same basic fashion: A constant volume of pressurized air is pumped into the aircraft cabin (or, more accurately, into the "pressure vessel"—the pressurized section of the fuselage) and allowed to vent overboard through an outflow valve.

The outflow valve can be modulated to allow more or less air to escape, thus varying the degree of cabin pressurization.

The source of pressurized air depends on the particular design. Aircraft with reciprocating engines are supplied pressurized air to the cabin by a supercharger of some kind—most likely, a turbosupercharger, although some older airplanes have mechanical superchargers for the job.

After leaving the compressor section or supercharger, the air must be cooled somehow. Most light airplanes use heat exchangers (intercoolers), which function very much like radiators.

Turbine-powered aircraft generally utilize high-pressure "bleed air" taken from one of the compressor stages of each engine. (In addition to cabin pressurization, bleed air also may be used for other purposes, such as to heat the cabin, defog the windshield and/or deice the leading edges of the wings.)

Bleed air in most jet transports is taken through a series of air-conditioning steps in a complex of components known collectively as "pacs" before being routed into the cabin.

The result of either design is the same: A fairly constant amount of air is supplied to the cabin.

Depending upon the system design, the amount of air allowed to flow overboard is controlled either manually or completely automatically, according to a predetermined schedule.

Some aircraft, such as the MD-80, have a normal system which operates automatically and a manual backup system which is controlled totally by the pilot.

But, in either case, what is being controlled is the outflow valve. Its movement will range from fully closed to fully open, depending on need.

Besides venting through an outflow valve, most pressurized aircraft cabins leak air through a variety of other sources, such as door seals or ducting.

Thus, no pressure vessel is really airtight. However, in normal circumstances, there is enough excess air being pumped into the cabin to mask the effects of these small leaks.

"Max Diff"

A system's differential pressure limit—the maximum allowable pressure difference between the air inside and outside of the cabin (informally called "max diff")—determines how high an aircraft can go while maintaining the desired cabin altitude.

Most jet aircraft have systems with normal differential pressure limits somewhere around 8.7 psi, which allows an approximate 8,000-foot cabin altitude at Flight Level 410.

Pressurization systems on singles and light twins typically operate at much lower differential pressure limits.

The Cessna P210, for example, has a differential pressure limit of 3.35 psi, allowing for a 12,100-foot cabin altitude at its maximum certified altitude of 23,000 feet.

The Malibu operates at a somewhat higher differential pressure limit, allowing it to maintain an 8,000-foot cabin altitude at the maximum ceiling of 25,000 feet.

Pressurization systems are not designed to maintain a sea-level cabin altitude at all times. While a sea-level cabin altitude might be possible to maintain at 10,000 feet MSL in a certain aircraft, a more typical cabin altitude will be somewhere around 8,000 feet at FL 350.

Although it would be possible to design a system that could maintain sea-level cabin pressure at very high altitudes, this is not necessarily desirable. The resulting differential pressure would be significantly higher, making the effects of an explosive decompression that much more dramatic and requiring a stronger, heavier and more expensive fuselage design.

One reason aircraft such as the P210 and Malibu have not been designed to fly above 25,000 feet is that above that level, the FARs require a supplemental oxygen system and beefier windows in case of decompression.

Failure Modes

Pressurization system malfunctions commonly involve some kind of failure of the "controller"—the part of the system that signals the flow-control valve to change position.

Other mechanical problems, such as sticking outflow valves or leaks and ruptures in the lines supplying pressurized air to the cabin, can upset the system, as well.

In the not-too-distant past, when smoking was allowed on most domestic airline flights, a common sight was a long brown streak of tar and nicotine on the fuselages, emanating from the outflow valves.

The gummy deposits clogged the outflow valves and associated linkage, and required constant attention from the maintenance folks. (The same deposits also fouled up temperature sensors in the cabin, making it difficult for flight crews to judge whether the passengers were comfortable. Luckily, the backup manual temperature-sensing system—the flight attendants—are never shy about speaking their mind on this subject.)

Like any other aircraft system, pressurization systems work best when they receive their fair share of preventive maintenance.

Transport-category aircraft are designed with redundant pressurization systems and supplemental oxygen systems. Over the last decade, I have experienced about two dozen minor pressurization system faults in transports, all of which were basically non-events because of the backup systems. (In fact, the only times we've had passenger oxygen masks drop, the culprit has been my firm landing and not a pressurization problem.)

That same kind of redundancy is not true of all aircraft. The single pressurization system on some light aircraft can be totally disabled with the failure of the turbocharger or the loss of engine power.

This is something that the pilot-in-command needs to plan for when operating at high altitude. An oxygen system might not be required equipment for aircraft restricted to operations at 25,000 feet or below, but it makes sense to have one as a backup.

Considering that it is not always possible to complete an emergency descent right away (as when over mountainous terrain or in turbulent weather or heavy icing conditions), having the capability to maintain altitude with a failed pressurization system could be a lifesaver.

Sometimes, defects in the aircraft structure, itself, cause related pressurization problems. Two of the best known examples in recent years involved structural failures in airliners, with resultant explosive decompressions.

The "flip-top" Aloha Airlines B-737 and the United Airlines B-747 with a blown-out cargo door focused world attention on aging-aircraft problems. Each involved a catastrophic failure that severely damaged the aircraft and caused, among other things, complete loss of cabin pressure.

Both aircraft were landed successfully, although there were fatalities in each of the accidents.

Losing Pressure

Decompression is defined as the inability of the aircraft's pressurization system to maintain its designed pressure differential. There are degrees of decompression, depending upon how quickly it occurs.

An *explosive decompression* involves a change of cabin pressure faster than your lungs can decompress, resulting in possible lung damage.

Such an event might occur in just a fraction of a second and would result in dirt and debris, and even large objects, flying about the cabin. Fog might form due to the sudden change in relative humidity and the drop in temperature.

A somewhat less extreme variation is the *rapid decompression*, which still occurs quite quickly but at a rate allowing decompression of your lungs before decompression of the cabin.

Gradual loss of cabin pressure during a slow decompression can occur without any obvious signs until the problem is well advanced.

The biggest danger resulting from any type of decompression is hypoxia, and the only sure protection from hypoxia is adequate oxygen. Therefore, you must perform an immediate emergency descent and/or don an oxygen mask to avoid hypoxic symptoms.

In either case, the operative word is *immediate*. Your own time of useful consciousness (TUC) is affected by many variables, including altitude, health condition, age and whether you are a smoker or non-smoker.

At FL 250, TUC can vary from several minutes to just seconds, depending upon an individual's physiology. Unless a typical day for you includes running triathlete events through the Andes, figure you are on the low end of the scale.

Speaking of oxygen, if you haven't preflighted your oxygen system, it could turn out to be a useless collection of metal and plastic just when you need it most.

Proper preflight means checking that the supply is adequate for the planned flight. Masks should be connected to the supply before takeoff, and they should be within easy reach of occupants.

Depending on system design, you should configure the regulator or control valves so that oxygen flow is available immediately upon demand. If the oxygen supply valve is normally left in the closed position, be sure you completely understand where the valve is and how to turn it on if needed.

If the mask contains a built-in microphone, preflight it, as well. You will probably have to manipulate an additional switch on the audio panel to select the oxygen mask microphone. The time to learn how to communicate while wearing the mask is before the flight, not in the middle of an emergency descent.

If you happen to wear glasses, be sure the mask you fly with is one that can accommodate them. Despite advertising claims, not all masks can be worn comfortably while wearing glasses. Some will push glasses to a higher-than-normal position on your face, causing focus problems (especially with bifocal-type lenses).

Likewise, if you have a heavy beard, check that the mask can seal properly around it. If not, try another design.

Emergency Descent

With your mask donned and working properly (if available), you will have plenty to keep you busy after a decompression. As with other abnormal situations, prioritize what needs to be done: Fly the airplane, navigate and communicate.

Although a decompression can be a critical emergency, don't be in such a rush to get down that you misinterpret the situation.

I know of one air carrier crew that declared an emergency, thinking they had a decompression. In reality, they misread the cabin rate-of-climb indicator, which was showing a rapid cabin *descent*—an increase in pressure, not a loss of cabin pressure.

They accomplished an unnecessary emergency descent by the book, with enough resulting egg on the face to cater a fair-sized fly-in breakfast. (In their defense, I should mention that this particular kind of rate-of-climb gauge is easy to misread. A pegged-out climb or descent looks almost the same.)

So, think of this as a two-step process: assessing the problem and, if necessary, performing an emergency descent.

After verifying that cabin pressure is, indeed, decreasing (that the cabin is "climbing"), you should begin the descent immediately, if possible.

A turn off-airway will serve two purposes: First, it will probably take you away from other traffic which may be below you on the same route. Secondly, the turn will supply a positive G force that will help reduce the negative G force induced when nosing the aircraft over. (Negative Gs are more uncomfortable than positive Gs for most of us. In combination with being lightheaded from insufficient oxygen, negative Gs can increase your sense of disorientation.)

Control, Communicate

The cause of the decompression may not be immediately obvious to you. If you suspect that it was caused by a structural failure of some kind, you will want to be operating at your aircraft's turbulence-penetration speed.

If structural integrity is not suspect and the air is smooth, a speed closer to redline (or barber pole in a jet) may be more appropriate, since this will result in a more rapid altitude loss.

Use all available means of expediting the descent, such as extending spoilers, landing gear and flaps as recommended by the aircraft manufacturer. Have a specific level-off altitude in mind and be extremely aware of what kind of terrain is below and around you.

At night or in the clouds, it is easy to forget that the ground may be closer than you think. The unusually high descent rates combined with the distraction of the situation could cause you to descend into terrain.

Once you have aircraft control well in hand and are sure of your location and altitude relative to any cumulus granitus clouds, let the world know what you are doing.

Talk to Center and squawk 7700. Your transponder may, in fact, be the best means of communication you have, especially if a blown window or other structural failure produces noise levels too loud for voice communication, or if your oxygen mask does not have a built-in microphone.

As time permits, tell your passengers what is going on. They will be scared, confused and eager to hear from you.

Sometimes, chronic pressurization system problems are an early warning of a hidden problem in another part of the aircraft.

Take, for example, the following case, which involved an experienced, commercial pilot operating a twin-turboprop Swearingen SA-26AT Merlin:

The 45-year-old pilot was the lone occupant for the repositioning flight from Del Rio to McGregor, Texas. The flight began uneventfully enough in good VFR conditions.

But, as the Merlin climbed through 14,800 feet on its way to an assigned cruise altitude of FL 190, something happened. The pilot told Center he was experiencing a rapid decompression.

His next communication, two minutes later, was his last. He reported that the tail had come off the aircraft.

The airplane impacted in an inverted flat spin. The tail and a section of the empennage were found less than a mile from the main wreckage.

According to the NTSB report, a skin seam had split open along a 54-inch span, in an area where two pieces of L-shaped channels had been riveted together to form a stringer. Normally, the stringer would be made using a single piece of T-shaped channel.

The nonstandard stringer had been fabricated during repairs made following a gear-up landing seven years earlier. Subsequent analysis revealed that the rivets holding the "L" channels together had failed due to stresses induced each time the aircraft was pressurized. The repetitive pressurization cycles over the seven-year period finally caused the "repair" to give.

During the same period, the aircraft had been plagued by a series of chronic pressurization system problems. Unfortunately, the root cause of these problems—the nonstandard repair—was not discovered in time to avert the disaster.

Knowing how your pressurization system works and how to recognize and deal with malfunctions is critical to safe flight at high altitudes.

What about those of use who don't have the luxury of pressurization? In that case, of course, we have to rely on either built-in or portable oxygen systems.

Before we discuss the system itself, however, here are a few words on hypoxia. The important thing to keep in mind when reading this part of the chapter is that the FAR requirements for oxygen are about as realistic as those for instrument currency: the prudent pilot will do much more than the regulations demand to remain safe.

Oxygen Systems and Hypoxia

Despite the activity we engage in—whether it's exercising, relaxing or even thinking—we remain largely unaware of the transfer of oxygen from the air to our lungs and then into our bloodstream.

Oxygen is, of course, vital to our very existence. It nourishes every cell in our body.

But, respiration is not something one thinks about, since it is automatic and the necessary supply of oxygen is always available—at least, on the ground. Leave the surface of the Earth, however, and the story changes. Oxygen, that cornerstone of life, becomes increasingly scarce the higher we go.

Even at relatively low altitudes, and particularly at night, oxygen deficiency, known as hypoxia, impairs one's ability to see, to think and to respond. The situation is lethal because the rapid degeneration in mental and physical ability goes almost totally unnoticed.

The insidious nature of hypoxia makes it difficult to diagnose but even more difficult to attribute as a probable cause in resulting aircraft accidents. In fact, over the past ten years, NTSB and the FAA have attributed hypoxia as a probable cause in only six accidents and a few other incidents where high altitude had played an important role.

With the statistics so low, is hypoxia something to concern oneself about?

You bet. An SAE (Society of Automotive Engineers) report states, "Early onset of these altered mental functions, which are not recognized by the individual, represents serious hazards to the air crew and may be the direct or indirect cause of many accidents."

Although the FARs require commercial flight crews to use oxygen at levels above 10,000 feet, according to the FAA's Office of Aviation

Medicine, the first symptom of hypoxia occurs at 4,000 feet, in the form of diminished night vision.

At 8,000 to 9,000 feet, instruments and maps can easily be misread, and dimly lit ground features can be misinterpreted or unrecognized. To the pilot, it's just dark outside. But, that darkness could mask an oncoming aircraft or an obstruction, or lead to spatial disorientation.

Consider a likely scenario for a loss-of-control accident in IMC (instrument meteorological conditions) at night: The pilot is likely to be tired. He or she becomes disoriented. He misinterprets his instruments, vertigo sets in, and ... the aircraft and the pilot become a statistic.

In situations such as this, it is impossible to say that hypoxia was the cause. But, anything that leaves a pilot less than fully alert should be considered a factor in compromising safety.

Zero Tolerance

The U.S. Air Force has zero tolerance for compromise. Because the retina of the eye is more demanding of oxygen than any other part of the body, Air Force pilots are required to use supplemental oxygen at night *from the surface on up*.

Hypoxia also affects other brain activity. Slow response times may result in delayed reaction to an emergency or an inability to think through complex ATC instructions.

In order to function normally, therefore, it is vitally important to consider breathing supplemental oxygen. The question is: At what altitude should you begin to use oxygen?

Unfortunately, there is no clear-cut answer. Consider the following:

• A Piper Dakota crashed two hours after taking off from Tucson, Ariz. to fly to Carlsbad, N.M. During cruise, the pilot tried various altitudes between 10,000 and 16,000 feet in order to top weather.

Eventually, radar and radio contact were lost. Witnesses saw the aircraft in level flight at 3,000 feet before it pitched down and spun in. The NTSB listed hypoxia as a contributing factor.

• A Beech Bonanza which had been cruising at 11,500 feet crashed in the desert on a night flight from San Jose, Calif. to Salt Lake City, Utah. No evidence of mechanical failure or malfunction was found.

The NTSB report stated that the pilot had a prior history of problems with hypoxia. "The altitude at which he last reported was in the average sub-hypoxic range." Spatial disorientation was listed as the probable cause, with hypoxia a contributing factor.

• A 7,000-hour, 78-year-old pilot of a Cessna 182 was attempting an approach to Jackson, Wyo. at night in deteriorating weather. According to the NTSB report, anxiety and apprehension over the missed approach were influences in the ensuing crash.

Hypoxia was listed as a contributing factor, taking into consideration the age of the pilot, his mental state, the time he had spent at altitude, as well as the weather and light conditions.

• In one incident from the FAA's files, the pilot of a Mooney 252 climbing to altitude in daylight conditions failed to respond to ATC instructions. A military aircraft was scrambled, and it helped the pilot to descend and to make a safe landing. The pilot said he had had problems with his oxygen supply.

Different Strokes

Even the slightest degradation in pilot ability erodes safety margins. The question you must ask yourself is, "To what degree am I willing to compromise safety?"

Hypoxia affects individuals in different ways, to different degrees, at different altitudes. An individual's requirement for oxygen is directly affected by that person's health and medical history.

In addition, increased physical or mental activity—including problem-solving, stress and anxiety—requires increasingly greater quantities of oxygen. In fact, severe exertion or stress could require eight times the amount of oxygen one needs when sitting at rest.

If the demand for oxygen is high and the ambient supply is limited, hypoxia has a greater impact.

Fatigue, depressant drugs (even in small amounts), traces of alcohol in the blood (although "legal" according to the regulations) or carbon monoxide poisoning induced by smoking tobacco or inhaling exhaust gases will exacerbate the effects of hypoxia.

According to the SAE report, "Individuals who smoke should consider themselves at an altitude 2,000 to 3,000 feet above the non-smoker...."

The regulations do not take these individual differences into consideration. FAR 91.211 stipulates that pilots use supplemental oxygen for any portion of a flight in excess of 30 minutes from 12,500 feet through 14,000 feet, and at all times above 14,000 feet.

If, as this regulation implies, the effects of hypoxia are insignificant at altitudes below 12,500 feet, why is FAR 135.89 even more restrictive?

This regulation states that, during an air taxi or commercial operation, pilots of unpressurized aircraft must use supplemental oxygen for any portion of a flight in excess of 30 minutes from 10,000 through 12,000 feet, and at all times above 12,000. (If cabin pressure in a pressurized aircraft should rise above 10,000 feet for any reason, the same rules apply.)

Of course, the stricter provisions of FAR 135 (and 121, for scheduled airline operations) reflect the FAA's intention to provide a greater level of safety for paying passengers.

Considering the oxygen requirements of FAR 135—and the fact that most pressurized airliners and corporate jets are designed to fly with cabin altitudes of 5,000 to 6,000 feet or less—it would appear that general aviation pilots could reduce the risk of hypoxia by using supplemental oxygen at levels far below what is stipulated in FAR 91.

Beyond the Regs

The SAE report, which is circulated by the FAA's Office of Aviation Medicine, concurs.

It states that, at 10,000 feet, "there is definite but unrecognizable hypoxia. It is the maximum altitude at which an individual should consider his judgment and ability minimally acceptable."

The report continues, "It should be noted again that the most rapid and serious changes without [the use of supplemental] oxygen occur between 10,000 and 15,000 feet." Approaching 14,000 feet, thought processes become "cloudy." At this altitude, the report notes, "an individual is considered appreciably handicapped."

At 16,000 feet, "the individual is considered 'considerably handi-capped,'" the report states. "Disorientation, belligerence or euphoric behavior and the complete lack of rational judgment [are] observed."

The report also states that the longer the period of oxygen depriva-tion, the more pronounced the symptoms become.

Consider a pilot under stress, confronting low fuel indications, unforecast adverse weather and instrument malfunctions. He has been flying at 13,000 feet for 25 minutes without oxygen prior to commencing a descent. He certainly is "legal," according to FAR 91 regulations; but, legality and safety clearly have taken divergent courses.

Does all of this suggest that we should be using oxygen if we fly above 6,000 or 8,000 feet? Not necessarily. What is important is to understand the effects of hypoxia and, certainly, not to be complacent about the possibility of hypoxia at altitudes well below those suggested by regulation.

By knowing that hypoxia can occur and knowing some of the symptoms, telltale signs might trigger alarms that result in early action before disaster strikes.

Benign Beginnings

Hypoxia usually is disguised initially as something benign.

Tingling in the legs, arms or neck isn't unusual if you've been sitting in one position for some time, as in the cockpit of an aircraft. Although easy to attribute to other causes, this is a classic symptom of hypoxia.

How about a lightheaded feeling or a headache? In the air, don't reach for an aspirin; descend or grab the oxygen mask.

What about when there are no overt symptoms at all? You're feeling great, confident, in charge. Dangerous? For sure. Euphoria and a sense of well-being also are classic hypoxia symptoms.

Having trouble setting the correct radio frequency? Loss of coordination and degraded judgment are other signs of oxygen deprivation.

During the day or night, while flying at 5,000 feet and higher, be aware of these subtle changes in ability and behavior.

Interestingly, much like fingerprints, each individual exhibits the same personal symptoms each time the hypoxia threshold is reached. One excellent way to discover your own personal symptoms is to take a "ride" in an altitude chamber as part of the FAA's Physiological Training program.

The FAA's Civil Aeromedical Institute in Oklahoma City, Okla. (405-954-4837) can arrange for such an opportunity either in Oklahoma City or at a military facility closer to you. Accident Prevention Specialists also have application forms available. The training costs only $20, and the experience could save your life one day.

Oxygen To Go

If you are flying a pressurized airplane, such as a Beech P58 Baron, Cessna P210 or Piper Malibu, supplemental oxygen is a concern only if the pressurization system fails.

If that should happen, there will be no question about what to do: Reach for the oxygen mask immediately and switch the system on. Remember, effective performance time at 22,000 feet is only five to ten minutes without supplemental oxygen. At 25,000 feet, you'll have less than three minutes of useful time in which to respond.

Many unpressurized, turbocharged singles and twins have built-in oxygen systems. If not, portable oxygen systems are available. These are also extremely useful in naturally aspirated, piston-engine aircraft. Scott, Puritan-Bennett, Ted Nelson, Aerox and Sky-Ox are among companies that market portable units, as well as built-in systems.

Having supplemental oxygen available means that at any time there is the slightest inkling of hypoxia, you can grab the mask and deal with what otherwise could become a nasty situation. Having oxygen aboard also allows you to take maximum advantage of your aircraft's performance capability.

The oxygen units most commonly available for piston-powered

general aviation aircraft are called *constant-flow* systems. That means that once the system is on, 100 percent oxygen flows continuously.

Although oxygen can be dispensed through a nasal cannula (like those used to administer oxygen to medical patients), most manufacturers recommend strongly against using them. Jim Kaletta, vice president of Scott Aviation, states flatly that "nose cannulas are not reliable." (More on cannulas later.)

Go With the Flow

Still, most pilots prefer to use masks, the most common variety of which is the rebreather mask.

This type of mask has an attached bag which mixes incoming oxygen from the tank with some ambient air plus a portion of exhaled breath (hence, the name rebreather). The user then inhales from the reservoir build-up in the bag.

A large portion of the gases exhaled contains oxygen not used by the lungs, and this is retained in the bag and mixed with the new supply of tank oxygen and ambient air. The remainder of the exhaled gas exits through flapper valves in the mask.

Another mask commonly used in aviation is the phase-dilution type. This allows only oxygen to enter the bag through a one-way valve. When the user exhales, gases from the lungs are vented outside.

FAR 23.1443 stipulates required minimum oxygen flows for fixed and portable systems at various altitudes. For example, at 15,000 feet, the minimum allowable flow rate is about 1.5 liters per minute. At 20,000 feet, the figure is about 2.0 liters per minute; and at 25,000 feet, it is about 2.5 liters per minute.

A manual or automatic regulator is incorporated in most oxygen systems to adjust the flow to that required at any given altitude. If it were not regulated, a constant-flow system designed for use at 25,000 feet would produce a flow of 2.5 liters per minute at *all* altitudes.

This, of course, would result in an excessive flow of oxygen at anything below 25,000 feet. Therefore, a regulator is used with most systems to increase or decrease the flow of oxygen approximately one-tenth of a liter per 1,000 feet.

Some automatic systems do not begin dispensing oxygen until 8,000 or 10,000 feet. That means that at night, at 6,000 feet, where oxygen might be desired, it just might not be available. The Scott automatic system installed in Mooneys and Beech Bonanzas will provide a regulated flow from the ground upward.

Portable systems are available both with and without altitude compensation or with manual regulators that are adjusted by the user for the given altitude. A 14-pound, 22-cubic-foot (623-liter) Scott portable oxygen system with a manual altitude compensator, for example, will provide one person with eight hours' worth of oxygen at 12,500 feet. The capacity of this system is reduced to 4.5 hours worth of oxygen for one user at 23,000 feet.

A 22-cubic-foot Puritan-Bennett system with a manual regulator provides about six hours of oxygen for one person at 12,000 feet and about three hours' worth at 23,000 feet.

Plan Ahead

The difference in the capacities of these two systems (probably due to the use of higher flow rates by Puritan-Bennett) points out the importance of using the manufacturer's numbers for accurate consumption calculations (with a caveat that we'll discuss later on).

Whether portable or fixed, oxygen systems add weight; and that means the pilot must consider the effect on payload.

A fully charged, 76-cubic-foot, built-in system will add 30 pounds to your aircraft's basic operating weight. Check weight and balance carefully, because on a long trip requiring full fuel, you may not be able to take the passenger or baggage load you thought you might.

If weight and balance checks out, think once again about the length of the journey. Depending on the number of passengers and the planned altitude, your oxygen range may be far less than your fuel range.

For most built-in systems, an oxygen duration chart is provided in the flight manual or owner's handbook. The information manual for a Mooney 231 with a 76-cubic-foot tank of oxygen, for example, indicates that the system can supply a pilot and one passenger for 6.2 hours at 24,000 feet. Add two more passengers, and maximum duration at 24,000 feet is reduced to 3.2 hours.

If the oxygen tank is not full, your duration will, of course, be less. Check the chart carefully against the pressure gauge indications. In a typical system, 900 pounds per square inch (psi) will provide half the duration of a full charge (1,800 psi), and 450 psi will provide about one quarter of the full tank duration.

Topping Up

When it's time to have your oxygen tank refilled, make certain that the supply tank has a greater pressure than the pressure you need in your own system.

If, for example, your gauge reads 1,300 psi and the supply bottle has only 1,500 psi of pressure, that's all you'll get; the supply bottle won't be able to bring the pressure in your bottle above that.

If you have higher pressure in your system than in the supply tank, the flow could reverse. So, check the FBO's pressure gauge before you top off.

Also remember that ambient temperature affects the amount of oxygen flowing into the aircraft cylinder. If you want to fill the tank to the equivalent of 1,850 psi at standard temperature, the actual filling pressure would be 1,775 psi at 30 F, or 2,000 psi if the temperature were 80 F.

While planning, although you should consult the oxygen-duration chart in your airplane manual or in the documentation that came with your portable oxygen system, don't necessarily count on the published figures.

Look for Leaks

If there are any leaks in the system, a considerable amount of oxygen will be dumped overboard.

Access valves in installed systems are prone to leak, whether or not the masks are plugged in.

Therefore, until you've gained enough experience to compare your actual flow rates against those in the "book," it will be wise to be conservative with your oxygen duration planning.

It's important to use the mask and plug combination designated for your system. Scott color-codes its plug couplings: A green plug will allow a flow three times that of the standard plug, for example.

With a constant-flow system not equipped with a regulator, you could possibly have an excess flow of oxygen, which would be fine from a breathing standpoint but disappointing in terms of duration. On the other hand, a standard plug at 23,000 feet might not provide sufficient oxygen flow.

This suggests a careful check of masks and couplings. Don't just plug anything in and expect it to work properly.

The mask, itself, could be the culprit in the system. If the edges aren't sealed against the skin, oxygen can leak out.

That means that bearded gentlemen may not receive the required flow of oxygen. And, it is for this reason that those with beards are not permitted to take part in the altitude chamber portion of the FAA's Physiological Training program.

Don't look at the bag attached to the mask for an indication of oxygen flow. The bag isn't intended to inflate greatly. So, don't worry if the bag appears to remain flaccid as you climb to 24,000 feet. The bag is not one of the flow-rate indicators that should be closely monitored.

As mentioned earlier, one way to avoid some of the drawbacks of the oxygen mask, such as discomfort and inability to talk, is to use a nasal cannula. Bear in mind that very few oxygen system manufacturers recommend their use, although some will sell them because the demand is there.

The nasal cannula is certainly more comfortable than a mask and doesn't require that the user be clean-shaven. You can also eat and talk normally, and you don't have to suffer the smell of rubber for hours at a time.

If you do use a cannula, remember that oxygen will be wasted if you aren't inhaling and that this will corrupt consumption figures. One type, called a "conserving" nasal cannula, incorporates a reservoir for trapping excess oxygen, and this improves duration figures slightly.

Although many suppliers will tell you that the cannula is approved for use up to 18,000 feet, that is technically incorrect. Actually, a cannula may be used with an aircraft oxygen system certificated to a maximum altitude of 18,000 feet.

Installations certificated for higher altitudes (FAR 23.1447) require that "each oxygen-dispensing unit must cover the nose and mouth of the user." That would preclude the use of nasal cannulas in turbocharged aircraft that can be operated above 18,000 feet, even though they are flown at lower altitudes.

In fact, your aircraft may have a maximum operating altitude of 16,000 feet but your oxygen system may have been certificated for much higher altitudes. In that case, use of a cannula would not be strictly legal.

Flow Indications

Most oxygen masks are supplied with a red/green flow indicator. The green indicator tells you that oxygen is flowing—but *not* how much.

Poor connections or the wrong plug could result in far smaller flows than required. At 25,000 feet, you could have an oxygen flow equivalent to that required at 5,000 feet and still see a green indication.

One way to solve the flow question is with a flow meter manufactured by the Ted Nelson Company. This device not only allows you to monitor the flow, but provides an adjustment to regulate the flow for altitude. This is a particular bonus for constant-flow systems without their own regulators.

Since every oxygen outlet may not be receiving the same amount of oxygen, the Nelson meter also allows the flow to be checked for each passenger.

Irrespective of the breathing system used, there are some general concerns about supplemental oxygen that everyone should be aware of.

Users should avoid moustache wax or greasy lipsticks. Oily substances such as these have been known to ignite when exposed to pure oxygen.

Obviously, smoking by anyone in the aircraft is out of the question completely, because oxygen is highly inflammable.

The availability of oxygen aboard any aircraft is not only an operational benefit for flights at high altitude but an important safety device well below those altitudes stipulated by regulation.

Hypoxia is insidious. Fatigue, stress, age, colds or congestion, or use of certain over-the-counter medications can bring on the ill effects of hypoxia much earlier than one might expect. At night, particularly, hypoxia takes an early toll on vision.

A Civil Aviation Aeromedical report states that occasional use of oxygen at low altitude, particularly at night, can act as a refresher. Pilots who regularly fly with oxygen equipment aboard say that ten minutes' use of oxygen prior to arrival at the destination can put you in an alert mental state for the approach and landing.

Remember the expression, "an accident looking for a place to happen." That certainly describes hypoxia. Hypoxia erodes the margin of safety to the point at which any intervening circumstance could lead to disaster. Oxygen is the only antidote, and it comes with a host of other advantages, as well.

Deicing Systems

*N*ow *we take a look at a highly IFR-specific system: deice. There are several systems, including bleed air (found only on turbine-powered aircraft), the "traditional" pneumatic boots, experimental electro-mechanical systems not currently in service, and the relatively new TKS weeping wing, which is actually an anti-ice, not a deice, system.*

Most aircraft that have deice systems use boots, and that's what we'll be covering here.

There's a lot of confusion about what boots actually do for you, leagally. Does the fact that an airplane you're considering for purchase is equipped with boots make it legal for flight into known icing? Not necessarily...first up we have a brief look at the ins and outs of the FARs.

Known Ice Legalities

To a buyer shopping the ads in *Trade-A-Plane*, the phrase "known ice" implies a list of equipment that, at a minimum, usually includes pneumatic boots and prop de-icers. Probably, a heated windshield or alcohol de-icing system is also part of the package, plus heated stall vanes and perhaps heated fuel vents, too.

However, there are plenty of light twins sporting just this kind of equipment that aren't certified for flight into known ice. And in some cases, even if the AFM says the airplane is certified, it may not be.

But that doesn't mean the airplane's not legal to fly into ice. It just means that there's a distinction between being *certified* for known ice, and simply being *legal* to fly in it. Being certified and/or legal has little to do with how safe it might be to fly in ice of any kind.

The FARs governing flight into known ice are vague to the extent that when manufacturers, operators and pilots have tried to pin down the exact legality of flight in icing, they've found themselves on slippery slopes.

For Part 91 operations, there are no prohibitions against flight into known icing, with the exception of 91.527, which prohibits large and turbine-powered multi-engine aircraft from flying into "known or forecast moderate" icing without de-ice equipment. Your average single- or multi-engine flib is not mentioned at all in Part 91.

Common sense keeps most of us from boring into icing in unprotected airplanes but roundabout, there is a reg that makes it a sin, too. It's 91.9, which requires pilots to operate their aircraft within the manufacturer's published limitations. Virtually all singles and twins manufactured since about 1972 are placarded against flight in icing, unless equipped with specified de-icing or anti-icing equipment.

In a perverse twist of the FAR's intent, any airplane built before then is probably not specifically prohibited against flight into icing. Technically, then, you'd be legal (if foolish) to launch into known ice with no protection at all.

For-hire operators subject to Part 135 generally have things spelled out for them in clearer terms, but not when it comes to icing.

FAR 135.227 says that any for-hire airplane certified for known-icing (under FAR 25, appendix C) can be flown into "known or forecast severe icing." Airplanes that aren't specifically certified for known ice but are nonetheless equipped with wing, stabilizer, windshield and prop de-icers can be flown into known or forecast light to moderate icing.

What the regs and the AFMs don't say is that the distinction between light, moderate and severe is utterly meaningless because icing reports (and, to a certain extent, forecasts) are based entirely on pilot perceptions. An encounter that scares the crap out of a freight dog in an Aztec might be little more than light icing to a Boeing crew.

Just read the AIM's definition of severe icing: "The rate of accumulation is such that de-icing/anti-icing equipment fails to reduce or control the hazard." That means that it's perfectly legal to fly your known-ice airplane into any conditions you like, including severe. But no matter how bad the ice, it's not officially severe unless the de-icers can't handle the accumulation. Clear?

And just because the airplane has known-ice certification, doesn't mean that it was test flown in severe conditions for any length of time or possibly at all.

FAR 25 requires that known-ice aircraft be flown in certain icing conditions in order to meet certification. Temperature, altitude, droplet size and moisture content and exposure time are all specified in exhaustive detail.

Pilots who have flown certification trials say that these conditions amount to at least moderate conditions but there's no implied correlation to FAA icing forecasts and/or pireps on actual icing. After all, unprotected surfaces ice up too and this can take a severe toll on performance.

As part of the certification, the airplane's AFM must specifically list the de-icing equipment installed during certification and there's supposed to be a notation in the AFM explaining the known-ice capability. There may also be a placard saying as much. To be legal, the aircraft must have that very same equipment installed and in working order before flying into ice.

Some aircraft may appear to have all the required de-icing equipment but may be missing minor items. This equipment may never have been installed or it may have been removed at sometime, a fact which should be noted in the aircraft logs.

The Piper Navajo, for example, was certified with inboard and outboard boots. A Navajo AFM we recently reviewed indicated that the airplane was certified for known ice but it lacked inboard boots, nonetheless.

Under Part 135, that limits the aircraft to light to moderate conditions. For Part 91 operations, lacking specific limitations, it's good to go into anything. Piper claims that the pilot of a Navajo that's not certified for known ice can't file and fly into icing conditions but none of the manuals we've seen list this as a limitation.

So much for the rulebook. In the real world, of course, the concept of "known icing" is so vague it's almost meaningless.

Now, on to the actual equipment.

Basic Boots

Any airplane sophisticated enough to be equipped with de-icing, usually has a fat manual to explain the various systems. Unfortunately, all of the manuals we've seen seem to assume that pilots transitioning into de-ice-equipped aircraft already know how the de-icers work because few offer more than a page or two of explanation.

Learn by doing isn't a solution in this case. Even in a cold climate, de-icers don't get much use and it's not improbable for a pilot to make it through an entire winter without ever needing them. But when they are needed, de-icers are usually *badly* needed. And that's no time to find out that they don't work or that you've forgotten how to use them correctly.

Operating Principle

For all practical purposes, BF Goodrich is the sole manufacturer of pneumatic de-icing boots. A French company, Kleber-Industrie, makes similar systems for the European market but few of these find their way to the U.S. Goodrich first introduced pneumatic de-ice boots in 1930 and in the intervening 61 years, the basic operating principle has remained unchanged; brittle ice adhering to the leading edge is dislodged when the boots inflate and deflate. Except for substantial decreases in system weight, even the hardware itself hasn't changed all that much. Like their predecessors, modern boots consist of multi-celled rubber bladders glued (or screwed in some older installations) to the leading edges of the wing and tail surfaces. Because boots are traditionally black, many pilots mistakenly assume that the silver leading edges on newer airplanes like Beech's Star Ship are electrically heated blankets. Nope, they're regular pneumatic boots that just happen to be colored silver.

A boot begins life as giant, flat rubber envelope or carcase made of several layers of thin neoprene or Estane. The individual cells are formed by gluing or sewing span- or chord-wise seams. It's a popular misconception that Goodrich makes up boot material by the lineal mile and then just snips the proper length off a giant reel to fill a customer order. Each boot is made to fit a specific surface of an aircraft and although Goodrich does stock parts for common models, many replacement boots are custom orders.

Inflation and deflation is accomplished by pumping vacuum and pressure to the boots through small manifold hoses which pass through holes bored in the leading edge. For redundancy, most twins have two vacuum pumps and to handle the boots' considerable demand for pressure and vacuum, these are quite a bit larger than the 200-series pumps found in a typical single-engine airplane. Airborne 400-series pumps are the usual choice. Both pumps feed to a common manifold so in the event of failure, either one can run the entire system, plus the vacuum instruments.

Boot-equipped piston-singles, such as the Cessna 210 and Piper Malibu, sometimes have two pumps too. In the Malibu, the extra pump can run the boots but in other singles, the spare is usually there to run the vacuum instruments and/or to provide enough suction to compress the boots against the wing in the event that the primary pump fails.

The schematic for a light twin de-icing system has lots of plumbing, but basically the system is set up so that in normal flight, the boots are held tight against the leading edge by vacuum pressure. When de-ice is selected, the flow valves reverse and direct air from the pressure side of the vacuum pumps to inflate the boots.

In most systems, the order in which the boots inflate is controlled by a timer, thus when you activate the boots, the inflation cycle may start with the outboard boots, followed by the tail surfaces and finishing up with the inboard boots.

Sequential inflation eases the strain on the pumps and, in some systems, it improves ice-shedding efficiency. The Malibu's wing profile, for example, proved difficult to de-ice so Goodrich installed what it calls "clamshell" boots. These inflate individually (and in sequence) on the top and bottom surfaces rather than all at once, as most boots do.

Pre-Flight Check

Goodrich installs de-icing boots in a cavernous hangar at Akron-Canton Regional Airport at the rate of about 300 systems a year. It's steady work year round except for a flurry of activity during the early fall, when pilots sail into the first ice of the season only to discover that their boots don't work right or at all. Owners lucky enough to have an annual in August might escape this unpleasant discovery but when it comes to deferring maintenance through the summer, de-icers (boots and props) top the list of things to forget about.

AFMs are characteristically weak on pre-flight procedures for boots and prop de-icers; they offer almost no advice on diagnosing major and minor faults. Goodrich's Jim Dunn, who manages the Akron-Canton hangar, recommends that boots be tested several times during the summer and inspected thoroughly before the first cold clouds of fall arrive. Besides detecting any faults soon enough to fix them, says Dunn, occasionally exercising the system keeps the valves and plumbing limbered up.

At the very least, with the engine(s) running, cycle the boots several times and check them visually for proper operation. The better way, says Dunn, is to apply shop air to both sides of the system (no more than 18 PSI for high-pressure systems, 10 PSI for low pressure) with the engines shut down. While a helper in the cockpit cycles the boots, check each one visually for proper inflation and evidence of leaks. If there's a vertical boot, you'll need a ladder to inspect it properly.

What typically goes wrong? Not much, but then it doesn't take much to disable a boot or the entire system. Check the boot surfaces for punctures, abrasions and blown stitch lines. As long as punctures are less than 3/4 in. long and not closer than 1/8 in. to a stitch line, they can be repaired with cold patches. If the stitch line itself is blown, you'll have to pony up the dough for a new boot.

Pin Holes

Deferring the shop-air inspection increases the likelihood of overlooking tiny pin holes in the boot surfaces. However, if there are enough small holes, they'll make their presence known in flight through a phenomenon known as autoinflation.

All or a portion of the boot will inflate because the pumps can't hold vacuum pressure against the leaks; airflow over the wing cause the boot to inflate partially. Loose connections, tattered hoses or a stuck flow valve can also cause autoinflation.

If holes are the problem, they should be patched as soon as possible, otherwise moisture may migrate into the boots and it's almost impossible to expel. Collect enough moisture in a boot and you may find that it will freeze at altitude and won't inflate when you need it most. Of course, on the ground, the boot will thaw and appear to operate normally. Dunn says he's seen some de-icers so sodden with water from pin holes that they squirt like lawn sprinklers when they're brought in for replacement.

You can locate the holes by brushing soapy water onto the boots after applying shop air. Mark the holes and patch them once the boot is dried off and cleaned up. Some older boots seem to have more patches than a cheap air mattress but that doesn't necessarily mean the de-icers are ready for retirement. Goodrich specs allow for quite a bit of patching, more, in fact, than many aircraft owners would consider cosmetically acceptable.

A shop-air inspection will also reveal problems with valves and plumbing that wouldn't necessarily show up during an engines-up pre-flight check. Failures in any of these elements can cause slow inflation, no inflation or lack of deflation, even though the pumps and boots are perfectly serviceable.

Cycling the boots regularly will exercise the valves and reveal any that may be malfunctioning. Goodrich says that disassembling and cleaning will often cure a sticky valve.

Can you overdo the test cycling? Not as far as Goodrich is concerned. They say the boots will degrade from sunlight, ozone, rain erosion and hangar rash long before they'll wear out from being cycled.

The vacuum pumps are another matter, however. If the de-icer plumbing is leaky or otherwise malfunctioning, the high vacuum load will heat up the pump vanes and ultimately accelerate wear.

A Word About Props

Since it doesn't do much good to fling ice off the wings while the props pick up a load, most known-ice airplanes also have electro-thermal prop de-icers. These are known generically as hot props but that's actually a misnomer because Goodrich makes two prop de-ice systems; one is known as the dual-element, four-cycle or standard system and another by the trade name HotProp.

Both consist of electro-thermal pads glued to the inboard portions of the prop and connected to the aircraft electrical system via wiring harnesses and brushes which ride on a slip ring located just behind the spinner.

The two systems look the same but they work a bit differently. The standard system de-icers are divided into two elements, an inboard (closest to the prop hub) and an outboard. As with boots, a timer is used to heat the elements in sequence, beginning with the outboard elements on one prop (about 34 seconds, depending on the system) followed by the inboard elements on the same prop, then repeating on the opposite-side prop. Sequential heating keeps the current draw reasonable and it accounts for the fact that loosened ice tends to move outward on the rotating prop.

The HotProp system on a twin heats all elements on one prop for 90 seconds, followed by all elements on other prop for 90 seconds. On a single, a HotProp cycles on and off every 90 seconds.

Warm to the Touch

As an occasional pre-flight procedure (at least once before icing season), activate the system very briefly on the ground with the engines off. Each de-icer should feel warm to the touch and should heat up and cool off in the sequence described here or in the AFM. Obviously, if any of the elements don't heat, the system will need to be checked out. Local hot spots signal a damaged de-icer, which may have to be replaced. Fortunately, compared to boots, prop de-icers are cheap and can be replaced piecemeal.

Activating the prop de-ice occasionally in flight even when it's not needed is good practice, too. Goodrich's Dunn says that when current flows through the system, minute amounts of silver contained in the carbon brushes are deposited on the slip ring, lubricating it and reducing wear. Monitor the system ammeter during test cycling and actual use. It should indicate in the green band during heating sequences (10 amps for 14-volt systems, 5 amps for 28-volt systems). If the ammeter shows no draw, the system probably isn't getting power or the timer is bad. Low current during any heating cycle may indicate a bad de-icer element or a bad connection at the slip ring.

Chopping Ice

If AFMs are any indication, manufacturers have always assumed that using boots is so stone simple that little need be said about their operation. Indeed, the advice in most manuals we've seen boils down to this: when you see ice, activate the system. Beyond that, there's not much else you can do. However, just when to cycle the boots requires a little judgement and, depending on conditions, some experience.

The AFMs generally recommend cycling the de-icers when 1/4 to 1/2 inch of ice has accumulated on the leading edges. The type of ice and rate of build has some bearing on when to hit the switch. A brittle layer of mixed ice will pop off a lot easier than a mushy build-up of cloudy rime. Sometimes, you may have to let the ice harden or build a bit before the boot can flex enough to dislodge it. Cycling with too little ice on the leading edge or too frequently in moderate conditions may cause the accumulation to continue beyond the contour of the inflated boots, a condition known as bridging. If this occurs, the boots may be rendered useless and the only solution will be to get out of the icing conditions as soon as possible (a good idea anyway) or plan on an immediate landing.

Even if you go by the book, ice can be sticky stuff and sometimes long sections of ice just won't let go. Assuming the boots are inflating normally, Goodrich says keeping the boots clean (soap and water wash, isopropyl alcohol for bug hits) and treated with Icex improves shedding. Icex, a silicone-based product sold by Goodrich, is intended to be applied periodically during the icing season. It can be used in conjunction with three other products made specifically for boot care. AgeMaster No. 1, a rubber preservative, keeps the boots flexible and slows degradation from the elements. In response to customer requests for a cosmetic treatment to spruce up faded boots, Goodrich this year introduced ShineMaster Prep, a cleaner, and ShineMaster, a cosmetic treatment.

Some operators use ordinary car or floor wax in place of Icex. These may or may not work but Goodrich warns that such products may cause surface checking. Similarly, Goodrich doesn't recommend commercial rubber and plastic preservatives, which may actually shorten the life of the rubber.

As for the props, AFMs vary in their recommendations; some don't specify when to activate prop de-ice, others recommend turning it on (along with pitot and windshield) heat in any conditions where icing is possible. Preventative use makes the most sense for even though prop systems are considered de-ice rather than anti-ice devices, waiting until ice actually forms will cause unnecessary vibration and once the props are heated, the dislodged ice can bang into the fuselage and chip the paint.

There Are Limits

The manufacturers (and Goodrich) wisely make no claims about just how much ice a known-ice airplane can handle. If the airplane is legal and certified under Part 25, appendix C (see page 9), the manufacturer has demonstrated that the airplane can fly safely in a specified icing envelope. Pilots who have flown certification tests will tell you that the conditions set out in Part 25 constitute a significant amount of icing but that the envelope in no way corresponds to forecast data or actual icing reports. There are just too many variables, including aircraft type, length of time in the conditions, pilot proficiency and how well the de-ice system is operating.

De-icers on light airplanes are not bullet proof. There are conditions they can't handle, including the kind of severe icing found in thunderstorms and heavy freezing rain. The smart pilot recognizes de-icers for just what the are; reliable protection in light or perhaps moderate icing and a means to extricate himself from severe conditions.

Landing Gear

W e'll close the book with a few words on a more prosaic system: the landing gear. All airplanes have it, but most of us who fly IFR regularly do so in airplanes that have retractable gear.

As accident statistics and service difficulty records show, retractable gear is the underlying cause of a lot of headaches. When we look at the figures, sometimes we wonder if it's really worth it.

Some insight into your gear and how it does what it does can help keep you from doing horrible things to the paint on the belly of your airplane. Here's John Conrad with some tips.

Landing Gear Lessons

dd as it may seem, the most common major accident to occur at airports results from pilots landing airplanes with the wheels retracted. Aircraft manufacturers have tried horns, bells, whistles, lights, sirens and mechanical indicators to alert pilots to the situation, but airplanes continue to slide down the runway on flaps and curled prop tips.

A large percentage of the gear-up accidents are a direct result of the pilots' failure to put the landing gear handle in the "down" position and check for a gear-down indication prior to landing. This often happens in training situations, when pilots become overwhelmed and overlook this one important item. It also occurs often when pilots forget to retract the landing gear after takeoff and move the switch to the "up" position on downwind, thinking that they have put it down.

In such cases, a change in procedure causes the pilot to forget the landing gear. Written checklists are supposed to preclude this, but I am of the opinion that they exacerbate the problem. The pilot who completes the checklist feels he or she has done the proper thing to ensure the safety of the aircraft. But if he has accidentally skipped the landing gear check, he may feel warm and fuzzy, but the wheels are still up.

To avoid this possibility, the pilot needs to develop a simple procedure that can be followed regardless of other distractions. The procedure is simply this: Every time you cross the runway threshold, approach lights or boundary fence, check to see that you have a gear-down indication. Whether crosswind or no wind, short field or long, IFR or VFR, with one engine running or two engines running or no engines running, check for gear down *every time*.

For about 10 years, I flew nothing but retractable-gear aircraft. Then, when I checked out in a Cessna 182, I was positively neurotic because there were no green lights glowing at me on final. Intellectually, I knew the landing gear was down and welded, but I was uncomfortable without something to check when I was supposed to check it.

Beyond situations in which pilots simply forget to throw the switch or put the handle in the wrong position, there are lots of mechanical problems which can result in a gear-up landing that could otherwise be avoided. A thorough understanding of how your landing gear system works, and why it works, can help you avoid a short-field landing in a shower of sparks.

Motors and Gears

Probably the most common design utilizes an electric motor and a gearbox to crank the landing gear up and down. All older twin Cessnas, all Beechcraft singles and light twins, and many other aircraft use these devices.

The advantage is that they are relatively simple and usually don't require up-locks to keep the landing gear retracted in flight. The disadvantage is the complex mechanical linkages required to make them work.

The electric motor, itself, doesn't create enough power to raise or lower the gear. The system depends on the mechanical advantage achieved through the gearbox and the various levers in the system.

It is possible for this system to develop several hundred pounds of mechanical advantage at some points, so in essence what you have is a very powerful mechanical device grinding away in the bowels of the aircraft.

All of the parts, including landing gear doors and extension devices, are attached to one another mechanically. So, if something goes wrong or is bent, the entire system can literally grind to a halt. One stray screw left over from the annual inspection can become lodged and bring the entire program to a halt. Furthermore, because of the power in the system, a small malfunction can result in considerable damage before the circuit breaker blows.

There are two types of emergency-extension mechanisms associated with this type of system. One is a mechanical crank which simply does what the electric motor would have otherwise done. Obviously, if the system is jammed, you aren't going to be able to turn the crank, either. A less common method releases the electric motor and gear drive mechanism and allows the landing gear to free-fall into position. If something jams, you might have to become a mechanic to fix it.

In Beeches, for example, the entire landing gear retraction and timing mechanism is under the two front seats. The crank for emergency extension sticks out behind the seats. Should the motor fail, the pilot should slow down, pull the circuit breakers, extend the crank and then do the work of the electric motor. But if the linkage jams, the crank isn't going to work any better than the motor did. I heard of one pilot who removed the seats from a Bonanza, opened up the area where the landing gear mechanism was and removed a Swiss Army knife that had somehow found its way into the works. He then reassembled the airplane and landed.

Though few of us have the mechanical expertise to perform this bit of improvisation, a thorough understanding of the landing gear mechanics can help in an emergency. During the annual inspection, try to get a look at the workings of the landing gear so that you know what moves what and why. Ask the mechanic to perform a gear retraction while the aircraft inspection plates are removed so that you can see how it works. Some day you may need to know.

(One more word of caution for Beech pilots. If a passenger should kick the emergency crank out of the stowed position, it will spin like mad when the landing gear is lowered. Not only is this a great way to break an instep, but if the crank should foul something, it can jam the whole system. One pilot spent an hour and a half trying to cut away a sweater that had been wound around the crank.)

Motors and Pumps

Another common system for landing gear actuation uses an electric motor to run a hydraulic pump. The pressure from this pump is then routed through pipes and hoses to hydraulic rams which are connected to the landing gear legs.

Single-engine Cessnas and Pipers use this system, which has its own advantages and disadvantages. One of the big advantages is that the landing gear are not mechanically connected, so one jammed component cannot jam the whole system. Though there is dubious advantage to landing with one main landing gear retracted as opposed to landing with both retracted, if you can get the nose gear down, you can usually save the engine and propeller.

The disadvantage is complexity. There are really two separate systems, an electric and a hydraulic. A problem with either affects both. Electric systems, of course, are dependent upon the aircraft battery and alternator. Hydraulic systems are dependent upon the correct operation of the pump and a series of valves, switches and, in some cases, mechanical up-locks. There must also be an abundance of hydraulic fluid in the system and an absence of air, which can act as a shock absorber and make it difficult for the landing gear to lock in the down position. Air also can get into the pump and cause it to quit functioning altogether.

For backup, many electro-hydraulic systems provide a hand pump to generate hydraulic pressure. But like the crank which serves as a substitute for the motor, a hand pump which is used in the event of an electric pump failure will have no effect on a problem that is deeper in the system, such as a lack of fluid or an abundance of air in the system.

Most of these system are also equipped with a free-fall mechanism which either releases hydraulic pressure or opens the up-locks so that the landing gear can drop into place. It is essential that the aircraft be at the correct airspeed before the system is released. Otherwise, the landing gear could be caught in transit by the wind load on the wheels or landing gear doors.

It is also important to remember that most electro-hydraulic systems do not use up-locks but rely on hydraulic pressure to keep the landing gear retracted. If the pump fails, the landing gear will slowly extend.

Engine-Driven

Some aircraft have an engine-driven hydraulic pump, instead of an electrically driven one. This eliminates one opportunity for failure in that, other than the indicator lights, the system is completely independent of the electrical system.

Of course, if the engine isn't turning, the hydraulic pump won't work either. Navions are among the few single-engine GA airplanes that use this type of system, but most piston-engine warbirds have it. It is more commonly found in twins, such as the Piper Apache, Aztec and Aerostar. If the engine bearing the hydraulic pump malfunctions, the pilot's workload increases. One of the most demanding twins I've flown is the Aerostar. A hydraulic pump on the right engine is used to both retract the landing gear and keep them up in the wells. Should the right engine fail, the pilot can lower the landing gear once, but that's it. Considering the performance of the aircraft on one engine, the pilot better know what he is doing before the gear comes out. A backup pump was offered as an option on the Aerostar, and as far as I'm concerned, it is essential.

Indicators

Most modern aircraft use a series of lights to indicate the landing gear position and an electric horn to warn the pilot of an impending gear-up landing. These electrical devices can present the pilot with as many difficulties as mechanical retraction linkages.

Normally, there's a system of microswitches which are all too often stuck out on the landing gear legs where they can easily be damaged. For the green light to illuminate on the instrument panel, one or more switches need to be in exactly the right position. Here again, a few minutes spent exploring the system with a mechanic can eliminate a lot of tension on final when only two of the three lights are glowing.

Many aircraft are also equipped with a "gear in transit" light. On some aircraft, the absence of a gear in transit light is an "all clear," even if one of the green lights malfunctions. On other aircraft it is not. Likewise, the absence of a gear warning horn may mean that the landing gear is in the correct position or that the landing gear *handle* is in the correct position. You have to take the time to learn how your particular system is wired in order to make the correct decisions.

Of course, if you are in the habit of carrying power through the round-out, you might as well throw the gear warning horn out the window. The horn usually won't blow until the throttles are closed, which may be too late.

Believe it or not, some mechanical indicators are disconnected by pilots. For instance, the Ryan Navion was originally equipped with little gear-up indicators which popped up through the top of the wing. Most of them have been removed because they cost a quarter of a knot in airspeed. (It makes you wonder what people are thinking about.)

Mechanical difficulties abound in landing gear systems, but the most common problem is still pilot error. Lest I sound holier than thou, let me tell you about how I ended up on short final last year with the landing gear retracted. I was flying a Beech Baron into Mexico. As I approached Tepic, Nayarit after six hours of flying, I was tired and the weather was lousy. I barely had a 1,000-foot ceiling and I had to sneak through a pass to get into the valley where the airport was. I was watching for towers and power lines, and there was another airplane reported inbound. I was on final when the controller (to whom I will be eternally grateful) advised me to check my landing gear. Would I have caught the gear-up situation when I crossed the threshold and checked for the lights? I don't know. Would I have heard the landing gear warning horn as I closed the throttles, even though I was wearing heavy headphones? I don't know that either. All I know is that it can happen to anyone, given the right circumstances.

In summary, to avoid one of the most common aircraft accidents, the pilot needs to develop a habit of always checking for a gear-down indication when crossing the threshold. The pilot of a complex aircraft should take the time to learn all the intimate details of the complex systems. If you haven't seen your landing gear system opened up during an annual inspection, you have been remiss. Of course, a careful and thorough preflight inspection is essential to the continued safe operation of the landing gear system. If ever you make a hard landing or a crosswind landing with a substantial side load, have the landing gear examined before you retract them again. Good procedure, knowledge and healthy skepticism will keep you out of trouble.

Index